Progress Chart

This chart lists all the topics in the book. Once you have completed each page, stick a star in the correct box below.

Page	Topic	Star	Page	Topic	Star	Page	Topic	Star
2	Multiplying by 10, 100, and 1000	☆	13	Decimal addition	☆	24	Perimeter of shapes	☆
3	The simplest form of fractions	☆	14	Decimal addition	☆	25	Decimal place value	☆
4	Changing improper fractions to mixed numbers	☆	15	Decimal subtraction	☆	26	Speed problems	☆
5	Rounding decimals	☆	16	Decimal subtraction	☆	27	Conversion table	☆
6	Adding with different numbers of digits	☆	17	Multiplying larger numbers by ones	☆	28	Interpreting circle graphs	☆
7	Adding with different numbers of digits	☆	18	Multiplying larger numbers by ones	☆	29	Probability scale 0 to 1	☆
8	Subtracting one number from another	☆	19	Real-life multiplication problems	☆	30	Likely outcomes	☆
9	Subtracting one number from another	☆	20	Comparing and ordering decimals	☆	31	Naming quadrilaterals	☆
10	Real-life problems	☆	21	Converting units of measure	☆	32	Speed trials	☆
11	Everyday problems	☆	22	Converting units of measure	☆	33	All the 3s	☆
12	Everyday problems	☆	23	Areas of rectangles and squares	☆	34	All the 3s again	☆

Math made Easy

Grade 5
Ages 10-11

Canadian Editor
Marilyn Wilson

Multiplying by 10, 100, and 1000

Write the answers in the boxes.

472 x 10 = `4720`   324 x 100 = `32 400`   57 x 1000 = `57 000`

Write the answers in the boxes.

426 x 10 =		319 x 10 =		584 x 10 =
740 x 10 =		985 x 10 =		612 x 10 =
102 x 100 =		725 x 100 =		383 x 100 =
909 x 100 =		651 x 100 =		737 x 100 =
4000 x 10 =		5649 x 10 =		8714 x 10 =
6302 x 100 =		9711 x 100 =		4826 x 100 =

Find the number that has been multiplied by 100.

x 100 = 163 100   x 100 = 562 300

x 100 = 841 300   x 100 = 864 700

x 100 = 636 500   x 100 = 839 100

x 100 = 521 000   x 100 = 537 000

Write the answers in the boxes.

4732 x 1000 =   9105 x 1000 =

6211 x 1000 =   4711 x 1000 =

11 264 x 1000 =   84 322 x 1000 =

47 544 x 1000 =   75 543 x 1000 =

59 223 x 1000 =   84 326 x 1000 =

Find the number that has been multiplied by 1000.

x 1000 =   764 000   x 1000 = 9 810 000

x 1000 = 5 372 000   x 1000 = 6 141 000

x 1000 = 4 169 000   x 1000 = 8 399 000

The simplest form of fractions

Make these fractions equivalent by putting a number in the box.

$$\frac{70}{100} = \frac{7}{10} \qquad \frac{4}{12} = \frac{1}{3}$$

Make these fractions equivalent by putting a number in each box.

$$\frac{30}{100} = \frac{}{10} \qquad \frac{8}{100} = \frac{}{25} \qquad \frac{40}{100} = \frac{}{10} \qquad \frac{15}{100} = \frac{}{20}$$

$$\frac{5}{20} = \frac{}{4} \qquad \frac{25}{100} = \frac{}{4} \qquad \frac{12}{60} = \frac{}{5} \qquad \frac{8}{20} = \frac{}{5}$$

$$\frac{16}{40} = \frac{}{5} \qquad \frac{2}{6} = \frac{}{3} \qquad \frac{10}{60} = \frac{}{6} \qquad \frac{2}{12} = \frac{}{6}$$

$$\frac{9}{18} = \frac{}{2} \qquad \frac{10}{18} = \frac{}{9} \qquad \frac{4}{24} = \frac{}{6} \qquad \frac{7}{28} = \frac{}{4}$$

$$\frac{4}{6} = \frac{2}{} \qquad \frac{6}{10} = \frac{3}{} \qquad \frac{9}{15} = \frac{3}{} \qquad \frac{8}{12} = \frac{2}{}$$

$$\frac{18}{20} = \frac{9}{} \qquad \frac{21}{28} = \frac{3}{} \qquad \frac{6}{8} = \frac{3}{} \qquad \frac{5}{50} = \frac{1}{}$$

$$\frac{15}{25} = \frac{3}{} \qquad \frac{4}{16} = \frac{1}{} \qquad \frac{12}{20} = \frac{3}{} \qquad \frac{12}{18} = \frac{2}{}$$

$$\frac{3}{15} = \frac{1}{} \qquad \frac{9}{36} = \frac{1}{} \qquad \frac{9}{27} = \frac{1}{} \qquad \frac{30}{50} = \frac{3}{}$$

Make these rows of fractions equivalent by putting a number in each box.

$$\frac{1}{9} = \frac{}{18} = \frac{3}{} = \frac{}{36} = \frac{}{45} = \frac{6}{}$$

$$\frac{1}{10} = \frac{}{20} = \frac{3}{} = \frac{4}{} = \frac{}{50} = \frac{}{60}$$

$$\frac{3}{5} = \frac{12}{} = \frac{}{25} = \frac{18}{} = \frac{}{35} = \frac{24}{}$$

$$\frac{5}{6} = \frac{}{12} = \frac{15}{} = \frac{20}{} = \frac{25}{} = \frac{30}{}$$

$$\frac{1}{7} = \frac{}{14} = \frac{}{21} = \frac{}{28} = \frac{5}{} = \frac{}{42}$$

$$\frac{3}{11} = \frac{}{44} = \frac{}{77} = \frac{27}{} = \frac{}{110} = \frac{33}{}$$

Changing improper fractions to mixed numbers

Change this improper fraction to a mixed number.
(Remember you may need to cancel.) $\dfrac{27}{12} = 2\dfrac{\cancel{3}^{1}}{\cancel{12}_{4}} = 2\dfrac{1}{4}$

Change these mixed numbers to improper fractions.

$2\dfrac{3}{4} = \dfrac{11}{4}$ $\qquad\qquad$ $4\dfrac{1}{2} = \dfrac{9}{2}$

Change these improper fractions to mixed numbers.

$\dfrac{25}{3} =$ $\qquad\qquad$ $\dfrac{15}{12} =$ $\qquad\qquad$ $\dfrac{40}{7} =$

$\dfrac{17}{6} =$ $\qquad\qquad$ $\dfrac{11}{9} =$ $\qquad\qquad$ $\dfrac{12}{5} =$

$\dfrac{27}{5} =$ $\qquad\qquad$ $\dfrac{26}{3} =$ $\qquad\qquad$ $\dfrac{32}{5} =$

$\dfrac{9}{2} =$ $\qquad\qquad$ $\dfrac{19}{2} =$ $\qquad\qquad$ $\dfrac{15}{4} =$

$\dfrac{30}{4} =$ $\qquad\qquad$ $\dfrac{26}{8} =$ $\qquad\qquad$ $\dfrac{42}{9} =$

Change these mixed numbers to improper fractions.

$4\dfrac{3}{4} =$ $\qquad\qquad$ $9\dfrac{1}{2} =$ $\qquad\qquad$ $12\dfrac{1}{4} =$

$3\dfrac{2}{3} =$ $\qquad\qquad$ $6\dfrac{3}{4} =$ $\qquad\qquad$ $3\dfrac{9}{10} =$

$5\dfrac{1}{8} =$ $\qquad\qquad$ $3\dfrac{2}{5} =$ $\qquad\qquad$ $2\dfrac{5}{6} =$

$5\dfrac{1}{4} =$ $\qquad\qquad$ $3\dfrac{3}{8} =$ $\qquad\qquad$ $2\dfrac{11}{12} =$

$2\dfrac{7}{10} =$ $\qquad\qquad$ $4\dfrac{3}{10} =$ $\qquad\qquad$ $4\dfrac{1}{8} =$

$7\dfrac{3}{4} =$ $\qquad\qquad$ $8\dfrac{1}{2} =$ $\qquad\qquad$ $1\dfrac{5}{12} =$

Rounding decimals

Write these decimals to the nearest tenth.

9.21 is ____   4.38 is ____   2.47 is ____

3.48 is ____   8.17 is ____   6.28 is ____

7.14 is ____   3.91 is ____   2.56 is ____

8.41 is ____   2.36 is ____   1.53 is ____

Write these decimals to the nearest tenth.

9.35 is ____   8.71 is ____   6.05 is ____

1.19 is ____   3.65 is ____   4.21 is ____

8.55 is ____   7.35 is ____   9.14 is ____

6.83 is ____   2.15 is ____   6.34 is ____

Write these decimals to the nearest tenth.

25.61 is ____   14.35 is ____   11.24 is ____

16.85 is ____   24.34 is ____   71.36 is ____

26.85 is ____   11.54 is ____   37.25 is ____

92.42 is ____   95.65 is ____   27.36 is ____

45.17 is ____   36.75 is ____   22.05 is ____

Adding with different numbers of digits

Find the total for each problem.

```
   432        ¹¹176
 +  43       +  97
 ───────     ───────
   475         273
```

Remember to regroup if you need to.

Find the total for each problem.

```
   148        271        371        938
 +  31      +  17      +  24      +  31
 ─────      ─────      ─────      ─────
```

```
   942        747        633        101
 +  26      +  34      +  43      +  75
 ─────      ─────      ─────      ─────
```

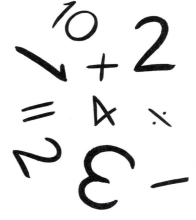

Write the answer in the box.

47 + 320 =

26 + 251 =

273 + 97 =

849 + 38 =

Write in the missing numbers in these problems.

```
   2 4 2        9 3 ▢        8 ▢ 5        6 ▢ 4
 +   2 7      +   3 8      +   1 2      +   6 3
 ─────────    ─────────    ─────────    ─────────
   2 ▢ 9        9 7 7        8 3 7        6 8 7
```

Find the answer to these problems. Use the space for working them out.

Tommy has saved $238. For his birthday he is given another $52. How much does he have now?

A circus sells 208 adult tickets and 86 children's tickets. How many tickets are sold altogether?

Adding with different numbers of digits

Work out the answer to each problem.

```
     1 11                      1 11
       987                    2 767
  +  423 123              +  12 844
     424 110                 15 611
```

Remember to regroup if you need to.

Work out the answer to each problem.

```
    3 587          8 537 227              27
+  17 628       +     86 518         +  9964
```

```
     436            387 177          6 770
+ 12 844        +     8 381     +  772 142
```

Write the answer in the box.

6 437 501 + 913 548 =

101 876 + 62 725 =

Write in the missing numbers in these sums.

```
   5  8                   21              6 7 5
+     8 4 9           +8 1 8 9        +    9 0 9
   6 2 3 6               8 5 1            7 6 6 1
```

Work out the answer to the problem. Use the space for working it out.

Jennifer has 1342 stamps in her collection. Dennis has 742.
How many do they have altogether?

Subtracting one number from another

Find the difference for each problem.

$$\begin{array}{r} \overset{7\ 13}{8\cancel{3}4} \\ -\ \ 44 \\ \hline 790 \end{array}$$

$$\begin{array}{r} \overset{3\ 12\ 11}{\cancel{4}\cancel{3}\cancel{1}} \\ -\ \ 84 \\ \hline 347 \end{array}$$

Find the difference for each problem.

$$\begin{array}{r} 835 \\ -\ 23 \\ \hline \end{array}$$
$$\begin{array}{r} 490 \\ -\ 70 \\ \hline \end{array}$$
$$\begin{array}{r} 175 \\ -\ 54 \\ \hline \end{array}$$
$$\begin{array}{r} 428 \\ -\ 67 \\ \hline \end{array}$$

$$\begin{array}{r} 587 \\ -\ 43 \\ \hline \end{array}$$
$$\begin{array}{r} 674 \\ -\ 62 \\ \hline \end{array}$$
$$\begin{array}{r} 389 \\ -\ 58 \\ \hline \end{array}$$
$$\begin{array}{r} 270 \\ -\ 30 \\ \hline \end{array}$$

$$\begin{array}{r} 483 \\ -\ 35 \\ \hline \end{array}$$
$$\begin{array}{r} 951 \\ -\ 28 \\ \hline \end{array}$$
$$\begin{array}{r} 746 \\ -\ 17 \\ \hline \end{array}$$
$$\begin{array}{r} 234 \\ -\ 16 \\ \hline \end{array}$$

Write the answer in the box.

$491 - 31 =$

$654 - 22 =$

$874 - 63 =$

$577 - 26 =$

Find the difference for each problem.

There are 565 children in a school. If 36 children are on a field trip, how many children are still at school?

A hardware store has 247 cans of paint. If they sell 29 cans, how many will they have left?

Subtracting one number from another

Work out the answer to each problem.

```
  1 16 16 7 15
  27 685          47 423
 –  8 726         – 5 351
  18 959           42 072
```

Work out the answer to each problem.

```
  68 231        62 411        11 684        37 481
 –  3 846      – 47 566      –  2 845      – 19 804
```

```
   7965          92 112        67 444         8818
 –  3976        – 46 489      – 29 545       – 7465
```

```
  52 812          2522          8529          6387
 – 37 341        – 1176        – 5892        – 2798
```

Write the answer in the box.

$$55\ 562 - 24\ 871 = $$

$$9118 - 8467 = $$

Work out the answer to the problem. Use the space for working it out.

2826 people went to see a rock concert. 135 had to leave early to catch their train. How many were left at the end?

Real-life problems

Toby has $525.95 in the bank and he spends $146.37 on his vacation. How much does he have left?

Toby has $379.58 left.

```
    4 11 15  8 15
   $525.95
 − $146.37
   $379.58
```

A rally driver drives 183 km on the first day of a race and 147 km on the second day. How many kilometres does he travel in the two days?

He drives 330 kilometres.

```
   1 1
   183 km
 + 147 km
   330 km
```

Mia spends $1525 on a new computer and $146 on a printer. How much does she spend altogether?

Derek has a board that is 3.46 m long to make a shelf to fit an alcove 2.63 m long. How much must he cut off his board in order for it to fit?

A family is on a vacation. If they travel 358 km in the first week and 388 km in the second week, how many kilometres have they travelled altogether?

If their car had already gone 17 028 km before the vacation, how many kilometres will it have gone by the end?

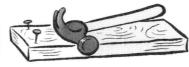

Two boxers are weighed before a boxing match. If the first has a mass of $84\frac{1}{2}$ kg and the second has a mass of 83 kg, what is the difference between their masses?

Everyday problems

An electrician buys 415 m of cable. If he uses
234 m, how much does he have left?

He has 181 m of cable left.

```
  3 11
  4̷1̷5 m
−  234 m
   181 m
```

Simon travels by train for 110 km, by bus
for 56 km and then walks the final 5 km.
How far does he travel?

Simon travels 171 km.

```
     1
   110 km
    56 km
+    5 km
   171 km
```

Mr. Hindley works 185 hours a month.
His wife works 73 hours a month. How many
hours do they work altogether in a month?

A school collects money for the local shelter. If the pupils
collect $275 in the first month, $210 in the second month, and
$136 in the third month, how much do they collect altogether?

Danny's car finishes the race in 12.75 seconds,
Rachelle's car finishes in 14.83 seconds.
Whose car won the race?

How much faster was the winning car?

A builder buys 8755 kg of sand, but uses only
6916 kg. How much does he have left?

Everyday problems

Rudy, Andrew, and Rachelle want to put their money together to buy a present for their brother. If Rudy gives $12.50, Andrew gives $14.75, and Rachelle gives $15.25, how much will they have to spend?

```
  11 1
  $12.50
  $14.75
+ $15.25
  $42.50
```

They will have $42.50 to spend.

A store has 130 kg of potatoes and sells 80 kg. How much does it have left?

```
  13
  130 kg
−  80 kg
   50 kg
```

The store has 50 kg left.

A bakery orders 145 kg of sugar, 565 kg of salt, and 926 kg of butter. What is the total mass of the order?

Mr. Jean-Paul travelled in a limo to the airport. After he paid a fare of $65, he had $125 left. How much money did he start with?

A vacation in Florida costs $394. A vacation in Majorca costs $876. How much cheaper is the Florida vacation?

Chamique is saving up to buy a guitar that costs $159.99. If she already has $65.37, how much more does she need?

Mr. Lorenzo's garden is 10 m long and 8 m wide. How much fence does he need to surround all four sides?

Decimal addition

Write in the answers to these problems.

$$\begin{array}{r} \overset{1}{4}7.\overset{1}{1}5 \\ +19.36 \\ \hline 66.51 \end{array} \qquad \begin{array}{r} \overset{1}{4}3.\overset{1}{9}9 \\ +12.76 \\ \hline 56.75 \end{array}$$

Write the answer to each problem.

53.72	84.17	29.36	23.56	62.49
+77.92	+68.21	+66.84	+79.14	+18.75

35.67	29.88	67.39	49.32	27.22
+12.99	+43.02	+81.70	+14.95	+38.84

Write the answer to each problem.

76.30	44.29	81.97	29.86	68.25
+22.97	+11.04	+69.14	+76.33	+84.36

83.90	45.83	52.17	84.93	72.83
+30.24	+45.71	+90.21	+29.37	+41.16

Write the answer to each problem.

37.89 + 82.15 =　　　　　32.44 + 21.88 =　　　　　37.19 + 28.24 =

68.67 + 29.82 =　　　　　21.99 + 79.32 =　　　　　52.45 + 34.58 =

84.77 + 39.12 =　　　　　63.84 + 29.81 =　　　　　34.43 + 25.64 =

33.97 + 24.62 =　　　　　76.39 + 43.78 =　　　　　52.38 + 38.43 =

Decimal addition

Write the sum for each problem.

$$\begin{array}{r} \overset{1\ \ 1}{296.48} \\ +\ 131.70 \\ \hline 428.18 \end{array}$$
$$\begin{array}{r} \overset{1\ 1}{73.00} \\ +\ 269.23 \\ \hline 342.23 \end{array}$$

Write the sum for each problem.

$$\begin{array}{r} 91.83 \\ +\ 37.84 \\ \hline \end{array}$$
$$\begin{array}{r} 64.71 \\ +\ 21.2 \\ \hline \end{array}$$
$$\begin{array}{r} 32.045 \\ +\ 4.99 \\ \hline \end{array}$$
$$\begin{array}{r} 306 \\ +\ 44.24 \\ \hline \end{array}$$

$$\begin{array}{r} 71.932 \\ +\ 55.26 \\ \hline \end{array}$$
$$\begin{array}{r} 842.01 \\ +\ 11.842 \\ \hline \end{array}$$
$$\begin{array}{r} 675.82 \\ +\ 105 \\ \hline \end{array}$$
$$\begin{array}{r} 37.82 \\ +\ 399.71 \\ \hline \end{array}$$

$$\begin{array}{r} 65.24 \\ +\ 605.27 \\ \hline \end{array}$$
$$\begin{array}{r} 178.935 \\ +\ 599.41 \\ \hline \end{array}$$
$$\begin{array}{r} 184.70 \\ +\ 372.81 \\ \hline \end{array}$$
$$\begin{array}{r} 443.27 \\ +\ 75 \\ \hline \end{array}$$

$$\begin{array}{r} 563 \\ +\ 413.98 \\ \hline \end{array}$$
$$\begin{array}{r} 703.95 \\ +\ 85.11 \\ \hline \end{array}$$
$$\begin{array}{r} 825.36 \\ +\ 249.857 \\ \hline \end{array}$$
$$\begin{array}{r} 529.3 \\ +\ 482.56 \\ \hline \end{array}$$

Write the sum for each problem.

421 + 136.25 =

92.31 + 241.73 =

501.8 + 361.93 =

558.32 + 137.945 =

27 + 142.07 =

75.31 + 293.33 =

153.3 + 182.02 =

491.445 + 105.37 =

253.71 + 62 =

829.2 + 63.74 =

Decimal subtraction

Write the difference for each problem.

64.92 − 26.35	64.21 − 16.02	73.71 −19.24	92.63 − 67.14
45.76 − 16.18	73.52 −39.27	98.98 −39.19	53.58 − 14.39
94.87 − 65.28	21.74 − 12.1	62.35 − 13.16	81.94 − 28.15
62.95 − 33.37	81.42 −25.04	48.52 − 14.49	61.55 − 13.26

Write the difference for each problem.

51.52 − 12.13 =

91.91 − 22.22 =

41.82 − 18.13 =

83.91 − 14.73 =

53.21 − 35.12 =

72.41 − 23.18 =

53.84 − 19.65 =

51.61 − 23.14 =

64.65 − 37.26 =

77.31 − 28.15 =

Decimal subtraction

Write the difference for each problem.

$$\begin{array}{r} {}^{7}\ ^{11}\\ 68.\!\not{1}7 \\ -11.40 \\ \hline 56.77 \end{array} \qquad \begin{array}{r} {}^{1}\ ^{10}\\ 39.\!\not{2}\not{0} \\ -13.15 \\ \hline 26.05 \end{array}$$

Work out the difference for each problem.

$$\begin{array}{r} 87.23 \\ -24.4 \\ \hline \end{array} \qquad \begin{array}{r} 95.15 \\ -31.356 \\ \hline \end{array} \qquad \begin{array}{r} 66.37 \\ -21.9 \\ \hline \end{array} \qquad \begin{array}{r} 85 \\ -26.32 \\ \hline \end{array}$$

$$\begin{array}{r} 72.28 \\ -1.3 \\ \hline \end{array} \qquad \begin{array}{r} 63.14 \\ -32 \\ \hline \end{array} \qquad \begin{array}{r} 99.235 \\ -33.70 \\ \hline \end{array} \qquad \begin{array}{r} 62.1 \\ -29.34 \\ \hline \end{array}$$

$$\begin{array}{r} 77.3 \\ -24.42 \\ \hline \end{array} \qquad \begin{array}{r} 55.492 \\ -27.66 \\ \hline \end{array} \qquad \begin{array}{r} 68 \\ -31.5 \\ \hline \end{array} \qquad \begin{array}{r} 35.612 \\ -13.207 \\ \hline \end{array}$$

$$\begin{array}{r} 82.35 \\ -23.40 \\ \hline \end{array} \qquad \begin{array}{r} 63.20 \\ -15.36 \\ \hline \end{array} \qquad \begin{array}{r} 53.64 \\ -23 \\ \hline \end{array} \qquad \begin{array}{r} 35.612 \\ -26.19 \\ \hline \end{array}$$

Write the difference for each problem.

$63.4 - 24.51 =$ $92.197 - 63.28 =$

$91.3 - 33 =$ $41.24 - 14.306 =$

$52.251 - 22.42 =$ $72.6 - 53.71 =$

$92.84 - 23 =$ $61.16 - 24.4 =$

$81.815 - 55.90 =$ $94.31 - 27.406 =$

Multiplying larger numbers by ones

Write the product for each problem.

$$
\begin{array}{r}
{\scriptstyle 13} \\
529 \\
\times \quad 4 \\
\hline
2116
\end{array}
\qquad
\begin{array}{r}
{\scriptstyle 131} \\
1273 \\
\times \quad 5 \\
\hline
6365
\end{array}
$$

Write the product for each problem.

724 x 2	831 x 3	126 x 3	455 x 4
161 x 4	282 x 5	349 x 5	253 x 6
328 x 6	465 x 6	105 x 4	562 x 4

Write the product for each problem.

4261 x 3	1582 x 3	3612 x 4	4284 x 4
5907 x 5	1263 x 5	1303 x 6	1467 x 6
6521 x 6	8436 x 6	1599 x 6	3761 x 6
5837 x 4	6394 x 5	8124 x 6	3914 x 6

Multiplying larger numbers by ones

Write the answer to each problem.

$$
\begin{array}{r}
\overset{1\,4}{417} \\
\times \quad 7 \\
\hline
2919
\end{array}
\qquad
\begin{array}{r}
\overset{1\,7\,4}{2185} \\
\times \quad 9 \\
\hline
19\,665
\end{array}
$$

Write the answer to each problem.

419 × 7	604 × 7	715 × 8	327 × 7
425 × 8	171 × 9	682 × 8	246 × 8
436 × 8	999 × 9	319 × 9	581 × 9

Work out the answer to each problem.

4331 × 7	2816 × 7	1439 × 8	2617 × 8
3104 × 8	4022 × 8	3212 × 9	2591 × 9
1710 × 9	3002 × 8	2468 × 7	1514 × 8
4624 × 7	2993 × 8	3894 × 8	4361 × 9

Real-life multiplication problems

There are 157 apples in a box.
How many will there be in three boxes?

471 apples

```
  12
 157
×   3
─────
 471
```

A stamp album can hold 550 stamps.
How many stamps will 5 albums hold?

A train can take 425 passengers.
How many can it take in four trips?

Mr Jenkins puts $256 a month into the bank.
How much will he have put in after six months?

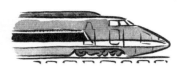

A theatre can seat 5524 people. If a play runs for 7 days, what is
the maximum number of people who will be able to see it?

A car costs $19 956. How much will it cost a
company to buy nine cars for its salespeople?

Installing a new window for a house costs $435. How
much will it cost to install 8 windows of the same size?

An airplane flies at a steady speed of 550 km/h.
How far will it travel in 7 hours?

Comparing and ordering decimals

Compare the decimals. Which decimal is greater?

2.2 and 3.1   0.45 and 0.6

Line them up vertically.

    2.2   0.45
    3.1   0.60

3>2, so 3.1>2.2   6>4, so 0.6>0.45

Compare the decimals. Which decimal is greater?

7.9 and 8.1   0.5 and 0.62   3.6 and 0.94   0.4 and 0.67

1.6 and 1.9   0.31 and 3.10   8.5 and 6.9   6.75 and 6.71

Find the greatest decimal.

2.9 and 2.75 and 2.6   0.97 and 1.09 and 1.3   4.9 and 3.87 and 4.75

Write the decimals in order from greatest to least.

0.33   3.1   0.3   24.95   23.9   24.5   7.5   6.95   7.58

Find the answer to each problem.

The Weather Bureau reported 5.18 centimetres of rain in March, 6.74 centimetres in April, and 5.23 centimetres in May. Which month had the least rainfall?

A postal worker walked 4.5 kilometres on Wednesday, 3.75 kilometres on Thursday, and 4.25 kilometres on Friday. Which day did she walk the farthest?

Converting units of measure

Convert 25 centimetres to millimetres.

$25 \times 10 =$ 250 mm

Convert 200¢ to dollars.

$200 \div 100 =$ $2

Convert these centimetres to millimetres.

40 cm		15 cm		9 cm	
12 cm		34 cm		62 cm	
43 cm		96 cm		105 cm	
92 cm		20 cm		426 cm	

Convert these millimetres to centimetres.

30 mm		100 mm		120 mm	
60 mm		90 mm		200 mm	
130 mm		10 mm		400 mm	

Convert these dollars to cents.

$35		$600		$15	
$12		$36		$95	
$72		$4		$250	

Convert these cents to dollars.

450¢		900¢		6000¢	
250¢		400¢		150¢	
100¢		300¢		750¢	

Converting units of measure

Convert 300 centimetres to metres.   Convert 4 kilometres to metres.

$300 \div 100 =$ 3 m $4 \times 1000 =$ 4000 m

Convert these centimetres to metres.

500 cm		900 cm		400 cm	
8000 cm		3000 cm		4000 cm	
9800 cm		8300 cm		6200 cm	
36 800 cm		94 200 cm		73 500 cm	

Convert these metres to centimetres.

47 m		29 m		84 m	
69 m		24 m		38 m	
146 m		237 m		921 m	

Convert these metres to kilometres.

5000 m		6000 m		9000 m	
15 000 m		27 000 m		71 000 m	
19 000 m		86 000 m		42 000 m	

Convert these kilometres to metres.

7 km		9 km		4 km	
23 km		46 km		87 km	
12 km		96 km		39 km	

Area of rectangles and squares

Find the area of this rectangle.

To find the area of a rectangle or square, we multiply length (l) by width (w).

Area = 800 cm²

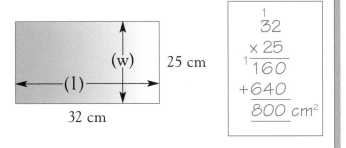

25 cm

(w)

(l)

32 cm

$$\begin{array}{r} \overset{1}{32} \\ \times\, 25 \\ \hline \overset{1}{160} \\ +640 \\ \hline 800 \text{ cm}^2 \end{array}$$

Find the area of these rectangles and squares.
You may need to do your work on a separate sheet.

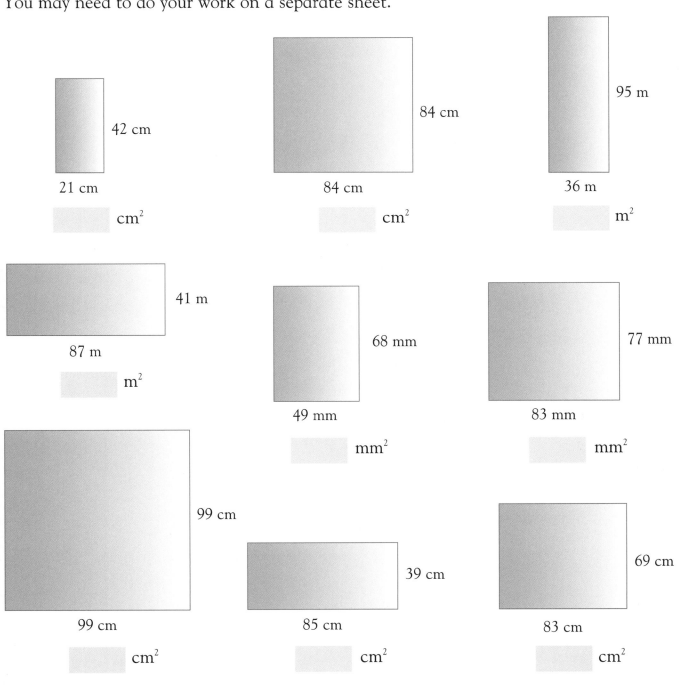

42 cm

21 cm

☐ cm²

84 cm

84 cm

☐ cm²

95 m

36 m

☐ m²

41 m

87 m

☐ m²

68 mm

49 mm

☐ mm²

77 mm

83 mm

☐ mm²

99 cm

99 cm

☐ cm²

39 cm

85 cm

☐ cm²

69 cm

83 cm

☐ cm²

Perimeter of shapes

Find the perimeter of this rectangle.

To find the perimeter of a rectangle or square, we add the two lengths and the two widths together.

12.4 cm

27.3 cm

1 1
27.3 cm
27.3 cm
12.4 cm
+ 12.4 cm
79.4 cm

79.4 cm

Find the perimeter of these rectangles and squares.
You may need to do your work on a separate sheet.

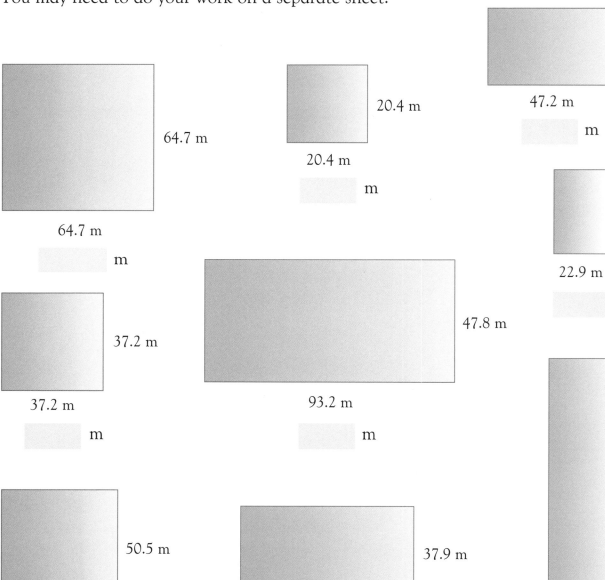

29.8 m

47.2 m

_____ m

64.7 m

64.7 m

_____ m

20.4 m

20.4 m

_____ m

36.8 m

22.9 m

_____ m

37.2 m

37.2 m

_____ m

47.8 m

93.2 m

_____ m

96.3 m

50.5 m

50.5 m

_____ m

37.9 m

65.2 m

_____ m

24.8 m

_____ m

Decimal place value

Work out the answer to the problem.

2.385
What is the value of the digit 8?

Ones		Tenths	Hundredths	Thousandths	Ten-thousandths
2.		3	8	5	0

2.3850
8 is in the hundredths place, so, its value is 8 hundredths.

Name the place of the digit 8 in each of the problems.

0.387	3.87	4.82	8.11

Name the value of the highlighted digit.

6.5937	5.371	7.403	0.42

6.24	3.611	1.062

Which number has a digit with the value 6 tenths?

Which number has a digit with the value 6 hundredths?

Which number has a digit with the value 6 ones?

How much greater is the second decimal than the first?

7.46	7.56		3.27	3.67		0.82	0.85
one tenth more							

Speed problems

How long will it take a bike rider to travel 36 km at a constant speed of 9 kilometres per hour?

4 hours

9)36

Time = Distance ÷ Speed

If a car travelled 150 km at a constant speed in 5 hours, at what speed was it travelling?

30 km/h

5)150

Speed = Distance ÷ Time

If a bus travels for 5 hours at 40 km/h, how far does it travel?

5 x 40 = 200 km

Distance = Speed x Time

A car travels along a road at a steady speed of 60 km/h. How far will it travel in 6 hours?

A train covers a distance of 480 km in 8 hours. If it travels at a constant speed, how fast is it travelling?

John walks at a steady speed of 3 km/h. How long will it take him to travel 24 kilometres?

A car travels at a constant speed of 65 km/h. How far will it have travelled in 4 hours?

Melanie completes a long distance run at an average speed of 6 km/h. If it takes her 3 hours, how far did she run?

Sarah cycles 30 km to her grandmother's house at a steady speed of 10 km/h. If she leaves home at 2:00 P.M., what time will she arrive?

Conversion table

This is part of a conversion table that shows how to change dollars to pesos when 10 Mexican pesos (10MN) equal $1.

Canadian Dollars	Mexican Pesos
1	10
2	20
3	30

How many pesos would you get for $2? **20MN**

How much is 25 pesos worth in dollars? **$2.50**

How many dollars would you get for 40MN?

How many dollars would you get for 85MN?

How much is 1MN worth?

Change $65 into pesos.

What is $3.50 in pesos?

Change 250MN into dollars.

How many pesos could you get for $0.40?

Canadian Dollars	Mexican Pesos
1	10
2	20
3	30
4	40
5	50
6	60
7	70
8	80
9	90
10	100

The rate then changes to 8MN to the dollar.
The conversion chart now looks like the one shown here.

How many pesos are worth $4?

How many dollars can you get for 56MN?

How many pesos are worth $9.50?

How many pesos can you get for $20?

How many dollars would you get for 120MN?

What is the value of 4MN?

Canadian Dollars	Mexican Pesos
1	8
2	16
3	24
4	32
5	40
6	48
7	56
8	64
9	72
10	80

32 children voted for their favourite ice-cream flavours.

How many children voted for chocolate?

$\frac{3}{8}$ of 32 is 12

12 children voted for chocolate.

12 children

How many children voted for fudge?

$\frac{1}{8}$ of 32 is 4

4 children voted for fudge.

4 children

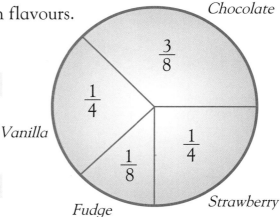

A class of 30 children voted for their favourite actor who has played James Bond.

How many voted for Sean Connery?

How many did not vote for George Lazenby?

How many more children voted for Pierce Brosnan than Roger Moore?

How many children altogether voted for Sean Connery and Roger Moore?

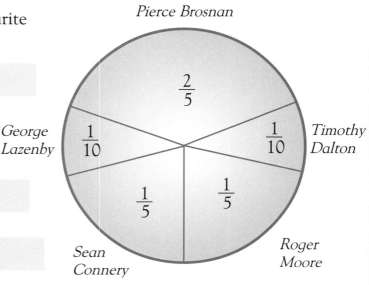

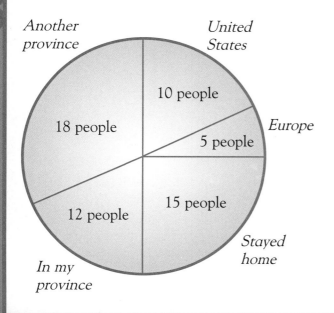

60 people were asked where they went on vacation last year. The circle graph shows the results.

What fraction of people vacationed in another province?

What fraction of people vacationed in the United States, or in Europe?

What fraction of people did not stay at home?

What fraction of people vacationed in their province or another province?

Probability scale 0 to 1

Look at this probability line.

Impossible = 0
Poor chance = 0.25
Fair = 0.5
Good chance = 0.75
Certain = 1

Write each letter in the correct place on the probability line.

a. It will be daylight in New Orleans at midnight.
b. The sun will come up tomorrow.
c. If I toss a coin it will come down heads.

a ↓   *c* ↓   *b* ↓

0   0.25   0.5   0.75   1

---

0   0.25   0.5   0.75   1

Write each letter in the correct place on the probability line.

a. If I cut a pack of cards I will get a red card.

b. If I cut a pack of cards I will get a diamond.

c. If I cut a pack of cards I will get a diamond, a spade, or a club.

d. If I cut a pack of cards I will get a diamond, a spade, a club, or a heart.

e. If I cut a pack of cards it will be a 15.

---

0   0.25   0.5   0.75   1

Write each letter in the correct place on the probability line.

a. Next week, Wednesday will be the day after Tuesday.

b. There will be 33 days in February next year.

c. It will snow in Vancouver in May.

d. It will snow in Newfoundland in January.

e. The next person to knock on the door will be a woman.

Likely outcomes

Throw one coin 20 times.

Keep a tally.

H	$\cancel{||||}$ $||||$
T	$\cancel{||||}$ $\cancel{||||}$ $|$

Put your results on a bar graph.

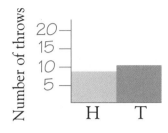

What do you notice?

Heads and tails come up roughly the same number of times because there are only two possible outcomes and they are equally likely.

Predict what you think the outcome will be if you tossed two coins 48 times.

2 heads _____ times   2 tails _____ times   1 of each _____ times

Now actually throw two coins 48 times and record your results on this tally chart.

2 Heads	
2 Tails	
1 of each	

Draw a bar graph to show your results.

Which result comes up the most often?

Can you explain why some results
are more probable than others?

Naming quadrilaterals

Name this shape.

Rhombus

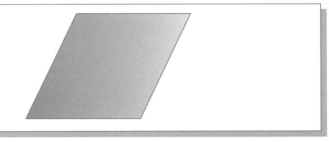

Name these shapes.

Sketch these shapes.

Parallelogram   Rectangle

Rhombus   Trapezoid

Speed trials

Write the answers as fast as you can, but get them right!

4 x 10 = 40   8 x 2 = 16   6 x 5 = 30

Write the answers as fast as you can, but get them right!

3 x 2 =	0 x 5 =	3 x 10 =	0 x 3 =
5 x 2 =	10 x 5 =	5 x 10 =	10 x 3 =
1 x 2 =	8 x 5 =	1 x 10 =	8 x 3 =
4 x 2 =	6 x 5 =	4 x 10 =	6 x 3 =
7 x 2 =	2 x 5 =	7 x 10 =	2 x 3 =
2 x 2 =	7 x 5 =	2 x 10 =	7 x 3 =
6 x 2 =	4 x 5 =	6 x 10 =	4 x 3 =
8 x 2 =	1 x 5 =	8 x 10 =	1 x 3 =
10 x 2 =	5 x 5 =	10 x 10 =	5 x 3 =
0 x 2 =	3 x 5 =	0 x 10 =	3 x 3 =
9 x 2 =	5 x 3 =	9 x 10 =	6 x 4 =
2 x 7 =	5 x 8 =	10 x 7 =	3 x 4 =
2 x 1 =	5 x 6 =	10 x 1 =	7 x 4 =
2 x 4 =	5 x 9 =	10 x 4 =	4 x 4 =
3 x 7 =	5 x 7 =	10 x 7 =	10 x 4 =
2 x 5 =	5 x 4 =	10 x 5 =	8 x 4 =
2 x 9 =	5 x 1 =	10 x 9 =	0 x 4 =
2 x 6 =	4 x 7 =	10 x 6 =	9 x 4 =
2 x 8 =	5 x 10 =	10 x 8 =	5 x 4 =
2 x 3 =	5 x 2 =	10 x 3 =	2 x 4 =

All the 3s

You will need to know these:

$1 \times 3 = 3$ $\qquad$ $2 \times 3 = 6$ $\qquad$ $3 \times 3 = 9$ $\qquad$ $4 \times 3 = 12$ $\qquad$ $5 \times 3 = 15$ $\qquad$ $10 \times 3 = 30$

How many altogether?

6 sets of three are ⬚ $\qquad$ six threes are ⬚ $\qquad$ $6 \times 3 =$ ⬚

How many altogether?

7 sets of three are ⬚ $\qquad$ seven threes are ⬚ $\qquad$ $7 \times 3 =$ ⬚

How many altogether?

8 sets of three are ⬚ $\qquad$ eight threes are ⬚ $\qquad$ $8 \times 3 =$ ⬚

How many altogether?

9 sets of three are ⬚ $\qquad$ nine threes are ⬚ $\qquad$ $9 \times 3 =$ ⬚

All the 3s again

Cover the three times table with a sheet of paper so you can't see the numbers.
Write the answers. Be as fast as you can, but get them right!

1 x 3 =	5 x 3 =	6 x 3 =
2 x 3 =	7 x 3 =	9 x 3 =
3 x 3 =	9 x 3 =	4 x 3 =
4 x 3 =	4 x 3 =	5 x 3 =
5 x 3 =	6 x 3 =	3 x 7 =
6 x 3 =	8 x 3 =	3 x 4 =
7 x 3 =	10 x 3 =	2 x 3 =
8 x 3 =	1 x 3 =	10 x 3 =
9 x 3 =	3 x 3 =	3 x 9 =
10 x 3 =	2 x 3 =	3 x 6 =
3 x 1 =	3 x 5 =	3 x 5 =
3 x 2 =	3 x 7 =	3 x 8 =
3 x 3 =	3 x 9 =	7 x 3 =
3 x 4 =	3 x 4 =	3 x 2 =
3 x 5 =	3 x 6 =	3 x 10 =
3 x 6 =	3 x 8 =	8 x 3 =
3 x 7 =	3 x 10 =	3 x 0 =
3 x 8 =	3 x 1 =	1 x 3 =
3 x 9 =	3 x 0 =	3 x 3 =
3 x 10 =	3 x 2 =	3 x 9 =

All the 4s

You should know these:

$1 \times 4 = 4$ $2 \times 4 = 8$ $3 \times 4 = 12$ $4 \times 4 = 16$ $5 \times 4 = 20$ $10 \times 4 = 40$

How many altogether?

6 sets of four are ▢   six fours are ▢ $6 \times 4 =$ ▢

How many altogether?

7 sets of four are ▢   seven fours are ▢ $7 \times 4 =$ ▢

How many altogether?

8 sets of four are ▢   eight fours are ▢ $8 \times 4 =$ ▢

How many altogether?

9 sets of four are ▢   nine fours are ▢ $9 \times 4 =$ ▢

All the 4s again

You should know all of the four times table by now.

1 x 4 = 4	2 x 4 = 8	3 x 4 = 12	4 x 4 = 16	5 x 4 = 20
6 x 4 = 24	7 x 4 = 28	8 x 4 = 32	9 x 4 = 36	10 x 4 = 40

Say these to yourself a few times.

Cover the four times table with a sheet of paper so you can't see the numbers.
Write the answers. Be as fast as you can, but get them right!

1 x 4 =	5 x 4 =	6 x 4 =
2 x 4 =	7 x 4 =	9 x 4 =
3 x 4 =	9 x 4 =	4 x 1 =
4 x 4 =	3 x 4 =	5 x 4 =
5 x 4 =	6 x 4 =	4 x 7 =
6 x 4 =	8 x 4 =	3 x 4 =
7 x 4 =	10 x 4 =	2 x 4 =
8 x 4 =	1 x 4 =	10 x 4 =
9 x 4 =	4 x 4 =	4 x 3 =
10 x 4 =	2 x 4 =	4 x 6 =
4 x 1 =	4 x 5 =	4 x 5 =
4 x 2 =	4 x 7 =	4 x 8 =
4 x 3 =	4 x 9 =	7 x 4 =
4 x 4 =	4 x 4 =	4 x 2 =
4 x 5 =	4 x 6 =	4 x 10 =
4 x 6 =	4 x 8 =	8 x 4 =
4 x 7 =	4 x 10 =	4 x 0 =
4 x 8 =	4 x 1 =	1 x 4 =
4 x 9 =	4 x 0 =	4 x 4 =
4 x 10 =	4 x 2 =	4 x 9 =

Speed trials

You should know all of the 1, 2, 3, 4, 5, and 10 times tables by now, but how quickly can you do them?
Ask someone to time you as you do this page.
Remember, you must be fast but also correct.

4 x 2 =	6 x 3 =	9 x 5 =
8 x 3 =	3 x 4 =	8 x 10 =
7 x 4 =	7 x 5 =	7 x 2 =
6 x 5 =	3 x 10 =	6 x 3 =
8 x 10 =	1 x 2 =	5 x 4 =
8 x 2 =	7 x 3 =	4 x 5 =
5 x 3 =	4 x 4 =	3 x 10 =
9 x 4 =	6 x 5 =	2 x 2 =
5 x 5 =	4 x 10 =	1 x 3 =
7 x 10 =	6 x 2 =	0 x 4 =
0 x 2 =	5 x 3 =	10 x 5 =
4 x 3 =	8 x 4 =	9 x 2 =
6 x 4 =	0 x 5 =	8 x 3 =
3 x 5 =	2 x 10 =	7 x 4 =
4 x 10 =	7 x 2 =	6 x 5 =
7 x 2 =	8 x 3 =	5 x 10 =
3 x 3 =	9 x 4 =	4 x 0 =
2 x 4 =	5 x 5 =	3 x 2 =
7 x 5 =	7 x 10 =	2 x 8 =
9 x 10 =	5 x 2 =	1 x 9 =

Some of the 6s

You should already know parts of the 6 times table because they are parts of the 1, 2, 3, 4, 5, and 10 times tables.

1 x 6 = 6   2 x 6 = 12   3 x 6 = 18
4 x 6 = 24   5 x 6 = 30   10 x 6 = 60

Find out if you can remember them quickly and correctly.

Cover the six times table with paper so you can't see the numbers.
Write the answers as quickly as you can.

What is three sixes?   What is ten sixes?

What is two sixes?   What is four sixes?

What is one six?   What is five sixes?

Write the answers as quickly as you can.

How many sixes make 12?   How many sixes make 6?

How many sixes make 30?   How many sixes make 18?

How many sixes make 24?   How many sixes make 60?

Write the answers as quickly as you can.

Multiply six by three.   Multiply six by ten.

Multiply six by two.   Multiply six by five.

Multiply six by one.   Multiply six by four.

Write the answers as quickly as you can.

4 x 6 =   2 x 6 =   10 x 6 =

5 x 6 =   1 x 6 =   3 x 6 =

Write the answers as quickly as you can.
A box contains six eggs. A man buys five boxes. How many eggs does he have?

A pack contains six sticks of gum.
How many sticks will there be in 10 packs?

The rest of the 6s

You need to learn these:

$6 \times 6 = 36$ $7 \times 6 = 42$ $8 \times 6 = 48$ $9 \times 6 = 54$

This work will help you remember the 6 times table.

Complete these sequences.

| 6 | 12 | 18 | 24 | 30 | | | | | |

$5 \times 6 = 30$ so $6 \times 6 = 30$ plus another $6 =$ [ ]

| 18 | 24 | 30 | | | | |

$6 \times 6 = 36$ so $7 \times 6 = 36$ plus another $6 =$ [ ]

| 6 | 12 | 18 | | | | | 48 | | 60 |

$7 \times 6 = 42$ so $8 \times 6 = 42$ plus another $6 =$ [ ]

| 6 | | 18 | 24 | 30 | | | | | |

$8 \times 6 = 48$ so $9 \times 6 = 48$ plus another $6 =$ [ ]

| | | | 24 | | | 42 | | | 60 |

Test yourself on the rest of the 6 times table.
Cover the above part of the page with a sheet of paper.

What is six sixes? [ ]   What is seven sixes? [ ]

What is eight sixes? [ ]   What is nine sixes? [ ]

$8 \times 6 =$ [ ] $7 \times 6 =$ [ ] $6 \times 6 =$ [ ] $9 \times 6 =$ [ ]

Practise the 6s

You should know all of the 6 times table now, but how quickly can you remember it?
Ask someone to time you as you do this page.
Remember, you must be fast but also correct.

1 x 6 =	2 x 6 =	7 x 6 =
2 x 6 =	4 x 6 =	3 x 6 =
3 x 6 =	6 x 6 =	9 x 6 =
4 x 6 =	8 x 6 =	6 x 4 =
5 x 6 =	10 x 6 =	1 x 6 =
6 x 6 =	1 x 6 =	6 x 2 =
7 x 6 =	3 x 6 =	6 x 8 =
8 x 6 =	5 x 6 =	0 x 6 =
9 x 6 =	7 x 6 =	6 x 3 =
10 x 6 =	9 x 6 =	5 x 6 =
6 x 1 =	6 x 3 =	6 x 7 =
6 x 2 =	6 x 5 =	2 x 6 =
6 x 3 =	6 x 7 =	6 x 9 =
6 x 4 =	6 x 9 =	4 x 6 =
6 x 5 =	6 x 2 =	8 x 6 =
6 x 6 =	6 x 4 =	10 x 6 =
6 x 7 =	6 x 6 =	6 x 5 =
6 x 8 =	6 x 8 =	6 x 0 =
6 x 9 =	6 x 10 =	6 x 1 =
6 x 10 =	6 x 0 =	6 x 6 =

Speed trials

You should know all of the 1, 2, 3, 4, 5, 6, and 10 times tables by now,
but how quickly can you remember them?
Ask someone to time you as you do this page.
Remember, you must be fast but also correct.

4 x 6 =	6 x 3 =	9 x 6 =
5 x 3 =	8 x 6 =	8 x 6 =
7 x 3 =	6 x 6 =	7 x 3 =
6 x 5 =	3 x 10 =	6 x 6 =
6 x 10 =	6 x 2 =	5 x 4 =
8 x 2 =	7 x 3 =	4 x 6 =
5 x 3 =	4 x 6 =	3 x 6 =
9 x 6 =	6 x 5 =	2 x 6 =
5 x 5 =	6 x 10 =	6 x 3 =
7 x 6 =	6 x 2 =	0 x 6 =
0 x 2 =	5 x 3 =	10 x 5 =
6 x 3 =	8 x 4 =	6 x 2 =
6 x 6 =	0 x 6 =	8 x 3 =
3 x 5 =	5 x 10 =	7 x 6 =
4 x 10 =	7 x 6 =	6 x 5 =
7 x 10 =	8 x 3 =	5 x 10 =
3 x 6 =	9 x 6 =	6 x 0 =
2 x 4 =	5 x 5 =	3 x 10 =
6 x 9 =	7 x 10 =	2 x 8 =
9 x 10 =	5 x 6 =	1 x 8 =

Some of the 7s

You should already know parts of the 7 times table because they are parts of the 1, 2, 3, 4, 5, 6 and 10 times tables.

  1 x 7 = 7   2 x 7 = 14   3 x 7 = 21   4 x 7 = 28
  5 x 7 = 35   6 x 7 = 42   10 x 7 = 70

Find out if you can remember them quickly and correctly.

Cover the seven times table with paper and write the answers to these questions as quickly as you can.

What is three sevens?

What is two sevens?

What is six sevens?

What is ten sevens?

What is four sevens?

What is five sevens?

Write the answers as quickly as you can.

How many sevens make 14?

How many sevens make 35?

How many sevens make 28?

How many sevens make 42?

How many sevens make 21?

How many sevens make 70?

Write the answers as quickly as you can.

Multiply seven by three.

Multiply seven by two.

Multiply seven by six.

Multiply seven by ten.

Multiply seven by five.

Multiply seven by four.

Write the answers as quickly as you can.

4 x 7 =   2 x 7 =   10 x 7 =

5 x 7 =   1 x 7 =   3 x 7 =

Write the answers as quickly as you can.

A bag has seven candies. Ann buys five bags. How many candies does she have?

How many days are there in six weeks?

42

The rest of the 7s

You should now know all of the 1, 2, 3, 4, 5, 6, and 10 times tables.

You need to learn only these parts of the seven times table.
7 x 7 = 49   8 x 7 = 56   9 x 7 = 63

This work will help you remember the 7 times table.

Complete these sequences.

7   14   21   28   35   42

6 x 7 = 42   so   7 x 7 = 42 plus another 7 =

21   28   35

7 x 7 = 49   so   8 x 7 = 49 plus another 7 =

7   14   21   56   70

8 x 7 = 56   so   9 x 7 = 56 plus another 7 =

7   21   28   35

Test yourself on the rest of the 7 times table.
Cover the section above with a sheet of paper.

What is seven sevens?   What is eight sevens?

What is nine sevens?   What is ten sevens?

8 x 7 =   7 x 7 =   9 x 7 =   10 x 7 =

How many days are there in eight weeks?

A package contains seven pens.
How many pens will there be in nine packets?

How many sevens make 56?

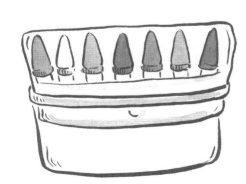

Practise the 7s

You should know all of the 7 times table now, but how quickly can you remember it?
Ask someone to time you as you do this page.
Remember, you must be fast but also correct.

1 x 7 =	2 x 7 =	7 x 6 =
2 x 7 =	4 x 7 =	3 x 7 =
3 x 7 =	6 x 7 =	9 x 7 =
4 x 7 =	8 x 7 =	7 x 4 =
5 x 7 =	10 x 7 =	1 x 7 =
6 x 7 =	1 x 7 =	7 x 2 =
7 x 7 =	3 x 7 =	7 x 8 =
8 x 7 =	5 x 7 =	0 x 7 =
9 x 7 =	7 x 7 =	7 x 3 =
10 x 7 =	9 x 7 =	5 x 7 =
7 x 1 =	7 x 3 =	7 x 7 =
7 x 2 =	7 x 5 =	2 x 7 =
7 x 3 =	7 x 7 =	7 x 9 =
7 x 4 =	7 x 9 =	4 x 7 =
7 x 5 =	7 x 2 =	8 x 7 =
7 x 6 =	7 x 4 =	10 x 7 =
7 x 7 =	7 x 6 =	7 x 5 =
7 x 8 =	7 x 8 =	7 x 0 =
7 x 9 =	7 x 10 =	7 x 1 =
7 x 10 =	7 x 0 =	6 x 7 =

Speed trials

You should know all of the 1, 2, 3, 4, 5, 6, 7, and 10 times tables by now, but how quickly can you remember them?
Ask someone to time you as you do this page.
Remember, you must be fast but also correct.

4 x 7 =	7 x 3 =	9 x 7 =
5 x 10 =	8 x 7 =	7 x 6 =
7 x 5 =	6 x 6 =	8 x 3 =
6 x 5 =	5 x 10 =	6 x 6 =
6 x 10 =	6 x 3 =	7 x 4 =
8 x 7 =	7 x 5 =	4 x 6 =
5 x 8 =	4 x 6 =	3 x 7 =
9 x 6 =	6 x 5 =	2 x 8 =
5 x 7 =	7 x 10 =	7 x 3 =
7 x 6 =	6 x 7 =	0 x 6 =
0 x 5 =	5 x 7 =	10 x 7 =
6 x 3 =	8 x 4 =	6 x 2 =
6 x 7 =	0 x 7 =	8 x 7 =
3 x 5 =	5 x 8 =	7 x 7 =
4 x 7 =	7 x 6 =	6 x 5 =
7 x 10 =	8 x 3 =	5 x 10 =
7 x 8 =	9 x 6 =	7 x 0 =
2 x 7 =	7 x 7 =	3 x 10 =
4 x 9 =	9 x 10 =	2 x 7 =
9 x 10 =	5 x 6 =	7 x 8 =

Some of the 8s

You should already know some of the 8 times table because it is part of the 1, 2, 3, 4, 5, 6, 7, and 10 times tables.

1 x 8 = 8	2 x 8 = 16	3 x 8 = 24	4 x 8 = 32
5 x 8 = 40	6 x 8 = 48	7 x 8 = 56	10 x 8 = 80

Find out if you can remember them quickly and correctly.

Cover the 8 times table with paper so you can't see the numbers.
Write the answers as quickly as you can.

What is three eights?   What is ten eights?

What is two eights?   What is four eights?

What is six eights?   What is five eights?

Write the answers as quickly as you can.

How many eights equal 16?   How many eights equal 40?

How many eights equal 32?   How many eights equal 24?

How many eights equal 56?   How many eights equal 48?

Write the answers as quickly as you can.

Multiply eight by three.   Multiply eight by ten.

Multiply eight by two.   Multiply eight by five.

Multiply eight by six.   Multiply eight by four.

Write the answers as quickly as you can.

6 x 8 =   2 x 8 =   10 x 8 =

5 x 8 =   7 x 8 =   3 x 8 =

Write the answers as quickly as you can.
A pizza has eight slices. John buys six pizzas.

How many slices does he have?

Which number multiplied by 8 gives the answer 56?

46

The rest of the 8s

You need to learn only these parts of the eight times table.
8 x 8 = 64   9 x 8 = 72

This work will help you remember the 8 times table.

Complete these sequences.

| 8 | 16 | 24 | 32 | 40 | 48 | | | | |

7 x 8 = 56   so   8 x 8 = 56 plus another 8 =

| 24 | 32 | 40 | | | | | |

8 x 8 = 64   so   9 x 8 = 64 plus another 8 =

| 8 | 16 | 24 | | | 64 | | 80 |

| 8 | | 24 | | 40 | | | |

Test yourself on the rest of the 8 times table.
Cover the section above with a sheet of paper.

What is seven eights?   What is eight eights?

What is nine eights?   What is eight nines?

8 x 8 =   9 x 8 =   8 x 9 =   10 x 8 =

What number multiplied by 8 gives the answer 72?

A number multiplied by 8 gives the answer 80. What is the number?

David puts out building bricks in piles of 8.
How many bricks will there be in 10 piles?

What number multiplied by 5 gives the answer 40?

How many 8s make 72?

Practise the 8s

You should know all of the 8 times table now, but how quickly can you remember it?
Ask someone to time you as you do this page.
Be fast but also correct.

1 x 8 =	2 x 8 =	8 x 6 =
2 x 8 =	4 x 8 =	3 x 8 =
3 x 8 =	6 x 8 =	9 x 8 =
4 x 8 =	8 x 8 =	8 x 4 =
5 x 8 =	10 x 8 =	1 x 8 =
6 x 8 =	1 x 8 =	8 x 2 =
7 x 8 =	3 x 8 =	7 x 8 =
8 x 8 =	5 x 8 =	0 x 8 =
9 x 8 =	7 x 8 =	8 x 3 =
10 x 8 =	9 x 8 =	5 x 8 =
8 x 1 =	8 x 3 =	8 x 8 =
8 x 2 =	8 x 5 =	2 x 8 =
8 x 3 =	8 x 8 =	8 x 9 =
8 x 4 =	8 x 9 =	4 x 8 =
8 x 5 =	8 x 2 =	8 x 6 =
8 x 6 =	8 x 4 =	10 x 8 =
8 x 7 =	8 x 6 =	8 x 5 =
8 x 8 =	8 x 8 =	8 x 0 =
8 x 9 =	8 x 10 =	8 x 1 =
8 x 10 =	8 x 0 =	6 x 8 =

Speed trials

You should know all of the 1, 2, 3, 4, 5, 6, 7, 8, and 10 times tables now,
but how quickly can you remember them?
Ask someone to time you as you do this page.
Be fast but also correct.

4 x 8 =	7 x 8 =	9 x 8 =
5 x 10 =	8 x 7 =	7 x 6 =
7 x 8 =	6 x 8 =	8 x 3 =
8 x 5 =	8 x 10 =	8 x 8 =
6 x 10 =	6 x 3 =	7 x 4 =
8 x 7 =	7 x 7 =	4 x 8 =
5 x 8 =	5 x 6 =	3 x 7 =
9 x 8 =	6 x 7 =	2 x 8 =
8 x 8 =	7 x 10 =	7 x 3 =
7 x 6 =	6 x 9 =	0 x 8 =
7 x 5 =	5 x 8 =	10 x 8 =
6 x 8 =	8 x 4 =	6 x 2 =
6 x 7 =	0 x 8 =	8 x 6 =
5 x 7 =	5 x 9 =	7 x 8 =
8 x 4 =	7 x 6 =	6 x 5 =
7 x 10 =	8 x 3 =	8 x 10 =
2 x 8 =	9 x 6 =	8 x 7 =
4 x 7 =	8 x 6 =	5 x 10 =
6 x 9 =	9 x 10 =	8 x 2 =
9 x 10 =	6 x 6 =	8 x 9 =

Some of the 9s

You should already know nearly all of the 9 times table because it is part of the 1, 2, 3, 4, 5, 6, 7, 8, and 10 times tables.

$1 \times 9 = 9$ $2 \times 9 = 18$ $3 \times 9 = 27$ $4 \times 9 = 36$ $5 \times 9 = 45$
$6 \times 9 = 54$ $7 \times 9 = 63$ $8 \times 9 = 72$ $10 \times 9 = 90$

Find out if you can remember them quickly and correctly.

Cover the nine times table so you can't see the numbers.
Write the answers as quickly as you can.

What is three nines?   What is ten nines?

What is two nines?   What is four nines?

What is six nines?   What is five nines?

What is seven nines?   What is eight nines?

Write the answers as quickly as you can.

How many nines equal 18?   How many nines equal 54?

How many nines equal 90?   How many nines equal 27?

How many nines equal 72?   How many nines equal 36?

How many nines equal 45?   How many nines equal 63?

Write the answers as quickly as you can.

Multiply nine by seven.   Multiply nine by ten.

Multiply nine by two.   Multiply nine by five.

Multiply nine by six.   Multiply nine by four.

Multiply nine by three.   Multiply nine by eight.

Write the answers as quickly as you can.

$6 \times 9 =$ $2 \times 9 =$ $10 \times 9 =$

$5 \times 9 =$ $3 \times 9 =$ $8 \times 9 =$

$0 \times 9 =$ $7 \times 9 =$ $4 \times 9 =$

The rest of the 9s

You need to learn only this part of the nine times table.

$$9 \times 9 = 81$$

This work will help you remember the 9 times table.

Complete these sequences.

| 9 | 18 | 27 | 36 | 45 | 54 | | | | |

$8 \times 9 = 72$ so $9 \times 9 = 72$ plus another 9 =

| 27 | 36 | 45 | | | | | |

| 9 | 18 | 27 | | | | | 72 | | 90 |

| 9 | | 27 | | 45 | | | | |

Look for a pattern in the nine times table.

1	x	9	=	09
2	x	9	=	18
3	x	9	=	27
4	x	9	=	36
5	x	9	=	45
6	x	9	=	54
7	x	9	=	63
8	x	9	=	72
9	x	9	=	81
10	x	9	=	90

Write down any patterns you can see. (There is more than one.)

_____

_____

_____

_____

_____

_____

Practise the 9s

You should know all of the 9 times table now, but how quickly can you remember it?
Ask someone to time you as you do this page.
Be fast and correct.

1 x 9 =	2 x 9 =	9 x 6 =
2 x 9 =	4 x 9 =	3 x 9 =
3 x 9 =	6 x 9 =	9 x 9 =
4 x 9 =	9 x 7 =	9 x 4 =
5 x 9 =	10 x 9 =	1 x 9 =
6 x 9 =	1 x 9 =	9 x 2 =
7 x 9 =	3 x 9 =	7 x 9 =
8 x 9 =	5 x 9 =	0 x 9 =
9 x 9 =	7 x 9 =	9 x 3 =
10 x 9 =	9 x 9 =	5 x 9 =
9 x 1 =	9 x 3 =	9 x 9 =
9 x 2 =	9 x 5 =	2 x 9 =
9 x 3 =	0 x 9 =	8 x 9 =
9 x 4 =	9 x 1 =	4 x 9 =
9 x 5 =	9 x 2 =	9 x 7 =
9 x 6 =	9 x 4 =	10 x 9 =
9 x 7 =	9 x 6 =	9 x 5 =
9 x 8 =	9 x 8 =	9 x 0 =
9 x 9 =	9 x 10 =	9 x 1 =
9 x 10 =	9 x 0 =	6 x 9 =

Speed trials

You should know all of the times tables by now, but how quickly can you remember them?
Ask someone to time you as you do this page.
Be fast and correct.

6 x 8 =	4 x 8 =	8 x 10 =
9 x 10 =	9 x 8 =	7 x 9 =
5 x 8 =	6 x 6 =	8 x 5 =
7 x 5 =	8 x 9 =	8 x 7 =
6 x 4 =	6 x 4 =	7 x 4 =
8 x 8 =	7 x 3 =	4 x 9 =
5 x 10 =	5 x 9 =	6 x 7 =
9 x 8 =	6 x 8 =	4 x 6 =
8 x 3 =	7 x 7 =	7 x 8 =
7 x 7 =	6 x 9 =	6 x 9 =
9 x 5 =	7 x 8 =	10 x 8 =
4 x 8 =	8 x 4 =	6 x 5 =
6 x 7 =	0 x 9 =	8 x 8 =
2 x 9 =	10 x 10 =	7 x 6 =
8 x 4 =	7 x 6 =	6 x 8 =
7 x 10 =	8 x 7 =	9 x 10 =
2 x 8 =	9 x 6 =	8 x 4 =
4 x 7 =	8 x 6 =	7 x 10 =
6 x 9 =	9 x 9 =	5 x 8 =
9 x 9 =	6 x 7 =	8 x 9 =

Times tables for division

Knowing the times tables can also help with division problems. Look at these examples.

3 x 6 = 18 which means that 18 ÷ 3 = 6 and that 18 ÷ 6 = 3
4 x 5 = 20 which means that 20 ÷ 4 = 5 and that 20 ÷ 5 = 4
9 x 3 = 27 which means that 27 ÷ 3 = 9 and that 27 ÷ 9 = 3

Use your knowledge of the times tables to work these division problems.

3 x 8 = 24 which means that 24 ÷ 3 =   and that 24 ÷ 8 =

4 x 7 = 28 which means that 28 ÷ 4 =   and that 28 ÷ 7 =

3 x 5 = 15 which means that 15 ÷ 3 =   and that 15 ÷ 5 =

4 x 3 = 12 which means that 12 ÷ 3 =   and that 12 ÷ 4 =

3 x 10 = 30 which means that 30 ÷ 3 =   and that 30 ÷ 10 =

4 x 8 = 32 which means that 32 ÷ 4 =   and that 32 ÷ 8 =

3 x 9 = 27 which means that 27 ÷ 3 =   and that 27 ÷ 9 =

4 x 10 = 40 which means that 40 ÷ 4 =   and that 40 ÷ 10 =

These division problems help practise the 3 and 4 times tables.

20 ÷ 4 =	15 ÷ 3 =	16 ÷ 4 =
24 ÷ 4 =	27 ÷ 3 =	30 ÷ 3 =
12 ÷ 3 =	18 ÷ 3 =	28 ÷ 4 =
24 ÷ 3 =	32 ÷ 4 =	21 ÷ 3 =

How many fours in 36?	Divide 27 by three.
Divide 28 by 4.	How many threes in 21?
How many fives in 35?	Divide 40 by 5.
Divide 15 by 3.	How many eights in 48?

54

Times tables for division

This page will help you remember times tables by dividing by 2, 3, 4, 5, and 10.

$20 \div 5 =$ 4 $18 \div 3 =$ 6 $60 \div 10 =$ 6

Complete the problems.

$40 \div 10 =$	$14 \div 2 =$	$32 \div 4 =$
$25 \div 5 =$	$21 \div 3 =$	$16 \div 4 =$
$24 \div 4 =$	$28 \div 4 =$	$12 \div 2 =$
$45 \div 5 =$	$35 \div 5 =$	$12 \div 3 =$
$10 \div 2 =$	$40 \div 10 =$	$12 \div 4 =$
$20 \div 10 =$	$20 \div 2 =$	$20 \div 2 =$
$6 \div 2 =$	$18 \div 3 =$	$20 \div 4 =$
$24 \div 3 =$	$32 \div 4 =$	$20 \div 5 =$
$30 \div 5 =$	$40 \div 5 =$	$20 \div 10 =$
$30 \div 10 =$	$80 \div 10 =$	$18 \div 2 =$
$40 \div 5 =$	$6 \div 2 =$	$18 \div 3 =$
$21 \div 3 =$	$15 \div 3 =$	$15 \div 3 =$
$14 \div 2 =$	$24 \div 4 =$	$15 \div 5 =$
$27 \div 3 =$	$15 \div 5 =$	$24 \div 3 =$
$90 \div 10 =$	$10 \div 10 =$	$24 \div 4 =$
$15 \div 5 =$	$4 \div 2 =$	$50 \div 5 =$
$15 \div 3 =$	$9 \div 3 =$	$50 \div 10 =$
$20 \div 5 =$	$4 \div 4 =$	$30 \div 3 =$
$20 \div 4 =$	$10 \div 5 =$	$30 \div 5 =$
$16 \div 2 =$	$100 \div 10 =$	$30 \div 10 =$

Times tables for division

This page will help you remember times tables by dividing by 2, 3, 4, 5, 6, and 10.

30 ÷ 6 = 5   12 ÷ 6 = 2   60 ÷ 10 = 6

Complete the problems.

18 ÷ 6 =   27 ÷ 3 =   48 ÷ 6 =

30 ÷ 10 =   18 ÷ 6 =   35 ÷ 5 =

14 ÷ 2 =   20 ÷ 2 =   36 ÷ 4 =

18 ÷ 3 =   24 ÷ 6 =   24 ÷ 3 =

20 ÷ 4 =   24 ÷ 3 =   20 ÷ 2 =

15 ÷ 5 =   24 ÷ 4 =   30 ÷ 6 =

36 ÷ 6 =   30 ÷ 10 =   25 ÷ 5 =

50 ÷ 10 =   18 ÷ 2 =   32 ÷ 4 =

8 ÷ 2 =   18 ÷ 3 =   27 ÷ 3 =

15 ÷ 3 =   36 ÷ 4 =   16 ÷ 2 =

16 ÷ 4 =   36 ÷ 6 =   42 ÷ 6 =

25 ÷ 5 =   40 ÷ 5 =   5 ÷ 5 =

6 ÷ 6 =   100 ÷ 10 =   4 ÷ 4 =

10 ÷ 10 =   16 ÷ 4 =   28 ÷ 4 =

42 ÷ 6 =   42 ÷ 6 =   14 ÷ 2 =

24 ÷ 4 =   48 ÷ 6 =   24 ÷ 6 =

54 ÷ 6 =   54 ÷ 6 =   18 ÷ 6 =

90 ÷ 10 =   60 ÷ 6 =   54 ÷ 6 =

30 ÷ 6 =   60 ÷ 10 =   60 ÷ 6 =

30 ÷ 5 =   30 ÷ 6 =   40 ÷ 5 =

Times tables for division

This page will help you remember times tables by dividing by 2, 3, 4, 5, 6, and 7.

$14 \div 7 =$ 2 $28 \div 7 =$ 4 $70 \div 7 =$ 10

Complete the problems.

$21 \div 7 =$	$18 \div 6 =$	$49 \div 7 =$
$35 \div 5 =$	$28 \div 7 =$	$35 \div 5 =$
$14 \div 2 =$	$24 \div 6 =$	$35 \div 7 =$
$18 \div 6 =$	$24 \div 4 =$	$24 \div 6 =$
$20 \div 5 =$	$24 \div 2 =$	$21 \div 3 =$
$15 \div 3 =$	$21 \div 7 =$	$70 \div 7 =$
$36 \div 4 =$	$42 \div 7 =$	$42 \div 7 =$
$56 \div 7 =$	$18 \div 3 =$	$32 \div 4 =$
$18 \div 2 =$	$49 \div 7 =$	$27 \div 3 =$
$15 \div 5 =$	$36 \div 4 =$	$16 \div 4 =$
$49 \div 7 =$	$36 \div 6 =$	$42 \div 6 =$
$25 \div 5 =$	$40 \div 5 =$	$45 \div 5 =$
$7 \div 7 =$	$70 \div 7 =$	$40 \div 4 =$
$63 \div 7 =$	$24 \div 3 =$	$24 \div 3 =$
$42 \div 7 =$	$42 \div 6 =$	$14 \div 7 =$
$24 \div 6 =$	$48 \div 6 =$	$24 \div 4 =$
$54 \div 6 =$	$54 \div 6 =$	$18 \div 3 =$
$28 \div 7 =$	$60 \div 6 =$	$56 \div 7 =$
$30 \div 6 =$	$63 \div 7 =$	$63 \div 7 =$
$35 \div 7 =$	$25 \div 5 =$	$48 \div 6 =$

Times tables for division

This page will help you remember times tables by dividing by 2, 3, 4, 5, 6, 7, 8, and 9.

$16 \div 8 =$ 2 $35 \div 7 =$ 5 $27 \div 9 =$ 3

Complete the problems.

$42 \div 6 =$	$81 \div 9 =$	$56 \div 7 =$
$32 \div 8 =$	$56 \div 7 =$	$45 \div 5 =$
$14 \div 7 =$	$72 \div 9 =$	$35 \div 7 =$
$18 \div 9 =$	$24 \div 8 =$	$18 \div 9 =$
$63 \div 7 =$	$27 \div 9 =$	$21 \div 3 =$
$72 \div 9 =$	$72 \div 9 =$	$28 \div 7 =$
$72 \div 8 =$	$42 \div 6 =$	$64 \div 8 =$
$56 \div 7 =$	$27 \div 3 =$	$32 \div 8 =$
$18 \div 6 =$	$14 \div 7 =$	$27 \div 9 =$
$81 \div 9 =$	$36 \div 4 =$	$16 \div 8 =$
$63 \div 9 =$	$36 \div 6 =$	$42 \div 6 =$
$45 \div 5 =$	$48 \div 8 =$	$45 \div 9 =$
$54 \div 9 =$	$21 \div 7 =$	$40 \div 4 =$
$70 \div 7 =$	$24 \div 3 =$	$24 \div 8 =$
$42 \div 7 =$	$40 \div 8 =$	$63 \div 7 =$
$30 \div 5 =$	$45 \div 9 =$	$24 \div 6 =$
$54 \div 6 =$	$54 \div 6 =$	$18 \div 6 =$
$56 \div 8 =$	$42 \div 7 =$	$56 \div 8 =$
$30 \div 5 =$	$63 \div 9 =$	$63 \div 9 =$
$35 \div 7 =$	$50 \div 5 =$	$48 \div 8 =$

Times tables practice grids

This is a times tables grid.

X	3	4	5
7	21	28	35
8	24	32	40

Complete each times tables grid.

X	1	3	5	7	9
2					
3					

X	4	6
6		
7		
8		

X	6	7	8	9	10
3					
4					
5					

X	10	7	8	4
3				
5				
7				

X	6	2	4	7
5				
10				

X	8	7	9	6
9				
7				

Times tables practice grids

Here are more times tables grids.

X	2	4	6
5			
7			

X	8	3	9	2
5				
6				
7				

X	2	3	4	5
8				
9				

X	10	9	8	7
6				
5				
4				

X	3	8
2		
3		
4		
5		
6		
7		

X	2	4	6	8
1				
3				
5				
7				
9				
0				

Times tables practice grids

Here are some other times tables grids.

X	8	9
7		
8		

X	9	8	7	6	5	4
9						
8						
7						

X	2	5	9
4			
7			
8			

X	2	3	4	5	7
4					
6					
8					

X	3	5	7
2			
8			
6			
0			
4			
7			

X	8	7	9	6
7				
9				
0				
10				
8				
6				

Speed trials

Try this final test.

27 ÷ 3 =

7 x 9 =

64 ÷ 8 =

90 ÷ 10 =

6 x 8 =

45 ÷ 9 =

3 x 7 =

9 x 5 =

48 ÷ 6 =

7 x 7 =

3 x 9 =

56 ÷ 8 =

36 ÷ 4 =

24 ÷ 3 =

36 ÷ 9 =

6 x 7 =

4 x 4 =

32 ÷ 8 =

49 ÷ 7 =

25 ÷ 5 =

56 ÷ 7 =

4 x 9 =

18 ÷ 2 =

6 x 8 =

21 ÷ 3 =

9 x 7 =

36 ÷ 4 =

4 x 6 =

45 ÷ 5 =

8 x 5 =

42 ÷ 6 =

7 x 4 =

35 ÷ 7 =

9 x 3 =

24 ÷ 8 =

8 x 2 =

36 ÷ 9 =

6 x 10 =

80 ÷ 10 =

6 x 9 =

16 ÷ 2 =

54 ÷ 9 =

14 ÷ 2 =

9 x 9 =

15 ÷ 3 =

8 x 8 =

24 ÷ 4 =

7 x 8 =

30 ÷ 5 =

6 x 6 =

42 ÷ 6 =

9 x 5 =

49 ÷ 7 =

8 x 6 =

72 ÷ 8 =

9 x 7 =

54 ÷ 9 =

7 x 6 =

10 ÷ 10 =

7 x 7 =

16 ÷ 8 =

7 x 9 =

63 ÷ 7 =

Line of symmetry

If a plane figure is cut into two equal parts, the line of the cut is called a line of symmetry.

Draw as many lines of symmetry as you can find on each of these shapes.

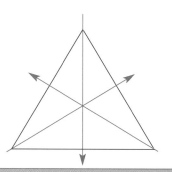

Draw a line of symmetry on each of these shapes.

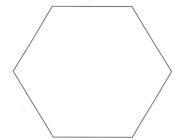

Draw as many lines of symmetry as you can find on each of these shapes.

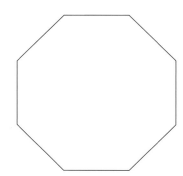

Ordering large numbers

Write these numbers in order, starting with the least.

256	654 327	39 214	147 243	9631
256	*9631*	*39 214*	*147 243*	*654 327*

Write these numbers in order, starting with the least.

72 463	730 241	261	5247	643 292

641 471	260 453	59 372	657 473	4290

327 914	647 212	47 900	3825	416

593 103	761	374 239	91 761	1425

600 200	500 200	5200	50 200	52 000

6437	643	64 370	6430	643 000

9900	999	900 200	920 200	9 200 000

In a country's election
O'Neil got 900 550 votes,
Schneider got 840 690 votes,
Rojas got 8 406 900 votes,
Marsalis got 7 964 201 votes and
Samperi got 859 999 votes.

Place the candidates in order.

1st _____

2nd _____

3rd _____

4th _____

5th _____

64

Rounding whole numbers

Round to the nearest hundred.

873		295		7348		3561	
16 537		4855		569		1200	
22 851		227		782		452	

Round to the nearest ten-thousand.

23 478		418 700		58 397		351 899	
109 544		31 059		67 414		33 500	
89 388		801 821		134 800		45 010	

Round to the nearest ten.

87		397		52		65	
1392		15		12 489		2861	
75		715		34		18 149	

Round to the nearest thousand.

3284		112 810		10 518		83 477	
8499		225 500		4500		6112	
1059		93 606		6752		2550	

Choosing units of measure

Circle the units that are the closest estimate.

The amount of orange juice in a full glass.

6 millilitres   (350 millilitres)   2 litres

Circle the units that are the closest estimate.

The mass of a box of cereal	750 grams	3 kilograms	2 tonnes
The length of a football field	20 centimetres	100 metres	1 kilometre
The area of a rug	20 sq centimetres	30 sq metres	1 sq kilometre
The amount of cough medicine in a bottle	120 millilitres	6 litres	1 litre
The distance from home plate to first base	120 centimetres	30 metres	6 metres
The mass of a package of sugar	2 grams	10 kilograms	1/2 tonne
The length of an airport runway	2 kilometres	50 metres	500 centimetres
The amount of water in a full pail	8 millilitres	2 millilitres	3 litres
The area of a place mat	200 sq centimetres	6 sq metres	1 sq kilometre

Comparing fractions

Which is greater, $\frac{2}{3}$ or $\frac{3}{4}$? $\boxed{\frac{3}{4}}$

The common denominator of 3 and 4 is 12.

So $\frac{2}{3} = \frac{8}{12}$ and $\frac{3}{4} = \frac{9}{12}$

$\frac{3}{4}$ is greater.

Which is greater?

$\frac{1}{4}$ or $\frac{1}{3}$ ___ $\frac{5}{6}$ or $\frac{7}{9}$ ___ $\frac{1}{2}$ or $\frac{5}{8}$ ___ $\frac{4}{9}$ or $\frac{1}{3}$ ___

$\frac{2}{5}$ or $\frac{3}{8}$ ___ $\frac{7}{10}$ or $\frac{8}{9}$ ___ $\frac{8}{10}$ or $\frac{7}{8}$ ___ $\frac{7}{12}$ or $\frac{2}{3}$ ___

$\frac{2}{3}$ or $\frac{5}{8}$ ___ $\frac{4}{15}$ or $\frac{1}{3}$ ___ $\frac{3}{5}$ or $\frac{2}{3}$ ___ $\frac{3}{8}$ or $\frac{1}{4}$ ___

Which two fractions in each row are equal?

$\frac{1}{4}$	$\frac{3}{8}$	$\frac{4}{12}$	$\frac{3}{12}$	$\frac{7}{8}$	$\frac{5}{8}$	
$\frac{5}{8}$	$\frac{6}{9}$	$\frac{7}{10}$	$\frac{8}{12}$	$\frac{1}{2}$	$\frac{3}{4}$	
$\frac{7}{12}$	$\frac{6}{14}$	$\frac{7}{14}$	$\frac{3}{8}$	$\frac{4}{8}$	$\frac{9}{12}$	
$\frac{3}{8}$	$\frac{3}{9}$	$\frac{2}{6}$	$\frac{4}{7}$	$\frac{9}{10}$	$\frac{6}{7}$	
$\frac{3}{10}$	$\frac{5}{15}$	$\frac{2}{10}$	$\frac{3}{15}$	$\frac{4}{10}$	$\frac{7}{15}$	

$\frac{2}{6}$ = $\frac{9}{12}$
=
$\frac{4}{10}$ $\frac{7}{15}$

Put these fractions in order starting with the least.

$\frac{1}{2}$ $\frac{5}{6}$ $\frac{2}{3}$ _____

$\frac{5}{8}$ $\frac{3}{4}$ $\frac{11}{12}$ _____

$\frac{2}{3}$ $\frac{8}{15}$ $\frac{3}{5}$ _____

67

Converting fractions to decimals

Convert these fractions to decimals.

$$\frac{3}{10} = \boxed{0.3}$$

(because the three goes in the tenths column)

$$\frac{7}{100} = \boxed{0.07}$$

(because the seven goes in the hundredths column)

Convert these fractions to decimals.

$\frac{6}{10} =$ ____ $\frac{9}{100} =$ ____ $\frac{4}{100} =$ ____ $\frac{6}{100} =$ ____

$\frac{4}{10} =$ ____ $\frac{2}{10} =$ ____ $\frac{1}{10} =$ ____ $\frac{7}{100} =$ ____

$\frac{8}{100} =$ ____ $\frac{5}{10} =$ ____ $\frac{7}{10} =$ ____ $\frac{8}{10} =$ ____

$\frac{2}{100} =$ ____ $\frac{5}{100} =$ ____ $\frac{1}{100} =$ ____ $\frac{3}{10} =$ ____

Convert $\frac{1}{4}$ to a decimal.

To do this we have to divide the bottom number into the top.

When we run out of numbers we put in the
decimal point and enough zeros to finish the sum.
Be careful to keep the decimal point in your answer
above the decimal point in the sum.

$$\begin{array}{r} 0.25 \\ 4\overline{)1.00} \\ \underline{8} \\ 20 \\ \underline{20} \\ 0 \end{array}$$

Convert these fractions to decimals.

$\frac{1}{2} =$ ____ $\frac{3}{4} =$ ____ $\frac{2}{5} =$ ____ $\frac{1}{5} =$ ____

$\frac{4}{5} =$ ____ $\frac{3}{8} =$ ____ $\frac{3}{5} =$ ____ $\frac{1}{4} =$ ____

Adding fractions

Work out the answer to the problem.

$$\frac{1}{5} + \frac{3}{5} = \boxed{\frac{4}{5}} \qquad\qquad \frac{4}{9} + \frac{2}{9} = \frac{{}^2\cancel{6}}{\cancel{9}_3} = \boxed{\frac{2}{3}}$$

Remember to reduce to simplest form if you need to.

Work out the answer to each sum. Reduce to simplest form if you need to.

$\dfrac{2}{7} + \dfrac{3}{7} = \dfrac{}{7}$
$\qquad \dfrac{2}{9} + \dfrac{5}{9} = \dfrac{}{9}$
$\qquad \dfrac{1}{3} + \dfrac{1}{3} = \dfrac{}{3}$

$\dfrac{3}{10} + \dfrac{4}{10} = \dfrac{}{10}$
$\qquad \dfrac{1}{8} + \dfrac{2}{8} = \dfrac{}{8}$
$\qquad \dfrac{2}{9} + \dfrac{3}{9} = \dfrac{}{9}$

$\dfrac{2}{5} + \dfrac{1}{5} = \dfrac{}{}$
$\qquad \dfrac{1}{7} + \dfrac{5}{7} = \dfrac{}{}$
$\qquad \dfrac{4}{9} + \dfrac{1}{9} = \dfrac{}{9}$

$\dfrac{3}{20} + \dfrac{4}{20} = \dfrac{}{}$
$\qquad \dfrac{3}{100} + \dfrac{8}{100} = \dfrac{}{}$
$\qquad \dfrac{7}{10} + \dfrac{2}{10} = \dfrac{}{}$

$\dfrac{1}{6} + \dfrac{2}{6} = \dfrac{}{} = \dfrac{}{}$
$\qquad \dfrac{31}{100} + \dfrac{19}{100} = \dfrac{}{} = \dfrac{}{}$
$\qquad \dfrac{11}{20} + \dfrac{4}{20} = \dfrac{}{} = \dfrac{}{}$

$\dfrac{3}{10} + \dfrac{3}{10} = \dfrac{}{} = \dfrac{}{}$
$\qquad \dfrac{1}{12} + \dfrac{5}{12} = \dfrac{}{} = \dfrac{}{}$
$\qquad \dfrac{2}{6} + \dfrac{2}{6} = \dfrac{}{} = \dfrac{}{}$

$\dfrac{3}{8} + \dfrac{3}{8} = \dfrac{}{} = \dfrac{}{}$
$\qquad \dfrac{3}{8} + \dfrac{1}{8} = \dfrac{}{} = \dfrac{}{}$
$\qquad \dfrac{5}{12} + \dfrac{3}{12} = \dfrac{}{} = \dfrac{}{}$

$\dfrac{1}{4} + \dfrac{1}{4} = \dfrac{}{} = \dfrac{}{}$
$\qquad \dfrac{3}{20} + \dfrac{2}{20} = \dfrac{}{} = \dfrac{}{}$
$\qquad \dfrac{2}{6} + \dfrac{2}{6} = \dfrac{}{} = \dfrac{}{}$

$\dfrac{2}{7} + \dfrac{4}{7} = \dfrac{}{}$
$\qquad \dfrac{2}{9} + \dfrac{2}{9} = \dfrac{}{}$
$\qquad \dfrac{13}{20} + \dfrac{5}{20} = \dfrac{}{} = \dfrac{}{}$

$\dfrac{81}{100} + \dfrac{9}{100} = \dfrac{}{} = \dfrac{}{}$
$\qquad \dfrac{7}{20} + \dfrac{6}{20} = \dfrac{}{}$
$\qquad \dfrac{3}{8} + \dfrac{2}{8} = \dfrac{}{}$

$\dfrac{6}{10} + \dfrac{2}{10} = \dfrac{}{} = \dfrac{}{}$
$\qquad \dfrac{29}{100} + \dfrac{46}{100} = \dfrac{}{} = \dfrac{}{}$
$\qquad \dfrac{73}{100} + \dfrac{17}{100} = \dfrac{}{} = \dfrac{}{}$

Subtracting fractions

Write the answer to each problem.

$$\frac{4}{5} - \frac{2}{5} = \boxed{\frac{2}{5}} \qquad\qquad \frac{8}{9} - \frac{5}{9} = \frac{\cancel{3}^{1}}{\cancel{9}_{3}} = \boxed{\frac{1}{3}}$$

Reduce to simplest form if you need to.

Write the answer to each problem. Reduce to simplest form if you need to.

$$\frac{3}{5} - \frac{1}{5} = \frac{\boxed{}}{5} \qquad\qquad \frac{6}{7} - \frac{3}{7} = \frac{\boxed{}}{7} \qquad\qquad \frac{9}{10} - \frac{6}{10} = \frac{\boxed{}}{10}$$

$$\frac{7}{10} - \frac{4}{10} = \frac{\boxed{}}{\boxed{}} \qquad\qquad \frac{5}{9} - \frac{4}{9} = \frac{\boxed{}}{\boxed{}} \qquad\qquad \frac{2}{3} - \frac{1}{3} = \frac{\boxed{}}{\boxed{}}$$

$$\frac{7}{8} - \frac{3}{8} = \frac{\boxed{}}{\boxed{}} = \frac{\boxed{}}{\boxed{}} \qquad \frac{14}{20} - \frac{10}{20} = \frac{\boxed{}}{\boxed{}} = \frac{\boxed{}}{\boxed{}} \qquad \frac{5}{6} - \frac{1}{6} = \frac{\boxed{}}{\boxed{}} = \frac{\boxed{}}{\boxed{}}$$

$$\frac{11}{12} - \frac{5}{12} = \frac{\boxed{}}{\boxed{}} = \frac{\boxed{}}{\boxed{}} \qquad \frac{17}{20} - \frac{12}{20} = \frac{\boxed{}}{\boxed{}} = \frac{\boxed{}}{\boxed{}} \qquad \frac{9}{12} - \frac{3}{12} = \frac{\boxed{}}{\boxed{}} = \frac{\boxed{}}{\boxed{}}$$

$$\frac{8}{10} - \frac{6}{10} = \frac{\boxed{}}{\boxed{}} = \frac{\boxed{}}{\boxed{}} \qquad \frac{12}{12} - \frac{2}{12} = \frac{\boxed{}}{\boxed{}} = \frac{\boxed{}}{\boxed{}} \qquad \frac{9}{10} - \frac{3}{10} = \frac{\boxed{}}{\boxed{}} = \frac{\boxed{}}{\boxed{}}$$

$$\frac{8}{9} - \frac{2}{9} = \frac{\boxed{}}{\boxed{}} = \frac{\boxed{}}{\boxed{}} \qquad \frac{7}{8} - \frac{1}{8} = \frac{\boxed{}}{\boxed{}} = \frac{\boxed{}}{\boxed{}} \qquad \frac{9}{12} - \frac{5}{12} = \frac{\boxed{}}{\boxed{}} = \frac{\boxed{}}{\boxed{}}$$

$$\frac{3}{4} - \frac{2}{4} = \frac{\boxed{}}{\boxed{}} \qquad\qquad \frac{6}{8} - \frac{3}{8} = \frac{\boxed{}}{\boxed{}} \qquad\qquad \frac{18}{20} - \frac{8}{20} = \frac{\boxed{}}{\boxed{}} = \frac{\boxed{}}{\boxed{}}$$

$$\frac{4}{6} - \frac{2}{6} = \frac{\boxed{}}{\boxed{}} = \frac{\boxed{}}{\boxed{}} \qquad \frac{5}{12} - \frac{4}{12} = \frac{\boxed{}}{\boxed{}} \qquad\qquad \frac{3}{8} - \frac{2}{8} = \frac{\boxed{}}{\boxed{}}$$

$$\frac{5}{7} - \frac{1}{7} = \frac{\boxed{}}{\boxed{}} \qquad\qquad \frac{5}{16} - \frac{1}{16} = \frac{\boxed{}}{\boxed{}} = \frac{\boxed{}}{\boxed{}} \qquad \frac{90}{100} - \frac{80}{100} = \frac{\boxed{}}{\boxed{}} = \frac{\boxed{}}{\boxed{}}$$

Adding fractions

Write the answer to each problem.

$$\frac{3}{8} + \frac{5}{8} = \boxed{\frac{8}{8}} = 1 \qquad\qquad \frac{3}{4} + \frac{3}{4} = \frac{3\cancel{6}}{\cancel{4}2} = \boxed{\frac{3}{2}} = 1\boxed{\frac{1}{2}}$$

Write the answer to each problem.

$$\frac{7}{10} + \frac{6}{10} = \frac{\ }{10} = 1\frac{\ }{10}$$
$$\frac{6}{7} + \frac{5}{7} = \frac{\ }{7} = 1\frac{\ }{7}$$
$$\frac{2}{3} + \frac{2}{3} = \frac{\ }{3} = 1\frac{\ }{3}$$

$$\frac{5}{10} + \frac{6}{10} = \frac{\ }{\ } = \ \frac{\ }{\ }$$
$$\frac{8}{13} + \frac{5}{13} = \frac{\ }{\ } = \ $$
$$\frac{7}{8} + \frac{4}{8} = \frac{\ }{\ } = \ \frac{\ }{\ }$$

$$\frac{7}{8} + \frac{5}{8} = \frac{\ }{\ } = \frac{\ }{\ } = \ \frac{\ }{\ }$$
$$\frac{2}{5} + \frac{3}{5} = \frac{\ }{\ } = \ $$
$$\frac{5}{8} + \frac{5}{8} = \frac{\ }{\ } = \frac{\ }{\ } = \ \frac{\ }{\ }$$

$$\frac{10}{20} + \frac{15}{20} = \frac{\ }{\ } = \frac{\ }{\ } = \ \frac{\ }{\ }$$
$$\frac{2}{3} + \frac{1}{3} = \frac{\ }{\ } = \ $$
$$\frac{5}{6} + \frac{5}{6} = \frac{\ }{\ } = \frac{\ }{\ } = \ \frac{\ }{\ }$$

$$\frac{5}{6} + \frac{3}{6} = \frac{\ }{\ } = \frac{\ }{\ } = \ \frac{\ }{\ }$$
$$\frac{6}{12} + \frac{7}{12} = \frac{\ }{\ } = \ \frac{\ }{\ }$$
$$\frac{8}{10} + \frac{6}{10} = \frac{\ }{\ } = \frac{\ }{\ } = \ \frac{\ }{\ }$$

$$\frac{12}{20} + \frac{10}{20} = \frac{\ }{\ } = \frac{\ }{\ } = \ \frac{\ }{\ }$$
$$\frac{3}{10} + \frac{7}{10} = \frac{\ }{\ } = \ $$
$$\frac{75}{100} + \frac{75}{100} = \frac{\ }{\ } = \frac{\ }{\ } = \ \frac{\ }{\ }$$

$$\frac{10}{20} + \frac{16}{20} = \frac{\ }{\ } = \frac{\ }{\ } = \ \frac{\ }{\ }$$
$$\frac{4}{5} + \frac{4}{5} = \frac{\ }{\ } = \ \frac{\ }{\ }$$
$$\frac{11}{21} + \frac{17}{21} = \frac{\ }{\ } = \frac{\ }{\ } = \ \frac{\ }{\ }$$

Adding fractions

Write the answer to each problem.

$$\frac{2}{3} + \frac{1}{6} = \frac{4}{6} + \frac{1}{6} = \frac{5}{6}$$

$$\frac{3}{4} + \frac{5}{6} = \frac{9}{12} + \frac{10}{12} = \frac{19}{12} = 1\frac{7}{12}$$

Work out the answer to each problem. Rename as a mixed number if you need to.

$$\frac{2}{5} + \frac{7}{10} = \frac{\ }{\ } + \frac{\ }{\ } = \frac{\ }{\ } = \square \frac{\ }{\ }$$

$$\frac{3}{4} + \frac{7}{10} = \frac{\ }{\ } + \frac{\ }{\ } = \frac{\ }{\ } = \square \frac{\ }{\ }$$

$$\frac{1}{4} + \frac{5}{6} = \frac{\ }{\ } + \frac{\ }{\ } = \frac{\ }{\ } = \square \frac{\ }{\ }$$

$$\frac{3}{4} + \frac{7}{8} = \frac{\ }{\ } + \frac{\ }{\ } = \frac{\ }{\ } = \square \frac{\ }{\ }$$

$$\frac{2}{3} + \frac{1}{4} = \frac{\ }{\ } + \frac{\ }{\ } = \frac{\ }{\ }$$

$$\frac{5}{6} + \frac{11}{12} = \frac{\ }{\ } + \frac{\ }{\ } = \frac{\ }{\ } = \square \frac{\ }{\ }$$

$$\frac{5}{7} + \frac{3}{14} = \frac{\ }{\ } + \frac{\ }{\ } = \frac{\ }{\ }$$

$$\frac{5}{8} + \frac{7}{10} = \frac{\ }{\ } + \frac{\ }{\ } = \frac{\ }{\ } = \square \frac{\ }{\ }$$

$$\frac{3}{4} + \frac{3}{5} = \frac{\ }{\ } + \frac{\ }{\ } = \frac{\ }{\ } = \square \frac{\ }{\ }$$

$$\frac{1}{2} + \frac{5}{9} = \frac{\ }{\ } + \frac{\ }{\ } = \frac{\ }{\ } = \square \frac{\ }{\ }$$

$$\frac{2}{3} + \frac{7}{9} = \frac{\ }{\ } + \frac{\ }{\ } = \frac{\ }{\ } = \square \frac{\ }{\ }$$

$$\frac{1}{3} + \frac{7}{8} = \frac{\ }{\ } + \frac{\ }{\ } = \frac{\ }{\ } = \square \frac{\ }{\ }$$

$$\frac{3}{8} + \frac{1}{6} = \frac{\ }{\ } + \frac{\ }{\ } = \frac{\ }{\ }$$

$$\frac{2}{3} + \frac{4}{5} = \frac{\ }{\ } + \frac{\ }{\ } = \frac{\ }{\ } = \square \frac{\ }{\ }$$

$$\frac{4}{5} + \frac{5}{6} = \frac{\ }{\ } + \frac{\ }{\ } = \frac{\ }{\ } = \square \frac{\ }{\ }$$

$$\frac{2}{3} + \frac{3}{10} = \frac{\ }{\ } + \frac{\ }{\ } = \frac{\ }{\ }$$

Subtracting fractions

Work out the answer to the problems.

$$\frac{7}{9} - \frac{1}{3} = \frac{7}{9} - \frac{3}{9} = \frac{4}{9}$$

$$\frac{7}{10} - \frac{3}{8} = \frac{28}{40} - \frac{15}{40} = \frac{13}{40}$$

Work out the answer to each problem. Reduce to the simplest form if you need to.

$$\frac{5}{8} - \frac{1}{2} = \underline{} - \underline{} = \underline{}$$

$$\frac{5}{6} - \frac{1}{4} = \underline{} - \underline{} = \underline{}$$

$$\frac{9}{10} - \frac{3}{8} = \underline{} - \underline{} = \underline{}$$

$$\frac{9}{10} - \frac{5}{8} = \underline{} - \underline{} = \underline{}$$

$$\frac{6}{7} - \frac{2}{5} = \underline{} - \underline{} = \underline{}$$

$$\frac{11}{12} - \frac{1}{6} = \underline{} - \underline{} = \underline{} = \underline{}$$

$$\frac{7}{12} - \frac{1}{6} = \underline{} - \underline{} = \underline{}$$

$$\frac{7}{10} - \frac{1}{4} = \underline{} - \underline{} = \underline{} = \underline{}$$

$$\frac{5}{9} - \frac{1}{3} = \underline{} - \underline{} = \underline{}$$

$$\frac{7}{9} - \frac{1}{4} = \underline{} - \underline{} = \underline{}$$

$$\frac{7}{16} - \frac{1}{8} = \underline{} - \underline{} = \underline{}$$

$$\frac{3}{7} - \frac{1}{5} = \underline{} - \underline{} = \underline{}$$

$$\frac{3}{8} - \frac{1}{6} = \underline{} - \underline{} = \underline{}$$

$$\frac{3}{5} - \frac{1}{4} = \underline{} - \underline{} = \underline{}$$

$$\frac{2}{3} - \frac{1}{2} = \underline{} - \underline{} = \underline{}$$

$$\frac{4}{5} - \frac{1}{4} = \underline{} - \underline{} = \underline{}$$

Adding mixed numbers

Work out the answer to each problem.

$$8\frac{10}{30} + 1\frac{3}{30} = \boxed{9\frac{13}{30}} = \boxed{9\frac{13}{30}}$$

$$3\frac{1}{4} + 1\frac{1}{6} = \boxed{3\frac{3}{12}} = \boxed{1\frac{1}{12}} = \boxed{4\frac{5}{12}}$$

Work out the answer to each problem.

$$2\frac{1}{8} + 3\frac{3}{8} = \boxed{} = \boxed{}$$

$$3\frac{5}{6} + 1\frac{1}{8} = \boxed{} + \boxed{} = \boxed{}$$

$$3\frac{3}{4} + 2\frac{1}{16} = \boxed{} + \boxed{} = \boxed{}$$

$$1\frac{2}{3} + 3\frac{2}{7} = \boxed{} + \boxed{} = \boxed{}$$

$$4\frac{1}{4} + 2\frac{1}{6} = \boxed{} + \boxed{} = \boxed{}$$

$$6\frac{1}{6} + 3\frac{2}{9} = \boxed{} + \boxed{} = \boxed{}$$

$$7\frac{5}{6} + 2\frac{1}{10} = \boxed{} + \boxed{} = \boxed{} = \boxed{}$$

$$1\frac{7}{12} + 4\frac{1}{12} = \boxed{} = \boxed{}$$

$$5\frac{1}{4} + 3\frac{2}{5} = \boxed{} + \boxed{} = \boxed{} = \boxed{}$$

$$3\frac{3}{8} + 1\frac{1}{4} = \boxed{} + \boxed{} = \boxed{}$$

$$6\frac{1}{4} + 2\frac{1}{4} = \boxed{} = \boxed{}$$

$$6\frac{2}{3} + 3\frac{1}{10} = \boxed{} + \boxed{} = \boxed{}$$

$$7\frac{1}{3} + 1\frac{2}{9} = \boxed{} + \boxed{} = \boxed{}$$

$$2\frac{2}{5} + 1\frac{3}{10} = \boxed{} + \boxed{} = \boxed{}$$

Subtracting mixed numbers

Work out the answer to the problems.

$$2\frac{7}{8} - 1\frac{5}{8} = \boxed{1\frac{2}{8}} = 1\frac{1}{4} \qquad\qquad 9\frac{9}{10} - 6\frac{5}{8} = \boxed{9\frac{36}{40}} - \boxed{6\frac{25}{40}} = \boxed{3\frac{11}{40}}$$

Work out the answer to each problem.

$$7\frac{3}{8} - 3\frac{1}{8} = \boxed{} = \boxed{} \qquad\qquad 2\frac{14}{15} - 1\frac{4}{9} = \boxed{} - \boxed{} = \boxed{}$$

$$2\frac{2}{3} - 1\frac{1}{6} = \boxed{} - \boxed{} = \boxed{} = \boxed{} \qquad\qquad 6\frac{4}{5} - 2\frac{1}{2} = \boxed{} - \boxed{} = \boxed{}$$

$$5\frac{11}{20} - 2\frac{1}{8} = \boxed{} - \boxed{} = \boxed{} \qquad\qquad 8\frac{11}{12} - 5\frac{5}{12} = \boxed{} = \boxed{}$$

$$9\frac{7}{9} - 3\frac{4}{6} = \boxed{} - \boxed{} = \boxed{} = \boxed{} \qquad\qquad 4\frac{7}{8} - 2\frac{1}{4} = \boxed{} - \boxed{} = \boxed{}$$

$$8\frac{2}{5} - 4\frac{1}{4} = \boxed{} - \boxed{} = \boxed{} \qquad\qquad 4\frac{5}{6} - 3\frac{1}{4} = \boxed{} - \boxed{} = \boxed{}$$

$$4\frac{2}{3} - 1\frac{2}{3} = \boxed{} = \boxed{} \qquad\qquad 9\frac{8}{9} - 3\frac{3}{4} = \boxed{} - \boxed{} = \boxed{}$$

$$3\frac{8}{15} - 2\frac{2}{5} = \boxed{} - \boxed{} = \boxed{} \qquad\qquad 2\frac{7}{9} - 1\frac{1}{5} = \boxed{} - \boxed{} = \boxed{}$$

Adding mixed numbers and fractions

Work out the answer to the problems.

$4\frac{3}{4} + \frac{3}{4} = 4\frac{6}{4} = 5\frac{2}{4} = 5\frac{1}{2}$

$3\frac{1}{2} + \frac{2}{3} = 3\frac{3}{6} + \frac{4}{6} = 3\frac{7}{6} = 4\frac{1}{6}$

Work out the answer to each problem.

$6\frac{2}{3} + \frac{2}{3} = \boxed{} = \boxed{}$

$4\frac{1}{4} + \frac{7}{8} = \boxed{} + \boxed{} = \boxed{} = \boxed{}$

$4\frac{5}{8} + \frac{7}{8} = \boxed{} = \boxed{}$

$3\frac{7}{10} + \frac{1}{2} = \boxed{} + \boxed{} = \boxed{} = \boxed{}$

$2\frac{3}{7} + \frac{8}{7} = \boxed{} = \boxed{}$

$1\frac{1}{2} + \frac{3}{4} = \boxed{} + \boxed{} = \boxed{} = \boxed{}$

$3\frac{5}{6} + \frac{2}{3} = \boxed{} + \boxed{} = \boxed{} = \boxed{}$

$5\frac{3}{4} + \frac{4}{5} = \boxed{} + \boxed{} = \boxed{} = \boxed{}$

$3\frac{7}{8} + \frac{1}{4} = \boxed{} + \boxed{} = \boxed{} = \boxed{}$

$3\frac{6}{7} + \frac{3}{4} = \boxed{} + \boxed{} = \boxed{} = \boxed{}$

$7\frac{7}{8} + \frac{1}{4} = \boxed{} + \boxed{} = \boxed{} = \boxed{}$

$4\frac{2}{3} + \frac{5}{8} = \boxed{} + \boxed{} = \boxed{} = \boxed{}$

$1\frac{9}{10} + \frac{2}{5} = \boxed{} + \boxed{} = \boxed{} = \boxed{}$

$8\frac{5}{6} + \frac{3}{5} = \boxed{} + \boxed{} = \boxed{} = \boxed{}$

Simple use of parentheses

Work out these problems.

$(4 + 6) - (2 + 1) =$ $10 - 3 = 7$

$(2 \times 5) + (10 - 4) =$ $10 + 6 = 16$

Remember to work out the parentheses first.

Work out these problems.

$(5 + 3) + (6 - 2) =$ $(3 - 1) + (12 - 1) =$

$(6 - 1) - (1 + 2) =$ $(9 + 5) - (3 + 6) =$

$(8 + 3) + (12 - 2) =$ $(14 + 12) - (9 + 4) =$

$(7 - 2) + (4 + 5) =$ $(9 - 3) - (4 + 2) =$

Now try these longer problems.

$(5 + 9) + (12 - 2) - (4 + 3) =$

$(10 + 5) - (2 + 4) + (9 + 6) =$

$(19 + 4) - (3 + 2) - (2 + 1) =$

$(24 - 5) - (3 + 7) - (5 - 2) =$

$(15 + 3) + (7 - 2) - (5 + 7) =$

Now try these. Be careful, the parentheses now have multiplication problems.

$(2 \times 3) + (5 \times 2) =$ $(3 \times 4) - (2 \times 2) =$

$(7 \times 2) + (3 \times 3) =$ $(5 \times 4) - (3 \times 2) =$

$(6 \times 4) - (4 \times 3) =$ $(9 \times 5) - (4 \times 6) =$

$(12 \times 4) - (8 \times 3) =$ $(7 \times 4) - (8 \times 2) =$

If the answer is 24, which of these problems gives the correct answer? Write the correct letter.

a $(3 + 5) + (3 \times 1)$ c $(3 \times 5) + (3 \times 3)$ e $(5 \times 7) - (2 \times 5)$

b $(3 \times 5) + (3 \times 2)$ d $(2 \times 5) + (2 \times 6)$ f $(6 + 7) + (12 - 2)$

Simple use of parentheses

Work out these problems.

$(7 + 3) \quad \times \quad (8 - 4) =$ $(5 - 2) \quad \times \quad (8 - 1) =$

$(9 + 5) \quad \div \quad (1 + 6) =$ $(14 - 6) \quad \times \quad (4 + 3) =$

$(14 + 4) \div (12 - 6) =$ $(9 + 21) \div (8 - 5) \quad =$

$(11 - 5) \quad \times \quad (7 + 5) =$ $(8 + 20) \div (12 - 10) =$

$(6 + 9) \quad \div \quad (8 - 3) \quad =$ $(14 - 3) \quad \times \quad (6 + 1) =$

$(10 + 10) \div (2 + 3) =$ $(9 + 3) \quad \times \quad (2 + 4) =$

Now try these.

$(4 \times 3) \quad \div \quad (1 \times 2) =$ $(5 \times 4) \quad \div \quad (2 \times 2) =$

$(8 \times 5) \quad \div \quad (4 \times 1) =$ $(6 \times 4) \quad \div \quad (3 \times 4) =$

$(2 \times 4) \quad \times \quad (2 \times 3) =$ $(3 \times 5) \quad \times \quad (1 \times 2) =$

$(8 \times 4) \quad \div \quad (2 \times 2) =$ $(6 \times 4) \quad \div \quad (4 \times 2) =$

If the answer is 30, which of these problems gives the correct answer?

a $(3 \times 5) \times (2 \times 2)$ d $(20 \div 2) \times (12 \div 3)$

b $(4 \times 5) \times (5 \times 2)$ e $(5 \times 12) \div (2 \times 5)$

c $(12 \times 5) \div (8 \div 4)$ f $(9 \times 5) \div (10 \div 2)$

If the answer is 8, which of these problems gives the correct answer?

a $(16 \div 2) \div (2 \times 1)$ d $(24 \div 6) \times (8 \div 4)$

b $(9 \div 3) \times (3 \times 2)$ e $(8 \div 4) \times (8 \div 1)$

c $(12 \times 4) \div (6 \times 2)$ f $(16 \div 4) \times (20 \div 4)$

Simple use of parentheses

Work out these problems.

$(5 + 3) + (9 - 2) =$ $8 + 7 = 15$

$(5 + 2) - (4 - 1) =$ $7 - 3 = 4$

$(4 + 2) \times (3 + 1) =$ $6 \times 4 = 24$

$(3 \times 5) \div (9 - 6) =$ $15 \div 3 = 5$

Remember to work out the parentheses first.

Work out these problems.

$(5 + 4) + (7 - 3) =$ $(9 - 2) + (6 + 4) =$

$(7 + 3) - (9 - 7) =$ $(15 - 5) + (2 + 3) =$

$(11 \times 2) - (3 \times 2) =$ $(15 \div 3) + (9 \times 2) =$

$(12 \times 2) - (3 \times 3) =$ $(6 \div 2) + (8 \times 2) =$

$(9 \times 3) - (7 \times 3) =$ $(15 \div 5) + (3 \times 4) =$

$(20 \div 5) - (8 \div 2) =$ $(5 \times 10) - (12 \times 4) =$

Now try these.

$(4 + 8) \div (3 \times 2) =$ $(6 \times 4) \div (3 \times 2) =$

$(9 + 5) \div (2 \times 1) =$ $(7 \times 4) \div (3 + 4) =$

$(3 + 6) \times (3 \times 3) =$ $(5 \times 5) \div (10 \div 2) =$

$(24 \div 2) \times (3 \times 2) =$ $(8 \times 6) \div (2 \times 12) =$

Write down the letters of all the problems that make 25.

a $(2 \times 5) \times (3 \times 2)$ d $(40 \div 2) + (10 \div 2)$

b $(5 \times 5) + (7 - 2)$ e $(10 \times 5) - (5 \times 5)$

c $(6 \times 5) - (10 \div 2)$ f $(10 \times 10) \div (10 - 6)$

Write down the letters of all the problems that make 20.

a $(10 \div 2) \times (4 \div 4)$ d $(20 \div 4) \times (8 + 2)$

b $(7 \times 3) - (3 \div 3)$ e $(10 \div 2) + (20 \div 2)$

c $(8 \times 4) - (6 \times 2)$ f $(14 \div 2) + (2 \times 7)$

Multiplying decimals

Work out these problems.

```
    1              4              3
   4.6            3.9            8.4
 x   3          x   5          x   8
 ┌──────┐      ┌──────┐      ┌──────┐
 │ 13.8 │      │ 19.5 │      │ 67.2 │
 └──────┘      └──────┘      └──────┘
```

Work out these problems.

```
    4.7            9.1            5.8            1.7            5.1
 x    3         x    3         x    3         x    2         x    2
 ────────       ────────       ────────       ────────       ────────


    7.4            3.6            6.5            4.2            3.8
 x    2         x    4         x    4         x    2         x    2
 ────────       ────────       ────────       ────────       ────────


    4.2            4.7            1.8            3.4            3.7
 x    4         x    4         x    5         x    5         x    5
 ────────       ────────       ────────       ────────       ────────


    2.5            2.4            5.3            7.2            5.1
 x    5         x    6         x    7         x    8         x    9
 ────────       ────────       ────────       ────────       ────────


    7.9            8.6            8.8            7.5            9.9
 x    9         x    9         x    8         x    8         x    6
 ────────       ────────       ────────       ────────       ────────


    6.8            5.7            6.9            7.5            8.4
 x    7         x    6         x    7         x    9         x    9
 ────────       ────────       ────────       ────────       ────────


    7.3            2.8            3.8            7.7            9.4
 x    8         x    7         x    8         x    7         x    9
 ────────       ────────       ────────       ────────       ────────
```

Multiplying decimals

Work out these problems.

11		31		42	
37.5		26.2		65.3	
x 2		x 5		x 9	
75.0		131.0		587.7	

Work out these problems.

53.3	93.2	51.4	34.6	35.2
x 2	x 2	x 2	x 3	x 3

46.5	25.8	16.4	47.1	37.4
x 4	x 4	x 3	x 5	x 5

12.4	46.3	17.5	36.5	72.4
x 5	x 5	x 6	x 6	x 7

37.5	20.3	73.4	92.6	47.9
x 7	x 7	x 7	x 6	x 6

53.9	75.6	28.8	79.4	99.9
x 8	x 8	x 8	x 8	x 9

37.9	14.8	35.4	46.8	27.2
x 9	x 9	x 9	x 8	x 7

39.5	84.2	68.5	73.2	47.6
x 6	x 9	x 8	x 9	x 6

Real-life problems

Carlos earns $3.50 a day on his paper route. How much does he earn per week?

$24.50

$$\begin{array}{r} {\scriptstyle 3} \\ \$3.50 \\ \times \quad 7 \\ \hline \$24.50 \end{array}$$

When Chanté subtracts the width of her closet from the length of her bedroom wall she finds she has 3.65 m of wall space left. If the closet is 0.87 m wide, what is the length of her bedroom wall?

4.52 m

$$\begin{array}{r} {\scriptstyle 1\ 1} \\ 3.65 \\ + \ 0.87 \\ \hline 4.52 \end{array}$$

Sophie buys her mother a bunch of flowers for $12.95 and her brothers some candy for $2.76. If she has $7.83 left, how much did she start with?

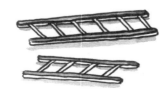

If Pedro were 7.5 cm taller, he would be twice as tall as Ian. Ian is 74.25 cm tall, so how tall is Pedro?

Sasha is making some shelves which are 75.5 cm long. If the wood she is using is 180 cm long, how many pieces will she need to make six shelves?

A café uses 27.5 litres of milk a day. If they have a weekly delivery of 180 litres, how much will they have left after six days?

Charles has 12.5 m of railway track. Gavin has 8.6 m and Kristy has 4.8 m. If they put their track together how long will their layout be?

Real-life problems

A novelist writes 9.5 pages of his book a day.
How many pages will he write in nine days?

85.5 pages

$$\begin{array}{r} {}^{4} \\ 9.5 \\ \times \quad 9 \\ \hline 85.5 \end{array}$$

After driving 147.7 km a driver stops at a service
station. If he has another 115.4 km to go, how long
will his trip be?

263.1 km

$$\begin{array}{r} {}^{1\,1} \\ 147.7 \\ + \ 115.4 \\ \hline 263.1 \end{array}$$

Mr. Mayfield divides his money equally
among four separate banks. If he has $98.65
in each bank, what is the total of his savings?

Mrs. Eldon buys two bottles of perfume; one contains
48.5 ml and the other contains 150.5 ml. How much
more perfume is in the larger of the two bottles?

A teacher spends 5.75 minutes grading
each story. How long would it take to
grade eight stories?

Eight tiles, each 15.75 cm wide, fit exactly
across the width of the bathroom wall. How
wide is the bathroom wall?

Terry has $8.50. If he spends $1.05 a day
over the next seven days, how much will he
have left at the end of the seven days?

A shop sells 427.56 kg of loose peanuts the
first week and 246.94 kg the second week.
How much did they sell over the two weeks?

Real-life problems

In a class of 30 children, 6 children are painting. What percent of children are painting?

$\frac{6}{30}$ of the children are painting and to change a fraction to a percent we multiply by 100.

20%

$$\frac{\cancel{6}^{1}}{\cancel{30}_{1}} \times \cancel{100}^{20} = 20$$

40% of a class is made up of girls. If there are 12 girls, how many children are in the class?

If 12 girls are 40% of the class, we divide 12 by 40 to find 1%. Then we multiply by 100 to find 100%.

30 children

$$\frac{\cancel{12}^{3}}{\cancel{40}_{10}} \times \cancel{100}^{10} = 30$$

A shop has 60 books by a new author. If the shop sells 45 books, what percent does it sell?

A school disco sells 65% of its tickets. If it had 120 tickets to start with, how many has it sold?

A school disco sells 65% of its tickets. If it had 120 tickets to start with, how many has it sold?

200 people go on a school trip. If 14% are adults, how many children go on the trip?

A shop sells 150 T-shirts but 12 are returned because they are faulty. What percent of the T-shirts was faulty?

A group of 120 children are asked their favourite colours.

15% like red. How many children like red?

20% like green. How many children like green?

30% like yellow. How many children like yellow?

35% like blue. How many children like blue?

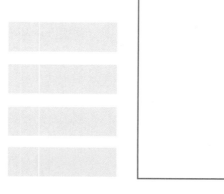

Conversions: length

Units of length	
10 millimetres	1 centimetre
1000 millimetres	1 metre
100 centimetres	1 metre
1000 metres	1 kilometre

This conversion table shows how to convert millimetres, centimetres, metres, and kilometres.

Brian's rope is 600 centimetres long. How many metres long is it?

600 ÷ 100 = 6   6 metres

Neilika's rope is 3 metres long. How many millimetres long is it?

3 x 100 = 300   300 centimetres long
300 x 10 = 3000   3000 millimetres long

Convert each measurement to centimetres.

10 millimetres	200 millimetres	48 millimetres	72 millimetres

Convert each measurement to metres.

600 centimetres	1200 centimetres	270 centimetres	3600 centimetres

Convert each measurement to millimetres.

4 centimetres	12 centimetres	8 centimetres	5 centimetres

Convert each measurement to centimetres.

6 metres	2 metres	7 metres	5 metres

Convert each measurement.

4 metres	5 kilometres	4 metres	1 kilometre
centimetres	metres	centimetres	centimetres

5840 centimetres	31 680 centimetres	1760 metres	352 metres
metres	kilometres	kilometres	kilometres

Conversions: capacity

Units of capacity	
1000 millilitres	1 litre

This conversion table shows how to convert millilitres and litres.

Katya's thermos holds 8 litres. How many millilitres does it hold?

Hannah's thermos holds 60 000 millilitres. How many litres does it hold?

| $8 \times 1000 = 8000$ | 8000 millilitres | | $60\ 000 \div 1000 = 60$ | 60 litres |

Convert each measurement to litres.

32 000 millilitres	16 000 millilitres	9600 millilitres	8000 millilitres

Convert each measurement to millilitres.

6 litres	12 litres	36 litres	50 litres

4 litres	12 litres	30 litres	16 litres

Convert each measurement to litres.

14 000 millilitres	32 000 millilitres	100 000 millilitres	20 000 millilitres

Convert each measurement.

3000 millilitres	5 litres	36 000 millilitres	72 litres
litres	millilitres	litres	millilitres

1 litre	24 000 millilitres	7 litres	11 000 millilitres
millilitres	litres	millilitres	litres

Fraction of a number

Work out to find the fraction of the number. Write the answer in the box.

$\frac{1}{6}$ of 42

$\frac{1}{6}$ x 42 = $\frac{42}{6}$ = 7

1 x 7 = 7

So, $\frac{1}{6}$ of 42 = 7

$\frac{3}{5}$ of 35

$\frac{1}{5}$ x 35 = $\frac{35}{5}$ = 7

3 x 7 = 21

So, $\frac{3}{5}$ of 35 = 21

$\frac{1}{4}$ of 100 = $\frac{100}{4}$ = 25

$\frac{1}{3}$ of 69 = $\frac{69}{3}$ = 23

Work out to find the fraction of the number. Write the answer in the box.

$\frac{1}{8}$ of 72 $\frac{1}{5}$ of 250 $\frac{1}{2}$ of 38

$\frac{1}{9}$ of 54 $\frac{1}{2}$ of 84 $\frac{1}{6}$ of 72

$\frac{1}{4}$ of 52 $\frac{1}{7}$ of 140 $\frac{1}{3}$ of 36

$\frac{1}{5}$ of 175 $\frac{1}{8}$ of 64 $\frac{1}{4}$ of 100

$\frac{1}{6}$ of 300 $\frac{1}{9}$ of 81 $\frac{1}{2}$ of 114

$\frac{1}{10}$ of 100 $\frac{1}{5}$ of 55 $\frac{1}{7}$ of 140

$\frac{3}{4}$ of 100 $\frac{2}{3}$ of 75 $\frac{4}{7}$ of 42

$\frac{2}{5}$ of 25 $\frac{5}{8}$ of 40 $\frac{2}{3}$ of 27

$\frac{5}{9}$ of 36 $\frac{2}{3}$ of 225 $\frac{5}{6}$ of 120

$\frac{3}{4}$ of 56 $\frac{5}{7}$ of 133 $\frac{2}{3}$ of 180

$\frac{4}{5}$ of 100 $\frac{2}{10}$ of 100 $\frac{3}{8}$ of 64

$\frac{2}{3}$ of 210 $\frac{4}{9}$ of 90 $\frac{7}{8}$ of 72

Showing decimals

Write the decimals on the number line.

0.4, 0.5, 0.6, 0.8, 0.9, 0.25, 0.45, 0.63

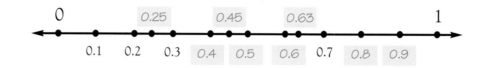

Write the decimals on the number line.

0.56, 0.2, 0.87, 0.45, 0.98, 0.6, 0.1

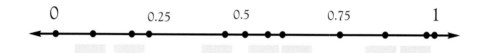

Write the decimals on the number line.

1.41, 1.8, 1.3, 1.98, 1.68, 1.2

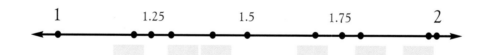

Write these decimals on the number line.

2.5, 3.75, 2.25, 3.1, 3.68, 4.2

Area of right-angled triangles

Find the area of this right-angled triangle.

Because the area of this triangle is
half the area of the rectangle shown,
we can find the area of the rectangle and
then divide it by two to find the area
of the triangle.
So the area = (8 cm x 4 cm) ÷ 2
= 32 cm² ÷ 2 = 16 cm²

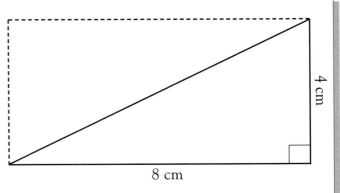

Area = 16 cm²

Find the area of these right-angled triangles.

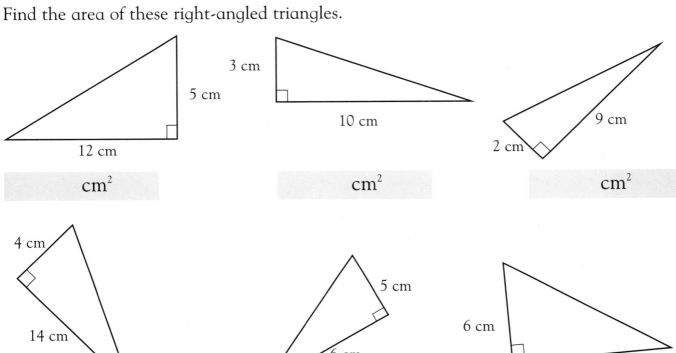

cm²   cm²   cm²

cm²   cm²   cm²

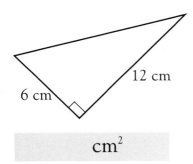
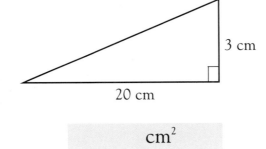
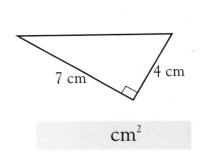

cm²   cm²   cm²

Speed problems

How long would it take to travel
120 km at 8 km/h?
(Time = Distance ÷ Speed)

15 hours

If a bus takes 3 hours to travel 150 km,
how fast is it going?
(Speed = Distance ÷ Time)

50 km/h

If a car travels at 60 km/h for 2 hours,
how far has it gone?
(Distance = Speed × Time)

120 km

$$\begin{array}{r} 60 \\ \times\ 2 \\ \hline 120 \end{array}$$

If a man walks for 6 kilometres at a
steady speed of 3 km/h, how long will
it take him?

A truck driver travels 120 km in 3 hours.
If he drove at a steady speed, how fast
was he going?

A car travels at a steady speed of 40 km/h.
How far will it travel in 4 hours?

Shane walks 10 km at 4 km/h. Damien
walks 12 km at 5 km/h. Which of them will
take the longest?

Courtney drives for 30 minutes at 50 km/h
and for 1 hour at 40 km/h. How far has he
travelled altogether?

A racing car travels 340 km in 120
minutes. What speed is it travelling at?

Conversion tables

Draw a table to convert dollars to cents.

$	cents
1	100
2	200
3	300

Complete the conversion chart below.

Weeks	Days
1	7
2	
	28
10	70

If there are 60 minutes in 1 hour, make a conversion chart for up to 10 hours.

Hours	Minutes

Reading bar graphs

Look at this graph.

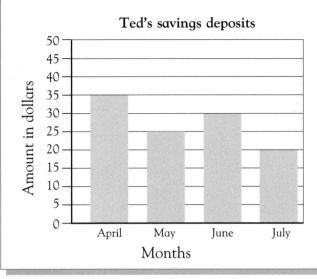

In which month did Ted save $25?

May

How much more money did Ted save in June than in July?

$10

Look at this graph.

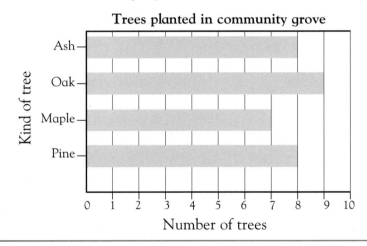

How many maple trees were planted?

The same number of ash trees were planted as what other kind of tree?

How many more oak trees were planted than maple trees?

Look at this graph.

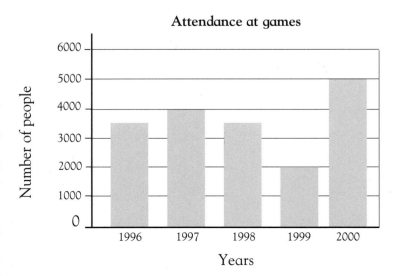

In which year did 4000 people attend the games?

How many more people attend the games in 2000 than in 1997?

The biggest increase in attendance was between which years?

Expanded form

What is the value of 3 in 2308?   *300*

Write 32 084 in expanded form.   *30 000 + 2000 + 80 + 4*

What is the value of 6 in these numbers?

26		162		36 904	
12 612		6130		567 902	
13 036		9764		17 632	

What is the value of 4 in these numbers?

14 300		942		8764	
10 408		1043		45 987	
6045		804 001		694	

Circle the numbers that have a 7 with the value of seventy thousand.

| 457 682 | 67 924 | 870 234 | 372 987 |
| 171 345 | 767 707 | 79 835 | 16 757 |

Write the numbers in expanded form.

34 897

508 061

50 810

8945

60 098

Cubes of small numbers

What is 2^3?

$2 \times 2 \times 2 = 8$

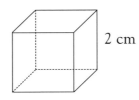 2 cm

What is the volume of this cube?

$2 \text{ cm} \times 2 \text{ cm} \times 2 \text{ cm} = 8 \text{ cm}^3$

You find the volume of a cube in the same way you work out the cube of a number.

Use extra paper here if you need to. What is...

3^3

4^3

6^3

5^3

1^3

2^3

What are the volumes of these cubes?

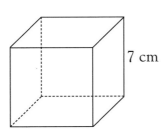 7 cm

cm^3

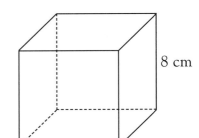 8 cm

cm^3

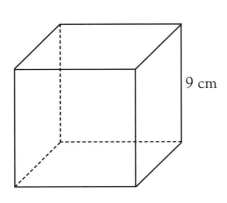 9 cm

cm^3

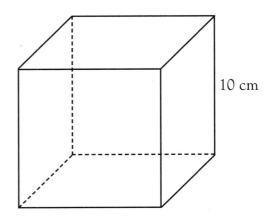 10 cm

cm^3

Multiplying fractions

Write the product.

$$\frac{3}{\underset{2}{8}} \times \frac{\overset{1}{4}}{7} = \boxed{\frac{3}{14}} \qquad \overset{1}{5} \times \frac{3}{\underset{2}{10}} = \boxed{\frac{3}{2} = 1\frac{1}{2}}$$

Write the product.

$\frac{1}{4} \times \frac{1}{4} = \boxed{}$ 　　　$\frac{3}{10} \times \frac{2}{6} = \boxed{}$ 　　　$6 \times \frac{3}{4} = \boxed{} = \boxed{}$

$8 \times \frac{1}{4} = \boxed{}$ 　　　$\frac{2}{5} \times \frac{5}{7} = \boxed{}$ 　　　$\frac{2}{5} \times \frac{5}{6} = \boxed{}$

$\frac{2}{5} \times \frac{2}{3} = \boxed{}$ 　　　$4 \times \frac{3}{16} = \boxed{}$ 　　　$\frac{3}{8} \times 10 = \boxed{} = \boxed{}$

$\frac{1}{3} \times 15 = \boxed{}$ 　　　$\frac{5}{9} \times \frac{1}{5} = \boxed{}$ 　　　$\frac{3}{4} \times \frac{4}{9} = \boxed{}$

$\frac{1}{4} \times \frac{2}{7} = \boxed{}$ 　　　$\frac{2}{9} \times \frac{3}{4} = \boxed{}$ 　　　$12 \times \frac{3}{10} = \boxed{} = \boxed{}$

$\frac{2}{3} \times \frac{1}{3} = \boxed{}$ 　　　$\frac{1}{12} \times 2 = \boxed{}$ 　　　$\frac{3}{4} \times \frac{1}{4} = \boxed{}$

$\frac{5}{6} \times 8 = \boxed{} = \boxed{}$ 　　　$7 \times \frac{1}{8} = \boxed{}$ 　　　$\frac{1}{6} \times \frac{5}{6} = \boxed{}$

$\frac{1}{2} \times 25 = \boxed{} = \boxed{}$ 　　　$\frac{7}{10} \times \frac{5}{7} = \boxed{}$ 　　　$4 \times \frac{3}{4} = \boxed{}$

More complex fraction problems

Find $\frac{3}{5}$ of $30.00.

Find $\frac{1}{5}$: $30 ÷ 5 = $6

$6 × 3 = $18

So, $\frac{3}{5}$ of $30 is $18

Find $\frac{7}{10}$ of 60 cm

Find $\frac{1}{10}$: 60 cm ÷ 10 = 6 cm

6 cm × 7 = 42 cm

So, $\frac{7}{10}$ of 60 cm is 42 cm

Find $\frac{3}{5}$ of these amounts.

40 cm

$50

$10.50

80 m

75 ml

45 kg

Find $\frac{7}{10}$ of these amounts.

48 m

$98.00

75 km

Find $\frac{2}{3}$ of these amounts.

48 cm

120 kg

$24.00

Finding percentages

Find 30% of 140.

$\dfrac{14\cancel{0}}{10\cancel{0}} \times 3\cancel{0} = 42$

(Divide by 100 to find 1% and then multiply by 30 to find 30%.)

Find 12% of 75.

$\dfrac{\cancel{75}^{3}}{\cancel{100}_{4}^{1}} \times \cancel{12}^{3} = 9$

(Divide by 100 to find 1% and then multiply by 12 to find 12%.)

Find 30% of these numbers.

620

240

80

160

Find 60% of these numbers.

60

100

160

580

Find 45% of these numbers.

80 g

40 cm

240 ml

600 km

Find 12% of these numbers.

$150

$600

125 m

775 m

Addition

Find each sum.

```
   5831        3724        9994         524
   8375        9942        7358        7034
+   219      +  623      +  471      +   95
  _____      _____      _____      _____
```

```
   7341        9328        7159         208
    299         347          39        4943
+  5143      + 8222      +  748      +   55
  _____      _____      _____      _____
```

Find each sum.

```
   8594        7362        3041        7641
    629         843         571          93
   9878        4732        5210        8521
+    96      +   53      +   71      +  843
  _____      _____      _____      _____
```

```
   8795        6043          27         146
    659           4         153        3714
   3212         147        8612          26
+   961      + 8948      +  127      + 5003
  _____      _____      _____      _____
```

98

More addition

Work out the answer to each problem.

```
  11  1                    12 1
  23 714                   11 541
   9 024                      861
+    348                   29 652
  33 086                 +      5
                           42 059
```

Remember to regroup if you need to.

Find each sum.

```
  17 203        29 521        65 214        25 046
     112         6 211           973            15
+  5 608      +     58      +  1 291      +    263
```

```
   6 958        73 009        11 536        87 019
      71             3            48           127
+ 16 911      +    581      +  2 435      +  5 652
```

Find each sum.

```
  79 622        64 599         6 940        72 148
   8 011           122           936           999
  47 391         6 375        58 274         7 481
+      7      +     91      +     36      + 21 685
```

```
  58 975        36 403             8            23
     858            73        22 849        99 951
   8 423           712           502           358
+     27      +  6 229      +  4 034      +  6 231
```

99

Dividing by ones

$477 \div 2$ can be written in two ways:

$$238\frac{1}{2}$$
$$2\overline{)477}$$

or

$$238 \text{ r } 1$$
$$2\overline{)477}$$

Work out the answers to these problems. Use fraction remainders.

$$2\overline{)479} \qquad 4\overline{)863} \qquad 5\overline{)579} \qquad 7\overline{)860}$$

$$2\overline{)175} \qquad 3\overline{)167} \qquad 9\overline{)457} \qquad 3\overline{)293}$$

Work out the answers to these problems. Use unit remainders.

$$2\overline{)705} \qquad 5\overline{)637} \qquad 4\overline{)330} \qquad 7\overline{)921}$$

Dividing by ones

361 ÷ 2 can be written in two ways:

$$180\frac{1}{2}$$ 180 r 1

or

2) 361   2) 361

Work out the answers to these problems. Use fraction remainders.

4) 320   7) 490   8) 349   9) 547

2) 807   2) 437   2) 943   3) 361

Work out the answers to these problems. Use unit remainders.

5) 417   9) 810   3) 303   4) 366

Dividing

$589 \div 5$ can be written in two ways:

$117\frac{4}{5}$

or

$117 \text{ r } 4$

$5\overline{)589}$ $5\overline{)589}$

Work out the answers to these problems. Use fractions remainders.

$8\overline{)435}$ $9\overline{)359}$ $7\overline{)452}$ $7\overline{)792}$

$8\overline{)937}$ $7\overline{)799}$ $9\overline{)289}$ $6\overline{)854}$

Work out the answers to these problems. Use unit remainders.

$9\overline{)653}$ $4\overline{)545}$ $8\overline{)952}$ $6\overline{)411}$

Everyday problems

A plumber has 6 m of copper tubing. If he uses 2.36 m, how much will he have left?

3.64 m

```
      9
    5 1010
    6.00
  - 2.36
    3.64
```

If he buys another 4.5 m of copper tubing, how much will he now have?

8.14 m

```
    1
    3.64
  + 4.50
    8.14
```

A man spends $35.65, $102.43, $68.99 and $36.50 in 4 different stores. How much money did he spend altogether?

A gas station has 10 400 litres of gasoline delivered on Monday, 13 350 litres on Tuesday, 14 755 litres on Wednesday, 9656 litres on Thursday, and 15 975 litres on Friday. How much did they have delivered from Monday through Friday?

If they sold 59 248 litres that week, how much gasoline did they have left?

Daniel runs 22.56 km in a charity fun run. Sandra runs 8420 m less. How far does Sandra run?

What is the combined distance run by Daniel and Sandra?

Dianne is 1 m 30 cm tall. Tania is 1 m 54 cm tall. How much taller is Tania?

Real-life problems

A man walks 18.34 km on Saturday and 16.57 km on Sunday. How far did he walk that weekend?

34.91 km

How much farther did he walk on Saturday?

1.77 km

```
    1   1
   18.34
 + 16.57
   34.91
        12
   7  ẑ 14
   18.34
 − 16.57
    1 .77
```

A rectangular field measures 103.7 m by 96.5 m. What is the perimeter of the field?

When Joe and Kerry stand on a scale it reads 91 kg. When Joe steps off, it reads 31.5 kg. How much does Joe weigh?

A rectangular room has an area of 32.58 m². When a carpet is put down there is still 7.99 m² of floor showing. What is the area of the carpet?

A brother's and sister's combined height is 270 cm. If the sister is $120\frac{1}{2}$ cm tall, how tall is the brother?

A province has 4 highways: Rte 1, which is 1246 km long; Rte 2 which is 339 km long; Rte 3 which is 1573 km long; and Rte 4 which is 48 km long. How much highway does the province have in total?

Jenny's aquarium holds $25\frac{1}{2}$ litres of water. She buys a new one that holds 32 litres. How much extra water do her fish have?

Real-life problems

Deborah's school bag has a mass of $6\frac{1}{2}$ kg.
Asha's has a mass of $4\frac{1}{2}$ kg. How much heavier is
Deborah's bag than Asha's?

2 kg

What is the total mass of the two bags?

11 kg

$$6\frac{1}{2}$$
$$-\ 4\frac{1}{2}$$
$$2$$

$$6\frac{1}{2}$$
$$+\ 4\frac{1}{2}$$
$$10\frac{2}{2} = 11$$

Mr Shaw needs to put weather stripping around four
sides of his front door. The door is 200 cm high and
90 cm wide. How many centimetres of weather
stripping does he need?

Bert earns $24 632 a year, Ernie earns
$34 321 a year, and Oscar earns $22 971 a
year. How much do they earn altogether?

How much more than Bert does
Ernie earn?

How much more than Oscar does
Bert earn?

How much more than Oscar does
Ernie earn?

An elevator says, "Maximum weight 636 kg."
If four people get in, weighing 90 kg, 60 kg, 115 kg, and
78 kg, how much more mass will the elevator hold?

Multiplication by 2-digit numbers

Work out the answer to each problem.

```
        26              95              32              78
  x     84        x     65        x     39        x     49
```

```
        97              94              32              47
  x     46        x     37        x     64        x     75
```

```
        28              47              36              45
  x     95        x     62        x     87        x     33
```

```
        46              29              85              63
  x     85        x     72        x     29        x     84
```

Division by ones

47 ÷ 2 can be written in two ways:

$$\begin{array}{r} 23 \\ 2\overline{)47} \\ \underline{4} \\ 7 \\ \underline{6} \\ 1 \end{array}$$

$23\frac{1}{2}$

or

$$\begin{array}{r} 23 \\ 2\overline{)47} \\ \underline{4} \\ 7 \\ \underline{6} \\ 1 \end{array}$$

23 r 1

Write the quotients for these problems with fraction remainders.

$2\overline{)17}$ $4\overline{)19}$ $3\overline{)16}$ $4\overline{)37}$

$3\overline{)29}$ $2\overline{)45}$ $5\overline{)87}$ $5\overline{)49}$

Write the quotients for these problems with unit remainders.

$2\overline{)73}$ $2\overline{)85}$ $2\overline{)39}$ $4\overline{)59}$

$4\overline{)71}$ $4\overline{)83}$ $5\overline{)29}$ $5\overline{)47}$

Dividing

$646 \div 3$ can be written in two ways:

$$215\tfrac{1}{3}$$ or $$215 \text{ r } 1$$

$$3\overline{)646}$$ $$3\overline{)646}$$

Work out the answer to each problem. Use fraction remainders.

$$4\overline{)377}$$ $$2\overline{)169}$$ $$7\overline{)158}$$ $$4\overline{)368}$$

$$5\overline{)197}$$ $$9\overline{)636}$$ $$2\overline{)325}$$ $$4\overline{)787}$$

Work out the answer to each problem. Use unit remainders.

$$5\overline{)947}$$ $$3\overline{)731}$$ $$7\overline{)878}$$ $$9\overline{)875}$$

Division of 3-digit decimal numbers

Work out these division sums.

$$
\begin{array}{r}
0.89 \\
3\overline{)2.67} \\
24 \\
\overline{27} \\
27 \\
\overline{0}
\end{array}
$$

0.89

$$
\begin{array}{r}
0.74 \\
4\overline{)2.96} \\
28 \\
\overline{16} \\
16 \\
\overline{0}
\end{array}
$$

0.74

Work out these division problems.

$2\overline{)2.94}$ $4\overline{)7.32}$ $4\overline{)6.12}$ $2\overline{)3.24}$

$2\overline{)9.98}$ $3\overline{)9.72}$ $4\overline{)6.24}$ $4\overline{)7.48}$

$4\overline{)2.24}$ $3\overline{)2.22}$ $3\overline{)2.25}$ $3\overline{)2.61}$

Division of 3-digit decimal numbers

Work out these division problems.

```
      1.99
  5)9.95
     5
    ___
     49
     45
    ___
      45
      45
     ___
       0
```
1.99

```
      1.61
  6)9.66
     6
    ___
     36
     36
    ___
       6
       6
      ___
       0
```
1.61

Work out these division problems.

5)8.15   5)9.25   5)6.35   6)9.12

6)2.16   7)8.82   7)4.83   8)5.92

8)8.72   9)8.19   9)5.67   6)6.36

Real-life problems

A builder uses 1600 kg of sand a day.
How much will he use in 5 days?

8000 kg

$$
\begin{array}{r}
{}^{3}1600 \\
\times\quad 5 \\
\hline
8000
\end{array}
$$

If he uses 9500 kg the next week,
how much more has he used than
the week before?

1500 kg

$$
\begin{array}{r}
9500 \\
-\ 8000 \\
\hline
1500
\end{array}
$$

An electrician uses 184 m of cable while
working on four houses. If he uses the same
amount on each house, how much does
he use on one house?

A family looks at vacations in two different resorts.
The first one costs $846.95. The second costs $932.
How much will the family save if they choose
the cheaper resort?

Doris has 5 sections of fence, each 96 cm
wide. If she puts them together, how much
of her yard can she fence off?

Shula goes on a sponsored walk and collects
$15.95 from her mother, $8.36 from her uncle,
$4.65 from her brother, and $2.75 from her aunt.
How much does she
collect altogether?

A taxi company has 9 cars.
If each car holds 40.4 litres of gasoline,
how many litres will it take to fill all
of the cars?

Rounding money

Round to the nearest dollar.

$3.95 rounds to $4

$2.25 rounds to $2

Round to the nearest ten dollars.

$15.50 rounds to $20

$14.40 rounds to $10

Round to the nearest dollar.

$2.60 rounds to	$8.49 rounds to	$3.39 rounds to
$9.55 rounds to	$1.75 rounds to	$4.30 rounds to
$7.15 rounds to	$6.95 rounds to	$2.53 rounds to

Round to the nearest ten dollars.

$37.34 rounds to	$21.75 rounds to	$85.03 rounds to
$71.99 rounds to	$66.89 rounds to	$52.99 rounds to
$55.31 rounds to	$12.79 rounds to	$15.00 rounds to

Round to the nearest hundred dollars.

$307.12 rounds to	$175.50 rounds to	$115.99 rounds to
$860.55 rounds to	$417.13 rounds to	$650.15 rounds to
$739.10 rounds to	$249.66 rounds to	$367.50 rounds to

Estimating sums of money

Round to the leading digit. Estimate the sum.

$3.26 → $3
+ $4.82 → + $5
is about $8

$68.53 → $70
+ $34.60 → + $30
is about $100

Round to the leading digit. Estimate the sum.

$52.61 →
+ $27.95 →
is about _____

$19.20 →
+ $22.13 →
is about _____

$70.75 →
+ $12.49 →
is about _____

$701.34 →
+ $100.80 →
is about _____

$339.50 →
+ $422.13 →
is about _____

$160.07 →
+ $230.89 →
is about _____

$25.61 →
+ $72.51 →
is about _____

$61.39 →
+ $19.50 →
is about _____

$18.32 →
+ $13.90 →
is about _____

$587.35 →
+ $251.89 →
is about _____

$109.98 →
+ $210.09 →
is about _____

$470.02 →
+ $203.17 →
is about _____

Round to the leading digit. Estimate the sum.

$75.95 + $17.95 →

$41.67 + $20.35 →

$49.19 + $38.70 →

$784.65 + $101.05 →

$516.50 + $290.69 →

$58.78 + $33.25 →

$82.90 + $11.79 →

$90.09 + $14.50 →

Estimating differences of money

Round the numbers to the leading digit. Estimate the differences.

$8.75 → $9
− $5.10 → − $5
is about $4

$61.47 → $60
− $35.64 → − $40
is about $20

Round the numbers to the leading digit. Estimate the differences.

$17.90 →
− $12.30 → ____
is about

$6.40 →
− $3.75 → ____
is about

$87.45 →
− $54.99 → ____
is about

$34.90 →
− $12.60 → ____
is about

$8.68 →
− $4.39 → ____
is about

$363.24 →
− $127.66 → ____
is about

$78.75 →
− $24.99 → ____
is about

$64.21 →
− $28.56 → ____
is about

$723.34 →
− $487.12 → ____
is about

Round the numbers to the leading digit. Estimate the differences.

$8.12 − $1.35
→   =

$49.63 − $27.85
→   =

$7.50 − $3.15
→   =

$85.15 − $42.99
→   =

$5.85 − $4.75
→   =

$634.60 − $267.25
→   =

$37.35 − $16.99
→   =

$842.17 − $169.54
→   =

$56.95 − $20.58
→   =

$628.37 − $252.11
→   =

Estimating sums and differences

Round the numbers to the leading digit. Estimate the sum or difference.

$$
\begin{array}{rcl}
3576 & \to & 4000 \\
+\ 1307 & \to & +1000 \\
\hline
\text{is about} & & 5000
\end{array}
\qquad
\begin{array}{rcl}
198\ 248 & \to & 200\ 000 \\
-\ 116\ 431 & \to & -\ 100\ 000 \\
\hline
\text{is about} & & 100\ 000
\end{array}
$$

Round the numbers to the leading digit. Estimate the sum or difference.

$$
\begin{array}{rcl}
685 & \to & \\
+\ 489 & \to & \underline{\hspace{2cm}} \\
\hline
\text{is about} & & \underline{\hspace{2cm}}
\end{array}
\qquad
\begin{array}{rcl}
21\ 481 & \to & \\
-\ 12\ 500 & \to & \underline{\hspace{2cm}} \\
\hline
\text{is about} & & \underline{\hspace{2cm}}
\end{array}
\qquad
\begin{array}{rcl}
7834 & \to & \\
+\ 3106 & \to & \underline{\hspace{2cm}} \\
\hline
\text{is about} & & \underline{\hspace{2cm}}
\end{array}
$$

$$
\begin{array}{rcl}
682\ 778 & \to & \\
+\ 130\ 001 & \to & \underline{\hspace{2cm}} \\
\hline
\text{is about} & & \underline{\hspace{2cm}}
\end{array}
\qquad
\begin{array}{rcl}
58\ 499 & \to & \\
-\ 22\ 135 & \to & \underline{\hspace{2cm}} \\
\hline
\text{is about} & & \underline{\hspace{2cm}}
\end{array}
\qquad
\begin{array}{rcl}
902\ 276 & \to & \\
-\ 615\ 999 & \to & \underline{\hspace{2cm}} \\
\hline
\text{is about} & & \underline{\hspace{2cm}}
\end{array}
$$

$$
\begin{array}{rcl}
46\ 801 & \to & \\
+\ 34\ 700 & \to & \underline{\hspace{2cm}} \\
\hline
\text{is about} & & \underline{\hspace{2cm}}
\end{array}
\qquad
\begin{array}{rcl}
9734 & \to & \\
-\ 8306 & \to & \underline{\hspace{2cm}} \\
\hline
\text{is about} & & \underline{\hspace{2cm}}
\end{array}
\qquad
\begin{array}{rcl}
65\ 606 & \to & \\
+\ 85\ 943 & \to & \underline{\hspace{2cm}} \\
\hline
\text{is about} & & \underline{\hspace{2cm}}
\end{array}
$$

$$
\begin{array}{rcl}
5218 & \to & \\
-\ 3673 & \to & \underline{\hspace{2cm}} \\
\hline
\text{is about} & & \underline{\hspace{2cm}}
\end{array}
\qquad
\begin{array}{rcl}
745 & \to & \\
+\ 451 & \to & \underline{\hspace{2cm}} \\
\hline
\text{is about} & & \underline{\hspace{2cm}}
\end{array}
\qquad
\begin{array}{rcl}
337\ 297 & \to & \\
-\ 168\ 931 & \to & \underline{\hspace{2cm}} \\
\hline
\text{is about} & & \underline{\hspace{2cm}}
\end{array}
$$

Write < or > for each problem.

329 + 495		800	11 569 – 6146		6000
563 – 317		300	8193 – 6668		1000
41 924 – 12 445		50 000	634 577 + 192 556		800 000
18 885 + 12 691		30 000	713 096 – 321 667		400 000

115

Estimating products

Round to the leading digit. Estimate the product.

3456 x 6
3000 x 6 = 18 000

73 x 46
70 x 50 = 3500

Round to the leading digit. Estimate the sum.

1908 x 8
_____ x 8 = _____

5 x 6099
5 x _____ = _____

7 x 1108
7 x _____ = _____

5239 x 9
_____ x 9 = _____

81 x 32
_____ x _____ = _____

19 x 62
_____ x _____ = _____

39 x 44
_____ x _____ = _____

94 x 12
_____ x _____ = _____

Estimate the product.

6 x 7243 _____

4785 x 4 _____

3 x 8924 _____

2785 x 5 _____

6298 x 4 _____

7 x 7105 _____

8 x 2870 _____

4176 x 7 _____

5 x 4803 _____

6777 x 9 _____

6 x 8022 _____

3785 x 4 _____

42 x 51 _____

54 x 28 _____

23 x 75 _____

16 x 32 _____

47 x 54 _____

59 x 52 _____

17 x 74 _____

33 x 22 _____

81 x 18 _____

31 x 91 _____

38 x 87 _____

46 x 77 _____

Estimating quotients

Round to compatible numbers. Estimate the quotient.

$3156 \div 6$
$3000 \div 6 =$ 500

$2159 \div 5$
$2500 \div 5 =$ 500

Round to compatible numbers. Estimate the quotient.

$1934 \div 8$
$\div 8 =$

$4066 \div 5$
$\div 5 =$

$1108 \div 4$
$\div 4 =$

$5657 \div 9$
$\div 9 =$

$3998 \div 6$
$\div 6 =$

$5525 \div 7$
$\div 7 =$

$1701 \div 3$
$\div 3 =$

$1304 \div 2$
$\div 2 =$

Estimate the quotient.

$4798 \div 7$ $8205 \div 9$ $5022 \div 5$

$3785 \div 4$ $5528 \div 6$ $2375 \div 8$

$1632 \div 3$ $4251 \div 4$ $4754 \div 9$

$7352 \div 8$ $1774 \div 2$ $3322 \div 7$

$3591 \div 6$ $2887 \div 5$ $5746 \div 2$

$3703 \div 3$ $2392 \div 6$ $6621 \div 8$

Rounding mixed numbers

Round to the closest whole number.

$2\frac{5}{6}$

$\frac{5}{6}$ is more than $\frac{1}{2}$,

so, $2\frac{5}{6}$ rounds up to 3.

$3\frac{2}{5}$

$\frac{2}{5}$ is less than $\frac{1}{2}$,

so, $3\frac{2}{5}$ rounds down to 3.

Circle the fractions that are more than $\frac{1}{2}$.

$\frac{3}{7}$ $\frac{2}{9}$ $\frac{6}{7}$ $\frac{5}{9}$ $\frac{3}{8}$ $\frac{1}{7}$ $\frac{2}{3}$ $\frac{4}{7}$

$\frac{7}{10}$ $\frac{2}{5}$ $\frac{1}{3}$ $\frac{5}{6}$ $\frac{3}{4}$ $\frac{2}{9}$ $\frac{5}{8}$ $\frac{3}{5}$

Circle the fractions that are less than $\frac{1}{2}$.

$\frac{1}{8}$ $\frac{3}{9}$ $\frac{4}{5}$ $\frac{2}{7}$ $\frac{3}{5}$ $\frac{2}{5}$ $\frac{7}{10}$ $\frac{2}{9}$

$\frac{3}{4}$ $\frac{1}{3}$ $\frac{4}{9}$ $\frac{3}{10}$ $\frac{5}{6}$ $\frac{1}{4}$ $\frac{3}{7}$ $\frac{5}{9}$

Round to the closest whole number.

$4\frac{3}{8}$ $2\frac{6}{7}$ $5\frac{3}{4}$ $3\frac{2}{9}$

$2\frac{5}{6}$ $1\frac{7}{8}$ $2\frac{2}{5}$ $5\frac{1}{7}$

$3\frac{1}{6}$ $5\frac{3}{8}$ $3\frac{3}{5}$ $7\frac{8}{13}$

$6\frac{3}{5}$ $1\frac{1}{4}$ $4\frac{5}{6}$ $9\frac{3}{4}$

$5\frac{2}{3}$ $3\frac{3}{7}$ $1\frac{6}{7}$ $6\frac{3}{4}$

Calculate the mean

What is the mean of 6 and 10? $(6+10) ÷ 2 = 8$

David is 9, Asha is 10, and
Daniel is 5. What is their mean age? $(9 + 10 + 5) ÷ 3 = 8$ years

---

Calculate the mean of these amounts.

9 and 5

5 and 7

8 and 12

19 and 21

6 and 8

11 and 7

13 and 15

40 and 60

Calculate the mean of these amounts.

5, 7, and 3

14, 10, and 6

7, 3, 5, and 9

16¢, 9¢, 12¢, and 3¢

11, 9, and 7

12, 8, and 4

$1, $1.50, $2.50, and $3

5 g, 7 g, 8 g, and 8 g

Calculate these answers.

The mean of two numbers is 7. If one of the numbers
is 6, what is the other number?

The mean of three numbers is 4. If two of the numbers
are 4 and 5, what is the third number?

The mean of four numbers is 12. If three of the numbers
are 9, 15, and 8, what is the fourth number?

Two children record their
last five spelling-test scores.

| Gayle | 17 | 18 | 16 | 14 | 15 |
| Sally | 19 | 20 | 12 | 13 | 11 |

Which child has the best mean score?

Mean, median, and mode

Sian throws a dice 7 times. Here are her results:
4, 2, 1, 2, 4, 2, 6

What is the mean? $(4 + 2 + 1 + 2 + 4 + 2 + 6) \div 7 = 3$

What is the median? Put the numbers in order of size and find the middle number, example, 1, 2, 2, 2, 4, 4, 6.

The median is 2.

What is the mode? The most common result, which is 2.

A school scoccer team scores the following number of goals in their first 9 matches:
2, 2, 1, 3, 2, 1, 2, 4, 1

What is the mean score?

What is the median score?

Write down the mode for their results.

The ages of the local hockey players are:
17, 15, 16, 19, 17, 19, 22, 17, 18, 21, 17

What is the mean of their ages?

What is their median age?

Write down the mode for their ages.

The results of Susan's last 11 spelling tests were:
15, 12, 15, 17, 11, 16, 19, 11, 3, 11, 13

What is the mean of her scores?

What is her median score?

Write down the mode for her scores.

Line graphs

Look at this graph.

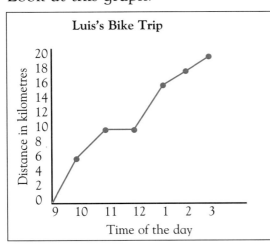

How many kilometres did Luis ride during the first hour of his trip?

> 6 kilometres

How many hours did Luis's trip take?

> 6 hours

How far did he travel in all?

> 20 kilometres

Luis stopped for lunch for one hour. What time did he stop?

Did Luis cover more distance between 12 and 1 or between 1 and 2?

Between which two hours did Luis travel 4 kilometres?

During which hours did Luis ride the fastest?

Did Luis travel farther before or after his lunch break?

How much longer did it take Luis to ride 10 kilometres after lunch?

Coordinates

Write the coordinates of:

A   (2, 4)

B   (3, 1)

C   (1, 1)

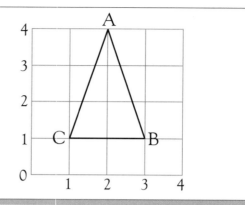

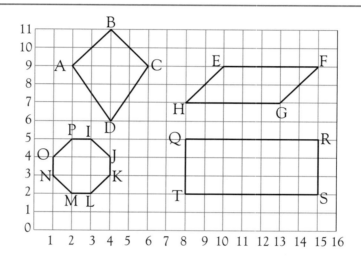

Write the coordinates of:

A	B	C	D	E
F	G	H	I	J
K	L	M	N	O
P	Q	R	S	T

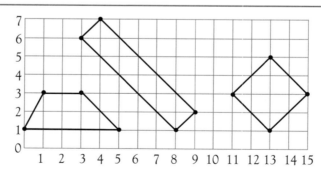

Plot these points on the grid, and connect them up in the right order.

(0, 1) (1, 3) (3, 3) (5, 1) (0, 1). What shape does this make?

(3, 6) (4, 7) (9, 2) (8, 1) (3, 6). What shape does this make?

(11, 3) (13, 5) (15, 3) (13, 1) (11, 3). What shape does this make?

Drawing angles

Acute angles are between 0° and 90°.   Obtuse angles are between 90° and 180°.

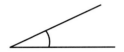

When you get to 180° you have a straight line.

Use a protractor to draw these angles. Remember to mark the angle you have drawn.

150°	135°
45°	110°
10°	20°

Reading and writing numbers

264 346 in words is Two hundred sixty-four thousand three hundred forty-six

One million three hundred twelve thousand five hundred two is 1 312 502

Write each of these numbers in words.

326 208

704 543

240 701

278 520

Write each of these in numbers.

Five hundred seventeen thousand forty-two

Six hundred ninety-four thousand seven hundred eleven

Eight hundred nine thousand two hundred three

Nine hundred thousand four hundred four

Write each of these numbers in words.

9 307 012

5 042 390

9 908 434

8 400 642

Write each of these in numbers.

Eight million two hundred fifty-one

Two million forty thousand four hundred four

Seven million three hundred two thousand one hundred one

Two million five hundred forty-one thousand five

Multiplying and dividing by 10

Write the answer in the box.

26 x 10 = <u>260</u>

40 ÷ 10 = <u>4</u>

Write the answer in the box.

76 x 10 =		43 x 10 =		93 x 10 =
66 x 10 =		13 x 10 =		47 x 10 =
147 x 10 =		936 x 10 =		284 x 10 =
364 x 10 =		821 x 10 =		473 x 10 =

Write the answer in the box.

30 ÷ 10 =		20 ÷ 10 =		70 ÷ 10 =
60 ÷ 10 =		50 ÷ 10 =		580 ÷ 10 =
310 ÷ 10 =		270 ÷ 10 =		100 ÷ 10 =
540 ÷ 10 =		890 ÷ 10 =		710 ÷ 10 =

Write the number that has been multiplied by 10.

x 10 = 370	x 10 = 640	x 10 = 740
x 10 = 810	x 10 = 100	x 10 = 830
x 10 = 7140	x 10 = 3070	x 10 = 5290
x 10 = 2640	x 10 = 8290	x 10 = 6480

Write the number that has been divided by 10.

÷ 10 = 3	÷ 10 = 2	÷ 10 = 9
÷ 10 = 42	÷ 10 = 93	÷ 10 = 74
÷ 10 = 57	÷ 10 = 38	÷ 10 = 86

Identifying patterns

Continue each pattern.

Steps of 9:	5 14 23	32	41	50	
Steps of 14:	20 34 48	62	76	90	

Continue each pattern.

n1	n2	n3					
21	38	55					
13	37	61					
7	25	43					
32	48	64					
12	31	50			107		
32	54	76					186
24	64	104					
4	34	64					
36	126	216		396			
12	72	132					
25	45	65			125		
22	72	122					
25	100	175					
60	165	270			585		
8	107	206					701
10	61	112					
26	127	228					733
48	100	152					

Recognizing multiples of 6, 7, and 8

Circle the multiples of 6.

8	(12)	15	(18)	20	(24)

Circle the multiples of 6.

8	22	14	18	36	40
16	38	44	25	30	60
6	21	19	54	56	24
12	48	10	20	35	26
42	39	23	28	36	32

Circle the multiples of 7.

7	17	24	59	42	55
15	20	21	46	12	70
14	27	69	36	47	49
65	19	57	28	38	63
33	34	35	37	60	56

Circle the multiples of 8.

40	26	15	25	38	56
26	8	73	41	64	12
75	58	62	24	31	72
12	80	32	46	38	78
16	42	66	28	48	68

Circle the number that is a multiple of 6 *and* 7.

18	54	42	21	28	63

Circle the numbers that are multiples of 6 *and* 8.

16	24	36	48	54	42

Circle the number that is a multiple of 7 *and* 8.

24	32	40	28	42	56

Factors of numbers from 1 to 30

The factors of 10 are   1   2   5   10

Circle the factors of 4.   (1)   (2)   3   (4)

Write all the factors of each number.

The factors of 26 are

The factors of 30 are

The factors of 9 are

The factors of 12 are

The factors of 15 are

The factors of 22 are

The factors of 20 are

The factors of 21 are

The factors of 24 are

Circle all the factors of each number.

Which numbers are factors of 14?   1   2   3   5   7   9   12   14

Which numbers are factors of 13?   1   2   3   4   5   6   7   8   9   10   11   13

Which numbers are factors of 7?   1   2   3   4   5   6   7

Which numbers are factors of 11?   1   2   3   4   5   6   7   8   9   10   11

Which numbers are factors of 6?   1   2   3   4   5   6

Which numbers are factors of 8?   1   2   3   4   5   6   7   8

Which numbers are factors of 17?   1   2   5   7   12   14   16   17

Which numbers are factors of 18?   1   2   3   4   5   6   8   9   10   12   18

Some numbers only have factors of 1 and themselves. They are called prime numbers. Write down all the prime numbers that are less than 30 in the box.

Recognizing equivalent fractions

Make each pair of fractions equal by writing a number in the box.

$$\frac{1}{2} = \frac{2}{4} \qquad\qquad \frac{1}{3} = \frac{2}{6}$$

Make each pair of fractions equal by writing a number in the box.

$\dfrac{1}{2} = \dfrac{}{10}$ $\dfrac{3}{4} = \dfrac{}{8}$ $\dfrac{1}{3} = \dfrac{}{9}$

$\dfrac{2}{3} = \dfrac{}{12}$ $\dfrac{6}{12} = \dfrac{}{6}$ $\dfrac{4}{8} = \dfrac{}{2}$

$\dfrac{1}{5} = \dfrac{}{10}$ $\dfrac{4}{12} = \dfrac{}{6}$ $\dfrac{3}{5} = \dfrac{}{10}$

$\dfrac{1}{4} = \dfrac{}{8}$ $\dfrac{6}{18} = \dfrac{}{3}$ $\dfrac{3}{12} = \dfrac{}{4}$

$\dfrac{3}{9} = \dfrac{1}{}$ $\dfrac{4}{10} = \dfrac{2}{}$ $\dfrac{3}{4} = \dfrac{9}{}$

$\dfrac{4}{16} = \dfrac{1}{}$ $\dfrac{15}{20} = \dfrac{3}{}$ $\dfrac{6}{12} = \dfrac{1}{}$

$\dfrac{3}{5} = \dfrac{6}{}$ $\dfrac{3}{6} = \dfrac{1}{}$ $\dfrac{9}{12} = \dfrac{3}{}$

Make each row of fractions equal by writing a number in each box.

$\dfrac{1}{2} = \dfrac{}{4} = \dfrac{3}{} = \dfrac{}{8} = \dfrac{}{10} = \dfrac{6}{}$

$\dfrac{1}{4} = \dfrac{2}{} = \dfrac{}{12} = \dfrac{4}{} = \dfrac{5}{} = \dfrac{}{24}$

$\dfrac{3}{4} = \dfrac{6}{} = \dfrac{}{12} = \dfrac{12}{} = \dfrac{}{20} = \dfrac{18}{}$

$\dfrac{1}{3} = \dfrac{}{6} = \dfrac{3}{} = \dfrac{4}{} = \dfrac{}{15} = \dfrac{12}{}$

$\dfrac{1}{5} = \dfrac{}{10} = \dfrac{}{15} = \dfrac{4}{} = \dfrac{5}{} = \dfrac{}{30}$

$\dfrac{2}{3} = \dfrac{}{6} = \dfrac{}{9} = \dfrac{8}{} = \dfrac{10}{} = \dfrac{14}{}$

Rounding decimals

Round each decimal to the nearest whole number.

3.4	3
5.7	6
4.5	5

If the whole number has 5 after it, round it to the whole number above.

Round each decimal to the nearest whole number.

6.2		2.5		1.5		3.8	
5.5		2.8		3.2		8.5	
5.4		7.9		3.7		2.3	
1.1		8.6		8.3		9.2	
4.7		6.3		7.3		8.7	

Round each decimal to the nearest whole number.

14.4		42.3		74.1		59.7	
29.9		32.6		63.5		96.4	
18.2		37.5		39.6		76.3	
40.1		28.7		26.9		12.5	
29.5		38.5		87.2		41.6	

Round each decimal to the nearest whole number.

137.6		423.5		426.2		111.8	
641.6		333.5		805.2		246.8	
119.5		799.6		562.3		410.2	
682.4		759.6		531.5		829.9	
743.4		831.1		276.7		649.3	

Real-life problems

Write the answer in the box.

Yasmin has $4.60 and she is given another $1.20.
How much money does she have?

$5.80

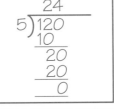

$$\begin{array}{r} \$4.60 \\ +\ \$1.20 \\ \hline \$5.80 \end{array}$$

David has 120 marbles.
He divides them equally among his 5 friends.
How many marbles
does each get?   24

$$\begin{array}{r} 24 \\ 5\overline{)120} \\ 10 \\ \hline 20 \\ 20 \\ \hline 0 \end{array}$$

Write the answer in the box.

Michael buys a ball for $5.50 and a flashlight for $3.65.
How much does he spend?

How much does he have left from $10?

The 32 children of a class bring in $5 each for a school trip.
What is the total of the amount brought in?

A set of 5 shelves can be made from a piece of wood 4 metres
long. What fraction of a metre will each shelf be?

Each of 5 children has $16.
How much do they have altogether?

If the above total were shared among 8 children, how much would
each child have?

Real-life problems

Find the answer to each problem.

A box is 16 cm wide. How wide will 6 boxes side by side be?

96 cm

$$\begin{array}{r} 3 \\ 16\ cm \\ \times\ 6 \\ \hline 96\ cm \end{array}$$

Josh is 1.20 m tall. His sister is 1.55 m tall. How much taller than Josh is his sister?

0.35 m

$$\begin{array}{r} 1.55\ m \\ -\ 1.20\ m \\ \hline 0.35\ m \end{array}$$

Find the answer to each problem.

A can contains 56 g of lemonade mix. If 12 g are used, how much is left?

A large jar of coffee has a mass of 280 g. A smaller jar has a mass of 130 g. How much heavier is the larger jar than the smaller jar?

There are 7 shelves of books. 5 shelves are 1.2 m long. 2 shelves are 1.5 m long. What is the total length of the 7 shelves?

A rock star can sign 36 photographs in a minute. How many can he sign in 30 seconds?

Shana has read 5 pages of a 20-page comic book. If it has taken her 9 minutes, how long is it likely to take her to read the whole comic book?

Problems involving time

Find the answer to this problem.

A train leaves the station at 7:30 A.M. and arrives at the end of the line at 10:45 A.M. How long did the journey take?

3 hours 15 minutes

7:30 → 10:30 = 3 h
10:30 → 10:45 = 15 min
Total = 3 h 15 min

Find the answer to each problem.

A film starts at 7:00 P.M. and finishes at 8:45 P.M. How long is the film?

A cake takes 2 hours 25 minutes to bake. If it begins baking at 1:35 P.M., at what time will the cake be done?

Sanjay needs to clean his bedroom and wash the car. It takes him 1 hour 10 minutes to clean his room and 45 minutes to clean the car. If he starts at 10:00 A.M., at what time will he finish?

A car is taken in for repair at 7:00 A.M. It is finished at 1:50 P.M. How long did the repairs take?

Claire has to be at school by 8:50 A.M. If she takes 1 hour 30 minutes to get ready, and the trip takes 35 minutes, at what time does she need to get up?

A bus leaves the bus station at 8:45 A.M. and arrives back at 10:15 A.M. How long has its trip taken?

Elapsed time

Write the answer in the box.

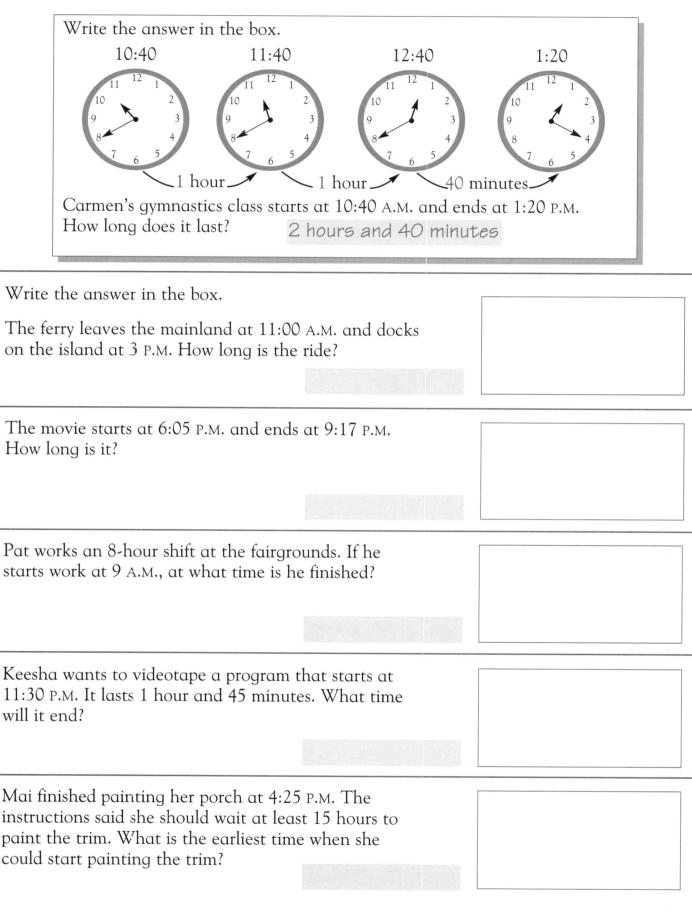

10:40   11:40   12:40   1:20

1 hour ➔   1 hour ➔   40 minutes ➔

Carmen's gymnastics class starts at 10:40 A.M. and ends at 1:20 P.M. How long does it last?

2 hours and 40 minutes

Write the answer in the box.

The ferry leaves the mainland at 11:00 A.M. and docks on the island at 3 P.M. How long is the ride?

The movie starts at 6:05 P.M. and ends at 9:17 P.M. How long is it?

Pat works an 8-hour shift at the fairgrounds. If he starts work at 9 A.M., at what time is he finished?

Keesha wants to videotape a program that starts at 11:30 P.M. It lasts 1 hour and 45 minutes. What time will it end?

Mai finished painting her porch at 4:25 P.M. The instructions said she should wait at least 15 hours to paint the trim. What is the earliest time when she could start painting the trim?

Recognizing multiples

Circle the multiples of 10.

14   (20)   25   (30)   47   (60)

Circle the multiples of 6.

| 20 | 48 | 56 | 72 | 25 | 35 |
| 1 | 3 | 6 | 16 | 26 | 36 |

Circle the multiples of 7.

| 14 | 24 | 35 | 27 | 47 | 49 |
| 63 | 42 | 52 | 37 | 64 | 71 |

Circle the multiples of 8.

| 25 | 31 | 48 | 84 | 32 | 8 |
| 18 | 54 | 64 | 35 | 72 | 28 |

Circle the multiples of 9.

17	81	27	35	92	106
45	53	108	90	33	95
64	9	28	18	36	98

Circle the multiples of 10.

| 15 | 35 | 20 | 46 | 90 | 100 |
| 44 | 37 | 30 | 29 | 50 | 45 |

Circle the multiples of 11.

24	110	123	54	66	90
45	33	87	98	99	121
43	44	65	55	21	22

Circle the multiples of 12.

136	134	144	109	108	132
24	34	58	68	48	60
35	29	72	74	84	94

Bar graphs

Use this bar graph to answer each question.

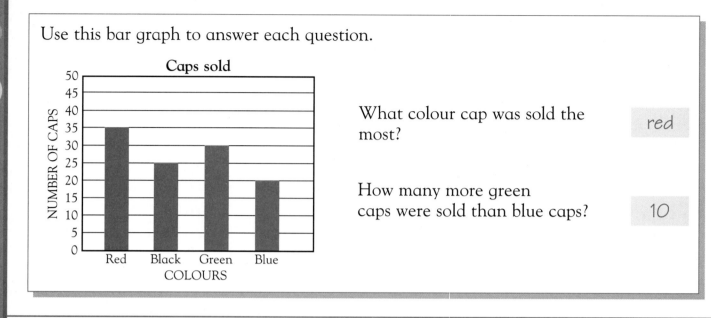

What colour cap was sold the most?

red

How many more green caps were sold than blue caps?

10

Use this bar graph to answer each question.

Tickets sold

How many tickets were sold on May 1?

How many more tickets were sold on May 2 than on May 4?

On which date were 90 tickets sold?

Use this bar graph to answer each question.

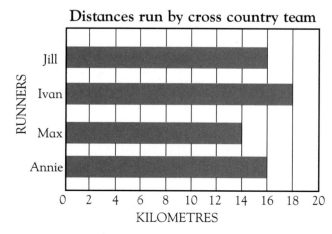

Which runner ran 14 kilometres?

Which runner ran the same distance as Annie?

How much farther did Ivan run than Max?

Triangles

Look at these different triangles.

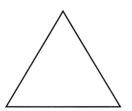 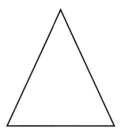 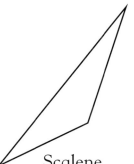 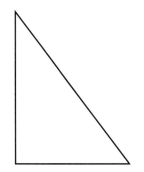

Equilateral
(all sides equal;
is also isosceles)

Isosceles
(two sides equal)

Scalene
(all sides different)

Right angle
(may be isosceles or
scalene, but one angle
must be a right angle)

1 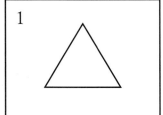　　2 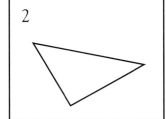　　3 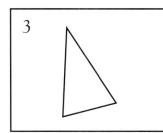　　4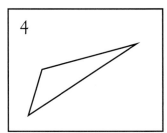

5 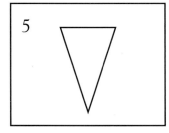　　6 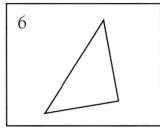　　7 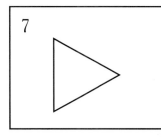　　8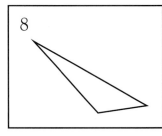

9 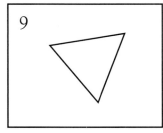　　10 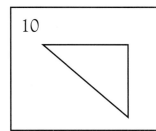　　11 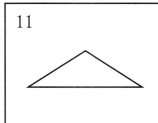　　12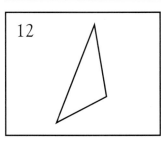

List the triangles that are:

Equilateral _____

Isosceles _____

Scalene _____

Right angle _____

Place value to 10 000 000

How many hundreds are there in 7000?   70   hundreds
(70 x 100 = 7000)

What is the value of the 9 in 694?   90   (because the 9 is in the tens column)

Write how many tens there are in:

400 _____ tens   600 _____ tens   900 _____ tens

200 _____ tens   1300 _____ tens   4700 _____ tens

4800 _____ tens   1240 _____ tens   1320 _____ tens

2630 _____ tens   5920 _____ tens   4350 _____ tens

What is the value of the 7 in these numbers?

76 _____   720 _____   137 _____

7122 _____   74 301 _____   724 _____

What is the value of the 3 in these numbers?

324 126 _____   3 927 141 _____   214 623 _____

8 254 320 _____   3 711 999 _____   124 372 _____

Write how many hundreds there are in:

6400 _____ hundreds   8500 _____ hundreds

19 900 _____ hundreds   36 200 _____ hundreds

524 600 _____ hundreds   712 400 _____ hundreds

What is the value of the 8 in these numbers?

8 214 631 _____   2 398 147 _____   463 846 _____

287 034 _____   8 110 927 _____   105 428 _____

Multiplying and dividing by 10

Write the answer in the box.

37 x 10 = 370   58 ÷ 10 = 5.8

Write the product in the box.

94 x 10 =   13 x 10 =   37 x 10 =

36 x 10 =   47 x 10 =   54 x 10 =

236 x 10 =   419 x 10 =   262 x 10 =

531 x 10 =   674 x 10 =   801 x 10 =

Write the quotient in the box.

92 ÷ 10 =   48 ÷ 10 =   37 ÷ 10 =

18 ÷ 10 =   29 ÷ 10 =   54 ÷ 10 =

345 ÷ 10 =   354 ÷ 10 =   723 ÷ 10 =

531 ÷ 10 =   262 ÷ 10 =   419 ÷ 10 =

Find the missing factor.

x 10 = 230   x 10 = 750   x 10 = 990

x 10 = 480   x 10 = 130   x 10 = 250

x 10 = 520   x 10 = 390   x 10 = 270

x 10 = 620   x 10 = 860   x 10 = 170

Find the dividend.

÷ 10 = 4.7   ÷ 10 = 6.8   ÷ 10 = 12.4

÷ 10 = 25.7   ÷ 10 = 36.2   ÷ 10 = 31.4

÷ 10 = 40.8   ÷ 10 = 67.2   ÷ 10 = 80.9

÷ 10 = 92.4   ÷ 10 = 32.7   ÷ 10 = 56.3

Appropriate units of measure

Choose the best units to measure the length of each item.

millimetres	centimetres	metres

desk	tooth	swimming pool
centimetres	millimetres	metres

Choose the best units to measure the length of each item.

centimetres	metres	kilometres

bed	bicycle	toothbrush	football field

shoe	driveway	sailboat	highway

The height of a door is about 2 _____.

The length of a pencil is about 17 _____.

The height of a flagpole is about 7 _____.

Choose the best units to measure the mass of each item.

grams	kilograms	tonnes

train	kitten	watermelon	tennis ball

shoe	bag of potatoes	elephant	washing machine

The mass of a hamburger is about 26 _____.

The mass of a bag of apples is about 2 _____.

The mass of a truck is about 4 _____.

Identifying patterns

Continue each pattern.

Intervals of 6:	1	7	13	19	25	31	37
Intervals of 3:	27	24	21	18	15	12	9

Continue each pattern.

0	10	20				
15	20	25				
5	7	9				
2	9	16				
4	7	10			19	
2	10	18		34		

Continue each pattern.

44	38	32				
33	29	25				
27	23	19				
56	48	40			16	
49	42	35				
28	25	22				10

Continue each pattern.

36	30	24		12		
5	14	23				
3	8	13				
47	40	33			12	
1	4	7				

Factors of numbers from 31 to 65

The factors of 40 are   1   2   4   5   8   10   20   40

Circle the factors of 56.

(1) (2)   3   (4)   5   6   (7) (8) (14) (28)   32   (56)

Find all the factors of each number.

The factors of 31 are

The factors of 47 are

The factors of 60 are

The factors of 50 are

The factors of 42 are

The factors of 32 are

The factors of 48 are

The factors of 35 are

The factors of 52 are

Circle all the factors of each number.

Which numbers are factors of 39?

    1   2   3   4   5   8   9   10   13   14   15   20   25   39

Which numbers are factors of 45?

    1   3   4   5   8   9   12   15   16   21   24   36   40   44   45

Which numbers are factors of 61?

    1   3   4   5   6   10   15   16   18   20   26   31   40   61

Which numbers are factors of 65?

    1   2   4   5   6   8   9   10   12   13   14   15   30   60   65

Some numbers have only factors of 1 and themselves. They are called prime numbers.
Write all the prime numbers between 31 and 65 in the box.

Greatest common factor

Circle the common factors.
Write the greatest common factor (GCF).

24: ①, ②, ③, 4, ⑥, 8, 12, 24
60: ①, ②, ③, 4, 5, ⑥, 8, 10, 12, 60   The GCF is 6
42: ①, ②, ③, ⑥, 7, 14

Find the factors. Circle the common factors.

45:                                    36:

28:                                    54:

Find the factors. Write the GCF.

35:                                    80:

The GCF is

32:                                    64:

The GCF is

12:                    24:   15:

The GCF is

54:                    72:   18:

The GCF is

Writing equivalent fractions

Make these fractions equal by writing the missing number.

$$\frac{20}{100} \quad = \quad \frac{2}{10} \quad = \quad \frac{1}{5}$$

$$\frac{5}{15} \quad = \quad \frac{1}{3}$$

Make these fractions equal by writing a number in the box.

$$\frac{10}{100} = \frac{\Box}{10} \qquad \frac{8}{100} = \frac{\Box}{25} \qquad \frac{4}{100} = \frac{\Box}{25}$$

$$\frac{2}{20} = \frac{\Box}{10} \qquad \frac{5}{100} = \frac{\Box}{20} \qquad \frac{6}{20} = \frac{\Box}{10}$$

$$\frac{3}{5} = \frac{\Box}{20} \qquad \frac{5}{6} = \frac{\Box}{12} \qquad \frac{2}{8} = \frac{\Box}{24}$$

$$\frac{2}{3} = \frac{\Box}{24} \qquad \frac{2}{18} = \frac{\Box}{9} \qquad \frac{4}{50} = \frac{\Box}{25}$$

$$\frac{11}{12} = \frac{\Box}{36} \qquad \frac{12}{15} = \frac{\Box}{5} \qquad \frac{8}{20} = \frac{\Box}{5}$$

$$\frac{2}{12} = \frac{1}{\Box} \qquad \frac{5}{20} = \frac{1}{\Box} \qquad \frac{5}{8} = \frac{10}{\Box}$$

$$\frac{7}{8} = \frac{21}{\Box} \qquad \frac{15}{100} = \frac{3}{\Box} \qquad \frac{6}{24} = \frac{1}{\Box}$$

$$\frac{5}{25} = \frac{1}{\Box} \qquad \frac{8}{20} = \frac{2}{\Box} \qquad \frac{15}{20} = \frac{3}{\Box}$$

$$\frac{5}{30} = \frac{1}{\Box} \qquad \frac{12}{14} = \frac{6}{\Box} \qquad \frac{1}{5} = \frac{4}{\Box}$$

$$\frac{9}{18} = \frac{1}{\Box} \qquad \frac{24}{30} = \frac{4}{\Box} \qquad \frac{25}{30} = \frac{5}{\Box}$$

$$\frac{1}{8} = \frac{\Box}{16} = \frac{3}{\Box} = \frac{\Box}{32} = \frac{\Box}{40} = \frac{6}{\Box}$$

$$\frac{20}{100} = \frac{\Box}{25} = \frac{2}{\Box} = \frac{1}{\Box} = \frac{\Box}{50} = \frac{\Box}{200}$$

$$\frac{2}{5} = \frac{6}{\Box} = \frac{\Box}{20} = \frac{10}{\Box} = \frac{\Box}{50} = \frac{40}{\Box}$$

$$\frac{1}{6} = \frac{\Box}{12} = \frac{3}{\Box} = \frac{4}{\Box} = \frac{5}{\Box} = \frac{6}{\Box}$$

$$\frac{2}{3} = \frac{\Box}{24} = \frac{\Box}{36} = \frac{\Box}{21} = \frac{6}{\Box} = \frac{\Box}{300}$$

Fraction models

Write the missing numbers to show what part is shaded.

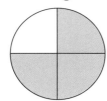

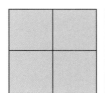

$\dfrac{3 \text{ shaded parts}}{4 \text{ parts}} = \dfrac{3}{4}$

$\dfrac{4}{4} = \boxed{1}$ and $\dfrac{2}{4} = \dfrac{1}{2}$

So, shaded part $= 1\dfrac{1}{2}$

Write the missing numbers to show what part is shaded.

   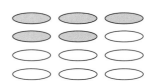

$\dfrac{}{9}$

$\dfrac{1}{}$

$\dfrac{}{}$

$\dfrac{}{}$

Write the fraction for the part that is shaded.

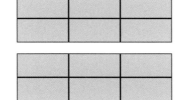 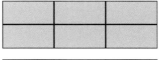 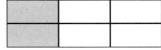

$\dfrac{}{}$ or $\dfrac{}{}$

$\dfrac{}{}$ or $\dfrac{}{}$

$\dfrac{}{}$ or $\dfrac{}{}$

Write the fraction for the part that is shaded.

$\dfrac{}{}$ or $\dfrac{}{}$

$\dfrac{}{}$ or $\dfrac{}{}$

$\dfrac{}{}$

Multiplying by one-digit numbers

Find each product. Remember to regroup.

$$\begin{array}{r} \tiny{1\ 1} \\ 465 \\ \times\ \ 3 \\ \hline 1395 \end{array}$$

$$\begin{array}{r} \tiny{3} \\ 391 \\ \times\ \ 4 \\ \hline 1564 \end{array}$$

$$\begin{array}{r} \tiny{3\ 4} \\ 278 \\ \times\ \ 5 \\ \hline 1390 \end{array}$$

Find each product.

$$\begin{array}{r} 563 \\ \times\ \ 3 \\ \hline \end{array}$$

$$\begin{array}{r} 910 \\ \times\ \ 2 \\ \hline \end{array}$$

$$\begin{array}{r} 437 \\ \times\ \ 3 \\ \hline \end{array}$$

$$\begin{array}{r} 812 \\ \times\ \ 2 \\ \hline \end{array}$$

$$\begin{array}{r} 572 \\ \times\ \ 4 \\ \hline \end{array}$$

$$\begin{array}{r} 831 \\ \times\ \ 3 \\ \hline \end{array}$$

$$\begin{array}{r} 406 \\ \times\ \ 5 \\ \hline \end{array}$$

$$\begin{array}{r} 394 \\ \times\ \ 6 \\ \hline \end{array}$$

Find each product.

$$\begin{array}{r} 318 \\ \times\ \ 3 \\ \hline \end{array}$$

$$\begin{array}{r} 223 \\ \times\ \ 4 \\ \hline \end{array}$$

$$\begin{array}{r} 542 \\ \times\ \ 4 \\ \hline \end{array}$$

$$\begin{array}{r} 217 \\ \times\ \ 3 \\ \hline \end{array}$$

$$\begin{array}{r} 127 \\ \times\ \ 4 \\ \hline \end{array}$$

$$\begin{array}{r} 275 \\ \times\ \ 5 \\ \hline \end{array}$$

$$\begin{array}{r} 798 \\ \times\ \ 6 \\ \hline \end{array}$$

$$\begin{array}{r} 365 \\ \times\ \ 6 \\ \hline \end{array}$$

$$\begin{array}{r} 100 \\ \times\ \ 5 \\ \hline \end{array}$$

$$\begin{array}{r} 372 \\ \times\ \ 4 \\ \hline \end{array}$$

$$\begin{array}{r} 881 \\ \times\ \ 4 \\ \hline \end{array}$$

$$\begin{array}{r} 953 \\ \times\ \ 3 \\ \hline \end{array}$$

Solve each problem.

A middle school has 255 students. A high school has 6 times as many students. How many children are there at the high school?

A train can carry 365 passengers. How many could it carry on

four trips?

six trips?

Multiplying by one-digit numbers

Find each product. Remember to regroup.

$$\begin{array}{r} \overset{33}{456} \\ \times \quad 6 \\ \hline 2736 \end{array}$$

$$\begin{array}{r} \overset{12}{823} \\ \times \quad 8 \\ \hline 6584 \end{array}$$

$$\begin{array}{r} \overset{44}{755} \\ \times \quad 9 \\ \hline 6795 \end{array}$$

Find each product.

$$\begin{array}{r} 394 \\ \times \quad 7 \\ \hline \end{array}$$
$$\begin{array}{r} 736 \\ \times \quad 7 \\ \hline \end{array}$$
$$\begin{array}{r} 827 \\ \times \quad 8 \\ \hline \end{array}$$
$$\begin{array}{r} 943 \\ \times \quad 9 \\ \hline \end{array}$$

$$\begin{array}{r} 643 \\ \times \quad 6 \\ \hline \end{array}$$
$$\begin{array}{r} 199 \\ \times \quad 6 \\ \hline \end{array}$$
$$\begin{array}{r} 821 \\ \times \quad 7 \\ \hline \end{array}$$
$$\begin{array}{r} 547 \\ \times \quad 8 \\ \hline \end{array}$$

$$\begin{array}{r} 501 \\ \times \quad 7 \\ \hline \end{array}$$
$$\begin{array}{r} 377 \\ \times \quad 8 \\ \hline \end{array}$$
$$\begin{array}{r} 843 \\ \times \quad 8 \\ \hline \end{array}$$
$$\begin{array}{r} 222 \\ \times \quad 9 \\ \hline \end{array}$$

$$\begin{array}{r} 471 \\ \times \quad 9 \\ \hline \end{array}$$
$$\begin{array}{r} 223 \\ \times \quad 8 \\ \hline \end{array}$$
$$\begin{array}{r} 606 \\ \times \quad 6 \\ \hline \end{array}$$
$$\begin{array}{r} 513 \\ \times \quad 7 \\ \hline \end{array}$$

$$\begin{array}{r} 500 \\ \times \quad 9 \\ \hline \end{array}$$
$$\begin{array}{r} 800 \\ \times \quad 9 \\ \hline \end{array}$$
$$\begin{array}{r} 900 \\ \times \quad 8 \\ \hline \end{array}$$
$$\begin{array}{r} 200 \\ \times \quad 9 \\ \hline \end{array}$$

Solve each problem.

A crate holds 550 apples. How many apples are there in 8 crates?

Keyshawn swims 760 laps each week. How many laps does he swim in 5 weeks?

Real-life problems

Find the answer to each problem.

Jacob spent $4.68 at the store and had $4.77 left.
How much did he have to start with?

$9.45

```
      1 1
    4.77
  +  4.68
  ───────
    9.45
```

Tracy receives a weekly allowance of $3.00 a week.
How much will she have if she saves all of it for 8 weeks?

$24.00

```
    3.00
  ×    8
  ───────
   24.00
```

Find the answer to each problem.

A theater charges $4 for each matinee
ticket. If it sells 360 tickets for a matinee
performance, how much does it take in?

David has saved $9.59. His sister
has $3.24 less. How much does
she have?

The cost for 9 children to go to a
theme park is $72. How much does
each child pay? If only 6 children
go, what will the cost be?

Paul has $3.69. His sister gives him
another $5.25, and he goes out and
buys a CD single for $3.99. How
much does he have left?

Ian has $20 in savings. He
decides to spend $\frac{1}{4}$ of it. How
much will he have left?

148

Real-life problems

Find the answer to each problem.

Nina has an hour to do her homework. She plans to spend $\frac{1}{3}$ of her time on math. How many minutes will she spend doing math?

20 minutes

1 hour is 60 minutes

$$3\overline{)60}^{\,20}$$

In gym class, David makes 2 long jumps of 1.78 m and 2.19 m. How far does he jump altogether?

3.97 m

$$
\begin{array}{r}
1 \\
1.78\,\text{m} \\
+\ 2.19\,\text{m} \\
\hline
3.97\,\text{m}
\end{array}
$$

Find the answer to each problem.

Moishe has a can of lemonade containing 400 ml. He drinks $\frac{1}{4}$ of it. How much is left?

David ran 40 m in 8 seconds. At that speed, how far did he run in 1 second?

A large jar of coffee contains 1.75 kg. If 1.48 kg is left in the jar, how much has been used?

A worker can fill 145 boxes of tea in 15 minutes. How many boxes can he fill in 1 hour?

Jennifer's computer is 41.63 cm wide and her printer is 48.37 cm wide. How much space does she have for books if her desk is 1.5 m wide?

Problems involving time

Find the answer to each problem.

Caitlin spends 35 minutes on her homework each day. How many minutes does she spend on her homework in one week from Monday through Friday?

175 minutes

$$\begin{array}{r} \overset{2}{35} \\ \times\ \ 5 \\ \hline 175 \end{array}$$

Jenny spends 175 minutes on her homework from Monday through Friday. How much time does she spend on homework each day?

35 minutes

$$5\overline{)175}\ ^{35}$$

Find the answer to each problem.

Amy works from 9 A.M. until 5 P.M. She has a lunch break from noon until 1 P.M. How many hours does she work in a 5-day week?

School children have a 15-minute break in the morning and a 10-minute break in the afternoon. How many minutes of break do they have in a week?

It takes 2 hours for one person to do a job. If John shares the work with 3 of his friends, how long will it take?

Mr. Tambo spent 7 days building a patio. If he worked a total of 56 hours and he divided the work evenly among the seven days, how long did he work each day?

It took Ben 45 hours to build a remote-controlled airplane. If he spent 5 hours a day working on it:

How many days did it take?

How many hours per day would he have needed to finish it in 5 days?

150

Multiplying and dividing

Write the answer in the box.

26 x 10 = 260   26 x 100 = 2600

400 ÷ 10 = 40   400 ÷ 100 = 4

Write the product in the box.

33 x 10 =   21 x 10 =   42 x 10 =

94 x 100 =   36 x 100 =   81 x 100 =

416 x 10 =   204 x 10 =   513 x 10 =

767 x 100 =   821 x 100 =   245 x 100 =

Write the quotient in the box.

120 ÷ 10 =   260 ÷ 10 =   470 ÷ 10 =

300 ÷ 100 =   800 ÷ 100 =   400 ÷ 100 =

20 ÷ 10 =   30 ÷ 10 =   70 ÷ 10 =

500 ÷ 100 =   100 ÷ 100 =   900 ÷ 100 =

Write the number that has been multiplied by 100.

x 100 = 5900   x 100 = 71 400

x 100 = 72 100   x 100 = 23 400

x 100 = 1100   x 100 = 47 000

x 100 = 8400   x 100 = 44 100

Write the number that has been divided by 100.

÷ 100 = 2   ÷ 100 = 8

÷ 100 = 21   ÷ 100 = 18

÷ 100 = 86   ÷ 100 = 21

÷ 100 = 10   ÷ 100 = 59

Identifying patterns

Continue each pattern.

Steps of 2:	$\frac{1}{2}$	$2\frac{1}{2}$	$4\frac{1}{2}$	$6\frac{1}{2}$	$8\frac{1}{2}$	$10\frac{1}{2}$
Steps of 5:	3.5	8.5	13.5	18.5	23.5	28.5

Continue each pattern.

$5\frac{1}{2}$	$10\frac{1}{2}$	$15\frac{1}{2}$			
$1\frac{1}{4}$	$3\frac{1}{4}$	$5\frac{1}{4}$			
$8\frac{1}{3}$	$9\frac{1}{3}$	$10\frac{1}{3}$		$12\frac{1}{3}$	
$55\frac{3}{4}$	$45\frac{3}{4}$	$35\frac{3}{4}$			
$42\frac{1}{2}$	$38\frac{1}{2}$	$34\frac{1}{2}$			$22\frac{1}{2}$
7.5	6.5	5.5			
28.4	25.4	22.4		16.4	
81.6	73.6	65.6			
6.3	10.3	14.3			
12.1	13.1	14.1			17.1
14.6	21.6	28.6			
$11\frac{1}{2}$	$10\frac{1}{2}$	$9\frac{1}{2}$			
8.4	11.4	14.4		20.4	
$7\frac{3}{4}$	$13\frac{3}{4}$	$19\frac{3}{4}$			$37\frac{3}{4}$
57.5	48.5	39.5			

Products with odd and even numbers

Find the products of these numbers.

3 and 4   The product of 3 and 4 is 12.   6 and 8   The product of 6 and 8 is 48.

Find the products of these odd and even numbers.

5 and 6

7 and 4

6 and 3

10 and 3

3 and 2

8 and 3

2 and 9

12 and 5

What do you notice about your answers? _____

_____

Find the products of these odd numbers.

5 and 7

5 and 11

9 and 5

13 and 3

3 and 9

7 and 3

11 and 7

1 and 5

What do you notice about your answers? _____

_____

Find the products of these even numbers.

2 and 4

6 and 2

10 and 2

6 and 10

4 and 6

4 and 8

4 and 10

6 and 8

What do you notice about your answers? _____

_____

Can you write a rule for the products with odd and even numbers?

_____

Factors of numbers from 66 to 100

The factors of 66 are   1   2   3   6   11   22   33   66

Circle the factors of 94.   (1)   (2)   28   32   43   (47)   71   86   (94)

Write the factors of each number in the box.

The factors of 70 are

The factors of 85 are

The factors of 69 are

The factors of 83 are

The factors of 75 are

The factors of 96 are

The factors of 63 are

The factors of 99 are

The factors of 72 are

Circle the factors of 68.

    1   2   3   4   5   6   7   8   9   11   12   17   34   35   62   68

Circle the factors of 95.

    1   2   3   4   5   15   16   17   19   24   37   85   90   95   96

Circle the factors of 88.

    1   2   3   4   5   6   8   10   11   15   22   25   27   44   87   88

Circle the factors of 73.

    1   2   4   5   6   8   9   10   12   13   14   15   30   60   73

A prime number only has two factors, 1 and itself.
Write all the prime numbers between 66 and 100 in the box.

Multiplying by two-digit numbers

Write the product for each problem.

```
    ¹            ²¹
    ¹
   56           45
 x 32         x 43
 ─────        ─────
  112          135
 1680         1800
 ─────        ─────
 1792         1935
```

Write the product for each problem.

56	23	47	84
x 23	x 24	x 25	x 22

73	52	64	51
x 34	x 35	x 33	x 32

Write the product for each problem.

41	65	72	84
x 62	x 54	x 68	x 71

92	57	38	26
x 63	x 82	x 94	x 75

Multiplying by two-digit numbers

Write the product for each problem.

```
   7          7
   6          6
  39         68
x 87       x 98
─────      ─────
 273        544
3120       6120
─────      ─────
3393       6664
```

Write the product for each problem.

87	76	99	85
x 98	x 78	x 69	x 98

88	67	94	89
x 95	x 76	x 69	x 47

Write the product for each problem.

87	46	58	73
x 79	x 67	x 59	x 98

95	58	78	96
x 67	x 88	x 97	x 79

Multiplying by 10, 100, and 1000

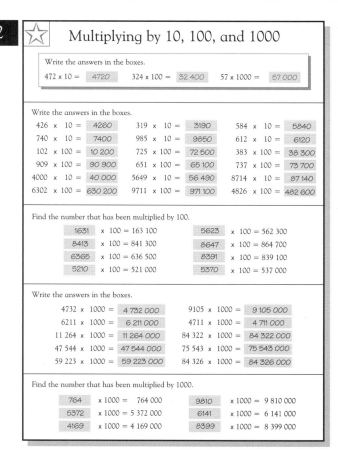

Write the answers in the boxes.

472 x 10 = 4720   324 x 100 = 32 400   57 x 1000 = 57 000

Write the answers in the boxes.

426 x 10 = 4260   319 x 10 = 3190   584 x 10 = 5840
740 x 10 = 7400   985 x 10 = 9850   612 x 10 = 6120
102 x 100 = 10 200   725 x 100 = 72 500   383 x 100 = 38 300
909 x 100 = 90 900   651 x 100 = 65 100   737 x 100 = 73 700
4000 x 10 = 40 000   5649 x 10 = 56 490   8714 x 10 = 87 140
6302 x 100 = 630 200   9711 x 100 = 971 100   4826 x 100 = 482 600

Find the number that has been multiplied by 100.

1631 x 100 = 163 100   5623 x 100 = 562 300
8413 x 100 = 841 300   8647 x 100 = 864 700
6365 x 100 = 636 500   8391 x 100 = 839 100
5210 x 100 = 521 000   5370 x 100 = 537 000

Write the answers in the boxes.

4732 x 1000 = 4 732 000   9105 x 1000 = 9 105 000
6211 x 1000 = 6 211 000   4711 x 1000 = 4 711 000
11 264 x 1000 = 11 264 000   84 322 x 1000 = 84 322 000
47 544 x 1000 = 47 544 000   75 543 x 1000 = 75 543 000
59 223 x 1000 = 59 223 000   84 326 x 1000 = 84 326 000

Find the number that has been multiplied by 1000.

764 x 1000 = 764 000   9810 x 1000 = 9 810 000
5372 x 1000 = 5 372 000   6141 x 1000 = 6 141 000
4169 x 1000 = 4 169 000   8399 x 1000 = 8 399 000

Children should realize that multiplying by 10, 100, or 1000 is the same as adding one, two, or three zeros. In the second and last sections, the child will need to divide the answer to find the number that has been multiplied.

3

The simplest form of fractions

Make these fractions equivalent by putting a number in the box.
$\frac{70}{100} = \frac{7}{10}$ $\frac{4}{12} = \frac{1}{3}$

Make these fractions equivalent by putting a number in each box.

$\frac{30}{100} = \frac{3}{10}$ $\frac{8}{100} = \frac{2}{25}$ $\frac{40}{100} = \frac{4}{10}$ $\frac{15}{100} = \frac{3}{20}$

$\frac{5}{20} = \frac{1}{4}$ $\frac{25}{100} = \frac{1}{4}$ $\frac{12}{60} = \frac{1}{5}$ $\frac{8}{20} = \frac{2}{5}$

$\frac{16}{40} = \frac{2}{5}$ $\frac{2}{6} = \frac{1}{3}$ $\frac{10}{60} = \frac{1}{6}$ $\frac{2}{12} = \frac{1}{6}$

$\frac{9}{18} = \frac{1}{2}$ $\frac{10}{18} = \frac{5}{9}$ $\frac{4}{24} = \frac{1}{6}$ $\frac{7}{28} = \frac{1}{4}$

$\frac{4}{6} = \frac{2}{3}$ $\frac{6}{10} = \frac{3}{5}$ $\frac{9}{15} = \frac{3}{5}$ $\frac{8}{12} = \frac{2}{3}$

$\frac{18}{20} = \frac{9}{10}$ $\frac{21}{28} = \frac{3}{4}$ $\frac{6}{8} = \frac{3}{4}$ $\frac{5}{50} = \frac{1}{10}$

$\frac{15}{25} = \frac{3}{5}$ $\frac{4}{16} = \frac{1}{4}$ $\frac{12}{20} = \frac{3}{5}$ $\frac{12}{18} = \frac{2}{3}$

$\frac{3}{15} = \frac{1}{5}$ $\frac{9}{36} = \frac{1}{4}$ $\frac{9}{27} = \frac{1}{3}$ $\frac{30}{50} = \frac{3}{5}$

Make these rows of fractions equivalent by putting a number in each box.

$\frac{1}{9} = \frac{2}{18} = \frac{3}{27} = \frac{4}{36} = \frac{5}{45} = \frac{6}{54}$

$\frac{1}{10} = \frac{2}{20} = \frac{3}{30} = \frac{4}{40} = \frac{5}{50} = \frac{6}{60}$

$\frac{3}{5} = \frac{12}{20} = \frac{15}{25} = \frac{18}{30} = \frac{21}{35} = \frac{24}{40}$

$\frac{5}{6} = \frac{10}{12} = \frac{15}{18} = \frac{20}{24} = \frac{25}{30} = \frac{30}{36}$

$\frac{1}{7} = \frac{2}{14} = \frac{3}{21} = \frac{4}{28} = \frac{5}{35} = \frac{6}{42}$

$\frac{3}{11} = \frac{12}{44} = \frac{21}{77} = \frac{27}{99} = \frac{30}{110} = \frac{33}{121}$

If children have problems with this page, explain to them that fractions remain the same as long as you multiply or divide the numerator and denominator by the same number.

Changing improper fractions to mixed numbers

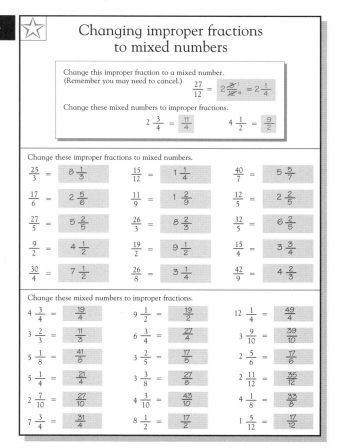

Change this improper fraction to a mixed number.
(Remember you may need to cancel.)
$\frac{27}{12} = 2\frac{3}{12} = 2\frac{1}{4}$

Change these mixed numbers to improper fractions.

$2\frac{3}{4} = \frac{11}{4}$ $4\frac{1}{2} = \frac{9}{2}$

Change these improper fractions to mixed numbers.

$\frac{25}{3} = 8\frac{1}{3}$ $\frac{15}{12} = 1\frac{1}{4}$ $\frac{40}{7} = 5\frac{5}{7}$

$\frac{17}{6} = 2\frac{5}{6}$ $\frac{11}{9} = 1\frac{2}{9}$ $\frac{12}{5} = 2\frac{2}{5}$

$\frac{27}{5} = 5\frac{2}{5}$ $\frac{26}{3} = 8\frac{2}{3}$ $\frac{32}{5} = 6\frac{2}{5}$

$\frac{9}{2} = 4\frac{1}{2}$ $\frac{19}{2} = 9\frac{1}{2}$ $\frac{15}{4} = 3\frac{3}{4}$

$\frac{30}{4} = 7\frac{1}{2}$ $\frac{26}{8} = 3\frac{1}{4}$ $\frac{42}{9} = 4\frac{2}{3}$

Change these mixed numbers to improper fractions.

$4\frac{3}{4} = \frac{19}{4}$ $9\frac{1}{2} = \frac{19}{2}$ $12\frac{1}{4} = \frac{49}{4}$

$3\frac{2}{3} = \frac{11}{3}$ $6\frac{3}{4} = \frac{27}{4}$ $3\frac{9}{10} = \frac{39}{10}$

$5\frac{1}{8} = \frac{41}{8}$ $3\frac{2}{5} = \frac{17}{5}$ $2\frac{5}{6} = \frac{17}{6}$

$5\frac{1}{4} = \frac{21}{4}$ $3\frac{3}{8} = \frac{27}{8}$ $2\frac{11}{12} = \frac{35}{12}$

$2\frac{7}{10} = \frac{27}{10}$ $4\frac{3}{10} = \frac{43}{10}$ $4\frac{1}{8} = \frac{33}{8}$

$7\frac{3}{4} = \frac{31}{4}$ $8\frac{1}{2} = \frac{17}{2}$ $1\frac{5}{12} = \frac{17}{12}$

In the first part, children should see that you can divide the denominator by the numerator and place the remainder over the denominator. Use card circles cut into equal parts to reinforce the idea, e.g. how many whole circles can you make from 17 quarter circles?

Rounding decimals

Write these decimals to the nearest tenth.

6.2 is 6.2   6.27 is 6.3

If the second decimal place is a 5, we round up the first decimal place to the next larger number.

6.25 is 6.3

Write these decimals to the nearest tenth.

9.21 is	9.2	4.38 is	4.4	2.47 is	2.5
3.48 is	3.5	8.17 is	8.2	6.28 is	6.3
7.14 is	7.1	3.91 is	3.9	2.56 is	2.6
8.41 is	8.4	2.36 is	2.4	1.53 is	1.5

Write these decimals to the nearest tenth.

9.35 is	9.4	8.71 is	8.7	6.05 is	6.1
1.19 is	1.2	3.65 is	3.7	4.21 is	4.2
8.55 is	8.6	7.35 is	7.4	9.14 is	9.1
6.83 is	6.8	2.15 is	2.2	6.34 is	6.3

Write these decimals to the nearest tenth.

25.61 is	25.6	14.35 is	14.4	11.24 is	11.2
16.85 is	16.9	24.34 is	24.3	71.36 is	71.4
26.85 is	26.9	11.54 is	11.5	37.25 is	37.3
92.42 is	92.4	95.65 is	95.7	27.36 is	27.4
45.17 is	45.2	36.75 is	36.8	22.05 is	22.1

If children experience difficulties, point out that the significant digit to look at is in the second decimal place. The use of a number line may be helpful where the child is still unsure. In the second section, the concept of .05 is introduced. This must be rounded up.

6

Adding with different numbers of digits

Find the total for each problem.

```
  432        176
+  43      +  97
  475        273
```

Remember to regroup if you need to.

Find the total for each problem.

```
  148        271        371        938
+  31      +  17      +  24      +  31
  179        288        395        969

  942        747        633        101
+  26      +  34      +  43      +  75
  968        781        676        176
```

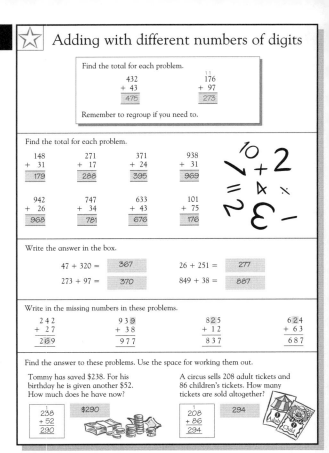

Write the answer in the box.

47 + 320 = 367   26 + 251 = 277

273 + 97 = 370   849 + 38 = 887

Write in the missing numbers in these problems.

```
  242        939        825        624
+  27      +  38      +  12      +  63
  269        977        837        687
```

Find the answer to these problems. Use the space for working them out.

Tommy has saved $238. For his birthday he is given another $52. How much does he have now?

```
  238
+  52
  290
```
$290

A circus sells 208 adult tickets and 86 children's tickets. How many tickets are sold altogether?

```
  208
+  86
  294
```
294

This page and the next should be straightforward. Any errors will probably be due to a failure to carry, or particularly in the second section, may occur where children have added digits with different place values.

7

Adding with different numbers of digits

Work out the answer to each problem.

```
      987          2 767
+ 423 123      + 12 844
  424 110         15 611
```

Remember to regroup if you need to.

Work out the answer to each problem.

```
   3 587      8 537 227          27
+ 17 628      +  86 518      + 9964
  21 215      8 623 745        9 991

     436        387 177        6 770
+ 12 844      +   8 381      + 772 142
  13 280        395 558        778 912
```

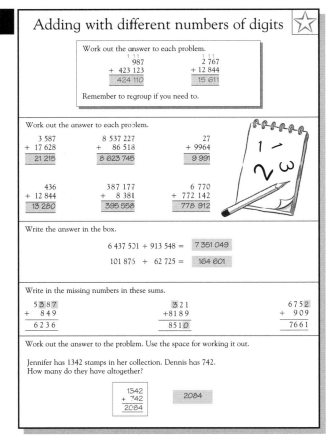

Write the answer in the box.

6 437 501 + 913 548 = 7 351 049

101 876 + 62 725 = 164 601

Write in the missing numbers in these sums.

```
  5387            321          6752
+  849          +8189         +  909
  6236           8510          7661
```

Work out the answer to the problem. Use the space for working it out.

Jennifer has 1342 stamps in her collection. Dennis has 742. How many do they have altogether?

```
  1342
+  742
  2084
```
2084

For problems in which the two numbers are not aligned vertically, ensure that children line up the digits in the ones place on the right side of the numbers. The most common error is not aligning the correct places.

Subtracting one number from another

Find the difference for each problem.

```
  834        431
-  44      -  84
  790        347
```

Find the difference for each problem.

```
  835        490        175        428
-  23      -  70      -  54      -  67
  812        420        121        361

  587        674        389        270
-  43      -  62      -  58      -  30
  544        612        331        240

  483        951        746        234
-  35      -  28      -  17      -  16
  448        923        729        218
```

Write the answer in the box.

491 – 31 = 460   654 – 22 = 632

874 – 63 = 811   577 – 26 = 551

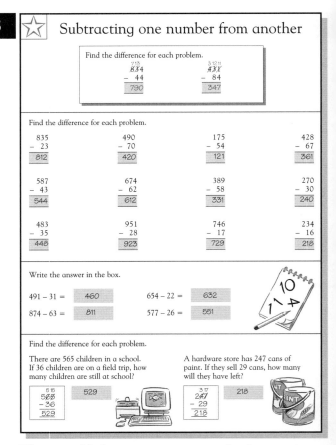

Find the difference for each problem.

There are 565 children in a school. If 36 children are on a field trip, how many children are still at school?

```
  565
-  36
  529
```
529

A hardware store has 247 cans of paint. If they sell 29 cans, how many will they have left?

```
  247
-  29
  218
```
218

The most likely errors to occur in the first section will involve subtractions where a larger digit has to be taken away from a smaller digit. Children often take the smaller digit that is on the top away from the larger digit on the bottom.

Subtracting one number from another ☆

Work out the answer to each problem.

$$\begin{array}{r} {}^{1\,16\,16\,7\,15} \\ 27\ \cancel{685} \\ -\ 8\ 726 \\ \hline 18\ 959 \end{array} \qquad \begin{array}{r} {}^{3\,12} \\ 47\ \cancel{423} \\ -\ 5\ 351 \\ \hline 42\ 072 \end{array}$$

Work out the answer to each problem.

$$\begin{array}{r} 68\ 231 \\ -\ 3\ 846 \\ \hline 64\ 385 \end{array} \qquad \begin{array}{r} 62\ 411 \\ -\ 47\ 566 \\ \hline 14\ 845 \end{array} \qquad \begin{array}{r} 11\ 684 \\ -\ 2\ 845 \\ \hline 8\ 839 \end{array} \qquad \begin{array}{r} 37\ 481 \\ -\ 19\ 804 \\ \hline 17\ 677 \end{array}$$

$$\begin{array}{r} 7965 \\ -\ 3976 \\ \hline 3989 \end{array} \qquad \begin{array}{r} 92\ 112 \\ -\ 46\ 489 \\ \hline 45\ 623 \end{array} \qquad \begin{array}{r} 67\ 444 \\ -\ 29\ 545 \\ \hline 37\ 899 \end{array} \qquad \begin{array}{r} 8818 \\ -\ 7465 \\ \hline 1353 \end{array}$$

$$\begin{array}{r} 52\ 812 \\ -\ 37\ 341 \\ \hline 15\ 471 \end{array} \qquad \begin{array}{r} 2522 \\ -\ 1176 \\ \hline 1346 \end{array} \qquad \begin{array}{r} 8529 \\ -\ 5892 \\ \hline 2637 \end{array} \qquad \begin{array}{r} 6387 \\ -\ 2798 \\ \hline 3589 \end{array}$$

Write the answer in the box.

55 562 − 24 871 = | 30 691

9118 − 8467 = | 651

Work out the answer to the problem. Use the space for working it out.

2826 people went to see a rock concert. 135 had to leave early to catch their train. How many were left at the end?

$$\begin{array}{r} {}^{7\,12} \\ 2\cancel{826} \\ -\ 135 \\ \hline 2691 \end{array} \qquad 2691$$

See the notes for page 7.

10

Real-life problems

Toby has $525.95 in the bank and he spends $146.37 on his vacation. How much does he have left?

Toby has $379.58 left.

$$\begin{array}{r} {}^{4\,11\,15\,8\,15} \\ \cancel{\$525.95} \\ -\ \$146.37 \\ \hline \$379.58 \end{array}$$

A rally driver drives 183 km on the first day of a race and 147 km on the second day. How many kilometres does he travel in the two days?

He drives 330 kilometres.

$$\begin{array}{r} {}^{1} \\ 183\ km \\ +\ 147\ km \\ \hline 330\ km \end{array}$$

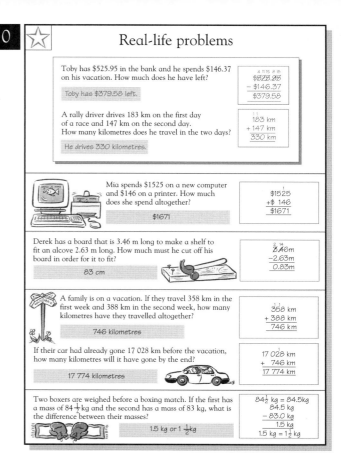

Mia spends $1525 on a new computer and $146 on a printer. How much does she spend altogether?

$1671

$$\begin{array}{r} {}^{1} \\ \$1525 \\ +\$\ 146 \\ \hline \$1671 \end{array}$$

Derek has a board that is 3.46 m long to make a shelf to fit an alcove 2.63 m long. How much must he cut off his board in order for it to fit?

83 cm

$$\begin{array}{r} {}^{2\ 14} \\ 3.\cancel{46}m \\ -2.63m \\ \hline 0.83m \end{array}$$

A family is on a vacation. If they travel 358 km in the first week and 388 km in the second week, how many kilometres have they travelled altogether?

746 kilometres

$$\begin{array}{r} {}^{1\ 1} \\ 358\ km \\ +\ 388\ km \\ \hline 746\ km \end{array}$$

If their car had already gone 17 028 km before the vacation, how many kilometres will it have gone by the end?

17 774 kilometres

$$\begin{array}{r} 17\ 028\ km \\ +\ 746\ km \\ \hline 17\ 774\ km \end{array}$$

Two boxers are weighed before a boxing match. If the first has a mass of $84\frac{1}{2}$ kg and the second has a mass of 83 kg, what is the difference between their masses?

1.5 kg or $1\frac{1}{2}$ kg

$$\begin{array}{r} 84\tfrac{1}{2}\ kg = 84.5kg \\ 84.5\ kg \\ -\ 83.0\ kg \\ \hline 1.5\ kg \\ 1.5\ kg = 1\tfrac{1}{2}\ kg \end{array}$$

In this page and the following two pages children can apply the skills of addition and subtraction to real-life problems, using various units of measurement. If the child is unsure which operation to use, discuss whether the answer will be larger or smaller.

11

Everyday problems

An electrician buys 415 m of cable. If he uses 234 m, how much does he have left?

He has 181 m of cable left.

$$\begin{array}{r} {}^{3\ 11} \\ 4\cancel{15}\ m \\ -\ 234\ m \\ \hline 181\ m \end{array}$$

Simon travels by train for 110 km, by bus for 56 km and then walks the final 5 km. How far does he travel?

Simon travels 171 km.

$$\begin{array}{r} 110\ km \\ 56\ km \\ +\ \ 5\ km \\ \hline 171\ km \end{array}$$

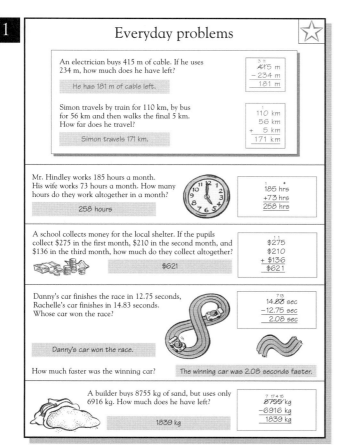

Mr. Hindley works 185 hours a month. His wife works 73 hours a month. How many hours do they work altogether in a month?

258 hours

$$\begin{array}{r} {}^{1} \\ 185\ hrs \\ +73\ hrs \\ \hline 258\ hrs \end{array}$$

A school collects money for the local shelter. If the pupils collect $275 in the first month, $210 in the second month, and $136 in the third month, how much do they collect altogether?

$621

$$\begin{array}{r} {}^{1\ 1} \\ \$275 \\ \$210 \\ +\ \$136 \\ \hline \$621 \end{array}$$

Danny's car finishes the race in 12.75 seconds, Rachelle's car finishes in 14.83 seconds. Whose car won the race?

Danny's car won the race.

$$\begin{array}{r} {}^{7\ 13} \\ 14.\cancel{83}\ sec \\ -12.75\ sec \\ \hline 2.08\ sec \end{array}$$

How much faster was the winning car?

The winning car was 2.08 seconds faster.

A builder buys 8755 kg of sand, but uses only 6916 kg. How much does he have left?

1839 kg

$$\begin{array}{r} {}^{7\ 14\ 15} \\ 8\cancel{755}\ kg \\ -6916\ kg \\ \hline 1839\ kg \end{array}$$

See the notes for page 10. Point out that an answer that will be larger will require addition, while one that will be smaller will require subtraction.

Everyday problems

Rudy, Andrew, and Rachelle want to put their money together to buy a present for their brother. If Rudy gives $12.50, Andrew gives $14.75, and Rachelle gives $15.25, how much will they have to spend?

They will have $42.50 to spend.

$$\begin{array}{r} {}^{1\ 1\ \ 1} \\ \$12.50 \\ \$14.75 \\ +\ \$15.25 \\ \hline \$42.50 \end{array}$$

A store has 130 kg of potatoes and sells 80 kg. How much does it have left?

The store has 50 kg left.

$$\begin{array}{r} {}^{13} \\ 130\ kg \\ -\ 80\ kg \\ \hline 50\ kg \end{array}$$

A bakery orders 145 kg of sugar, 565 kg of salt, and 926 kg of butter. What is the total mass of the order?

The total weight is 1636 kg.

$$\begin{array}{r} {}^{1\ 1} \\ 145\ kg \\ 565\ kg \\ +\ 926\ kg \\ \hline 1636\ kg \end{array}$$

Mr. Jean-Paul travelled in a limo to the airport. After he paid a fare of $65, he had $125 left. How much money did he start with?

He started with $190.

$$\begin{array}{r} {}^{1} \\ \$125 \\ +\ \$\ 65 \\ \hline \$190 \end{array}$$

A vacation in Florida costs $394. A vacation in Majorca costs $876. How much cheaper is the Florida vacation?

The Florida vacation is $482 cheaper.

$$\begin{array}{r} {}^{7\ 17} \\ \$\cancel{876} \\ -\ \$394 \\ \hline \$482 \end{array}$$

Chamique is saving up to buy a guitar that costs $159.99. If she already has $65.37, how much more does she need?

She needs $94.62 more.

$$\begin{array}{r} \$159.99 \\ -\$\ 65.37 \\ \hline \$\ 94.62 \end{array}$$

Mr. Lorenzo's garden is 10 m long and 8 m wide. How much fence does he need to surround all four sides?

He needs 36 m of fence.

$$\begin{array}{r} 10\ m \\ 10\ m \\ 8\ m \\ +\ 8\ m \\ \hline 36\ m \end{array}$$

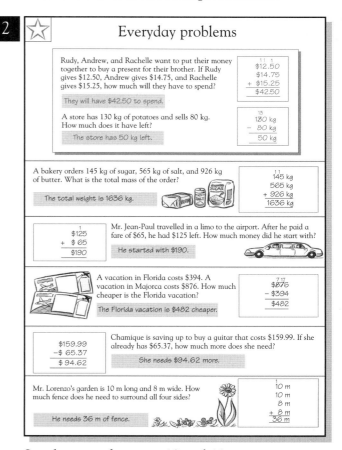

See the notes for pages 10 and 11.

13 — Decimal addition

13

Write in the answers to these problems.

```
 1 1            1 1
 47.15          43.99
+19.36         +12.76
 66.51          56.75
```

Write the answer to each problem.

53.72 +77.92 **131.64**	84.17 +68.21 **152.38**	29.36 +66.84 **96.20**	23.56 +79.14 **102.70**	62.49 +18.75 **81.24**
35.67 +12.99 **48.66**	29.88 +43.02 **72.90**	67.39 +81.70 **149.09**	49.32 +14.95 **64.27**	27.22 +38.84 **66.06**

Write the answer to each problem.

76.30 +22.97 **99.27**	44.29 +11.04 **55.33**	81.97 +69.14 **151.11**	29.86 +76.33 **106.19**	68.25 +84.36 **152.61**
83.90 +30.24 **114.14**	45.83 +45.71 **91.54**	52.17 +90.21 **142.38**	84.93 +29.37 **114.30**	72.83 +41.16 **113.99**

Write the answer to each problem.

37.89 + 82.15 = **120.04**   32.44 + 21.88 = **54.32**   37.19 + 28.24 = **65.43**

68.67 + 29.82 = **98.49**   21.99 + 79.32 = **101.31**   52.45 + 34.58 = **87.03**

84.77 + 39.12 = **123.89**   63.84 + 29.81 = **93.65**   34.43 + 25.64 = **60.07**

33.97 + 24.62 = **58.59**   76.39 + 43.78 = **120.17**   52.38 + 38.43 = **90.81**

This page and the next page should follow on from earlier addition work. On these two pages, children are dealing with two decimal places. The most likely mistakes will be errors involving carrying, or in the third section, where they are working horizontally.

---

14 — Decimal addition

14

Write the sum for each problem.

```
  1 1             1 1
 296.48           73.00
+131.70         +269.23
 428.18          342.23
```

Write the sum for each problem.

91.83 + 37.84 **129.67**	64.71 + 21.2 **85.91**	32.045 + 4.99 **37.035**	306 + 44.24 **350.24**
71.932 + 55.26 **127.192**	842.01 + 11.842 **853.852**	675.82 + 105 **780.82**	37.82 +399.71 **437.53**
65.24 + 605.27 **670.51**	178.935 + 599.41 **778.345**	184.70 + 372.81 **557.51**	443.27 + 75 **518.27**
563 +413.98 **976.98**	703.95 + 85.11 **789.06**	825.36 + 249.857 **1075.217**	529.3 + 482.56 **1011.86**

Write the sum for each problem.

421 + 136.25 = **557.25**   92.31 + 241.73 = **334.04**

501.8 + 361.93 = **863.73**   558.32 + 137.945 = **696.265**

27 + 142.07 = **169.07**   75.31 + 293.33 = **368.64**

153.3 + 182.02 = **335.32**   491.445 + 105.37 = **596.815**

253.71 + 62 = **315.71**   829.2 + 63.74 = **892.94**

Watch out for misalignment when children work on horizontal subtractions.

---

15 — Decimal subtraction

15

Write the difference for each problem.

```
     6 16             0 18
 59.76            57.18
-21.47           -22.09
 38.29            35.09
```

Write the difference for each problem.

64.92 − 26.35 **38.57**	64.21 − 16.02 **48.19**	73.71 −19.24 **54.47**	92.63 − 67.14 **25.49**
45.76 − 16.18 **29.58**	73.52 −39.27 **34.25**	98.98 −39.19 **59.79**	53.58 − 14.39 **39.19**
94.87 − 65.28 **29.59**	21.74 − 12.1 **9.64**	62.35 −13.16 **49.19**	81.94 − 28.15 **53.79**
62.95 − 33.37 **29.58**	81.42 −25.04 **56.38**	48.52 − 14.49 **34.03**	61.55 − 13.26 **48.29**

Write the difference for each problem.

51.52 − 12.13 = **39.39**   72.41 − 23.18 = **49.23**

91.91 − 22.22 = **69.69**   53.84 − 19.65 = **34.19**

41.82 − 18.13 = **23.69**   51.61 − 23.14 = **28.47**

83.91 − 14.73 = **69.18**   64.65 − 37.26 = **27.39**

53.21 − 35.12 = **18.09**   77.31 − 28.15 = **49.16**

On this page and the next two pages, the most likely errors will result from a failure to use decomposition where necessary (see notes for pages 8 and 9). Watch out for misalignment when children work on horizontal subtractions.

---

16 — Decimal subtraction

16

Write the difference for each problem.

```
    7 11            1 10
 68.17           39.20
-11.40          -13.15
 56.77           26.05
```

Work out the difference for each problem.

87.23 − 24.4 **62.83**	95.15 − 31.356 **63.794**	66.37 − 21.9 **44.47**	85 − 26.32 **58.68**
72.28 − 1.3 **70.98**	63.14 − 32 **31.14**	99.235 − 33.70 **65.535**	62.1 −29.34 **32.76**
77.3 − 24.42 **52.88**	55.492 − 27.66 **27.832**	68 − 31.5 **36.5**	35.612 −13.207 **22.405**
82.35 − 23.40 **58.95**	63.20 − 15.36 **47.84**	53.64 − 23 **30.64**	35.612 − 26.19 **9.422**

Write the difference for each problem.

63.4 − 24.51 = **38.89**   92.197 − 63.28 = **28.917**

91.3 − 33 = **58.3**   41.24 − 14.306 = **26.934**

52.251 − 22.42 = **29.831**   72.6 − 53.71 = **18.89**

92.84 − 23 = **69.84**   61.16 − 24.4 = **36.76**

81.815 − 55.90 = **25.915**   94.31 − 27.406 = **66.904**

On this page, the most common error will result from not writing the numbers to the same number of decimal places before subtracting.

17

Multiplying larger numbers by ones ☆

Write the product for each problem.

¹³ 529	¹³¹ 1273
x 4	x 5
2116	6365

Write the product for each problem.

724	831	126	455
x 2	x 3	x 3	x 4
1448	2493	378	1820

161	282	349	253
x 4	x 5	x 5	x 6
644	1410	1745	1518

328	465	105	562
x 6	x 6	x 4	x 4
1968	2790	420	2248

Write the product for each problem.

4261	1582	3612	4284
x 3	x 3	x 4	x 4
12 783	4746	14 448	17 136

5907	1263	1303	1467
x 5	x 5	x 6	x 6
29 535	6315	7818	8802

6521	8436	1599	3761
x 6	x 6	x 6	x 6
39 126	50 616	9594	22 566

5837	6394	8124	3914
x 4	x 5	x 6	x 6
23 348	31 970	48 744	23 484

Make sure that children understand the convention of multiplication problems, i.e. multiply the ones first, work left, and carry when necessary. This page will generally highlight gaps in knowledge of the 2, 3, 4, 5, and 6 multiplication tables.

18

☆ Multiplying larger numbers by ones

Write the answer to each problem.

¹⁴ 417	¹⁷⁴ 2185
x 7	x 9
2919	19 665

Write the answer to each problem.

419	604	715	327
x 7	x 7	x 8	x 7
2933	4228	5720	2289

425	171	682	246
x 8	x 9	x 8	x 8
3400	1539	5456	1968

436	999	319	581
x 8	x 9	x 9	x 9
3488	8991	2871	5229

Work out the answer to each problem.

4331	2816	1439	2617
x 7	x 7	x 8	x 8
30 317	19 712	11 512	20 936

3104	4022	3212	2591
x 8	x 8	x 9	x 9
24 832	32 176	28 908	23 319

1710	3002	2468	1514
x 9	x 8	x 7	x 8
15 390	24 016	17 276	12 112

4624	2993	3894	4361
x 7	x 8	x 8	x 9
32 368	23 944	31 152	39 249

Any problems encountered on this page will be similar to those of the previous page. Gaps in the child's knowledge of multiplication tables 7, 8, and 9 will be highlighted here.

19

Real-life multiplication problems ☆

There are 157 apples in a box. How many will there be in three boxes?

471 apples

¹² 157
x 3
471

A stamp album can hold 550 stamps. How many stamps will 5 albums hold?

2750 stamps

² 550
x 5
2750

A train can take 425 passengers. How many can it take in four trips?

1700 passengers

¹² 425
x 4
1700

Mr Jenkins puts $256 a month into the bank. How much will he have put in after six months?

$1536

³³ 256
x 6
1536

A theatre can seat 5524 people. If a play runs for 7 days, what is the maximum number of people who will be able to see it?

38 668 people

³ ¹² 5 524
x 7
38 668

A car costs $19 956. How much will it cost a company to buy nine cars for its salespeople?

$179 604

⁸⁸⁵⁵ 19 956
x 9
179 604

Installing a new window for a house costs $435. How much will it cost to install 8 windows of the same size?

$3480

²⁴ 435
x 8
3480

An airplane flies at a steady speed of 550 km/h. How far will it travel in 7 hours?

3850 kilometres

³ 550
x 7
3850

This page provides an opportunity for children to apply their skills of multiplication to real-life problems. As with previous multiplication work, gaps in the child's knowledge of multiplication facts will be highlighted here.

☆ Comparing and ordering decimals

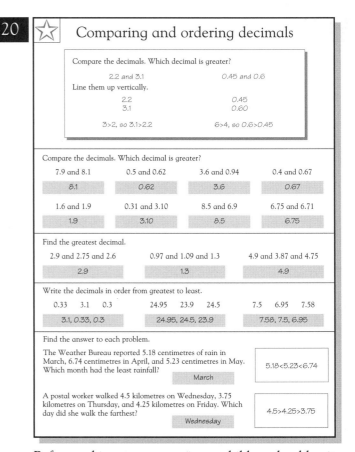

Compare the decimals. Which decimal is greater?

2.2 and 3.1   0.45 and 0.6

Line them up vertically.

2.2   0.45
3.1   0.60

3>2, so 3.1>2.2   6>4, so 0.6>0.45

Compare the decimals. Which decimal is greater?

7.9 and 8.1	0.5 and 0.62	3.6 and 0.94	0.4 and 0.67
8.1	0.62	3.6	0.67

1.6 and 1.9	0.31 and 3.10	8.5 and 6.9	6.75 and 6.71
1.9	3.10	8.5	6.75

Find the greatest decimal.

2.9 and 2.75 and 2.6	0.97 and 1.09 and 1.3	4.9 and 3.87 and 4.75
2.9	1.3	4.9

Write the decimals in order from greatest to least.

0.33 3.1 0.3	24.95 23.9 24.5	7.5 6.95 7.58
3.1, 0.33, 0.3	24.95, 24.5, 23.9	7.58, 7.5, 6.95

Find the answer to each problem.

The Weather Bureau reported 5.18 centimetres of rain in March, 6.74 centimetres in April, and 5.23 centimetres in May. Which month had the least rainfall?

March   5.18<5.23<6.74

A postal worker walked 4.5 kilometres on Wednesday, 3.75 kilometres on Thursday, and 4.25 kilometres on Friday. Which day did she walk the farthest?

Wednesday   4.5>4.25>3.75

Before making any comparisons, children should write out each of the numbers with the same number of decimal places, lining up the decimal points vertically.

Converting units of measure ☆

Convert 25 centimetres to millimetres.   Convert 200¢ to dollars.

25 x 10 = 250 mm   200 ÷ 100 = $2

Convert these centimetres to millimetres.

40 cm	400 mm	15 cm	150 mm	9 cm	90 mm
12 cm	120 mm	34 cm	340 mm	62 cm	620 mm
43 cm	430 mm	96 cm	960 mm	105 cm	1050 mm
92 cm	920 mm	20 cm	200 mm	426 cm	4260 mm

Convert these millimetres to centimetres.

30 mm	3 cm	100 mm	10 cm	120 mm	12 cm
60 mm	6 cm	90 mm	9 cm	200 mm	20 cm
130 mm	13 cm	10 mm	1 cm	400 mm	40 cm

Convert these dollars to cents.

$35	3500¢	$600	60 000¢	$15	1500¢
$12	1200¢	$36	3600¢	$95	9500¢
$72	7200¢	$4	400¢	$250	25 000¢

Convert these cents to dollars.

450¢	$4.50	900¢	$9.00	6000¢	$60.00
250¢	$2.50	400¢	$4.00	150¢	$1.50
100¢	$1.00	300¢	$3.00	750¢	$7.50

This page highlights problems with the relationship between millimetres and centimetres, and dollars and pennies. Use a ruler or money to explain. Look out for answers such as $7.5. Remind children that, with money, we use zero in the hundredths column.

22

☆ Converting units of measure

Convert 300 centimetres to metres.   Convert 4 kilometres to metres.

300 ÷ 100 = 3 m   4 x 1000 = 4000 m

Convert these centimetres to metres.

500 cm	5 m	900 cm	9 m	400 cm	4 m
8000 cm	80 m	3000 cm	30 m	4000 cm	40 m
9800 cm	98 m	8300 cm	83 m	6200 cm	62 m
36 800 cm	368 m	94 200 cm	942 m	73 500 cm	735 m

Convert these metres to centimetres.

47 m	4700 cm	29 m	2900 cm	84 m	8400 cm
69 m	6900 cm	24 m	2400 cm	38 m	3800 cm
146 m	14 600 cm	237 m	23 700 cm	921 m	92 100 cm

Convert these metres to kilometres.

5000 m	5 km	6000 m	6 km	9000 m	9 km
15 000 m	15 km	27 000 m	27 km	71 000 m	71 km
19 000 m	19 km	86 000 m	86 km	42 000 m	42 km

Convert these kilometres to metres.

7 km	7000 m	9 km	9000 m	4 km	4000 m
23 km	23 000 m	46 km	46 000 m	87 km	87 000 m
12 km	12 000 m	96 km	96 000 m	39 km	39 000 m

As with page 21, check that children understand the relationship between centimetres and millimetres, and metres and kilometres. If they are secure in this understanding, this should be a straightforward page of multiplying and dividing by 100 and 1000.

Area of rectangles and squares ☆

Find the area of this rectangle.

To find the area of a rectangle or square, we multiply length (l) by width (w).

Area = 800 cm²

```
   1
  32
x 25
 160
+640
 800 cm²
```

Find the area of these rectangles and squares.
You may need to do your work on a separate sheet.

42 cm / 21 cm: 882 cm²

84 cm / 84 cm: 7056 cm²

95 m / 36 m: 3420 m²

41 m / 87 m: 3567 m²

68 mm / 49 mm: 3332 mm²

77 mm / 83 mm: 6391 mm²

99 cm / 99 cm: 9801 cm²

39 cm / 85 cm: 3315 cm²

69 cm / 83 cm: 5727 cm²

For the exercises on this page, children need to multiply the two sides together to arrive at the area. If any answers are wrong, check the long multiplication, and if necessary, revise the method. Children may confuse area and perimeter, and add the sides together.

☆ Perimeter of shapes

Find the perimeter of this rectangle.

To find the perimeter of a rectangle or square, we add the two lengths and the two widths together.

12.4 cm / 27.3 cm

```
 1 1
27.3 cm
27.3 cm
12.4 cm
+12.4 cm
79.4 cm
```

79.4 cm

Find the perimeter of these rectangles and squares.
You may need to do your work on a separate sheet.

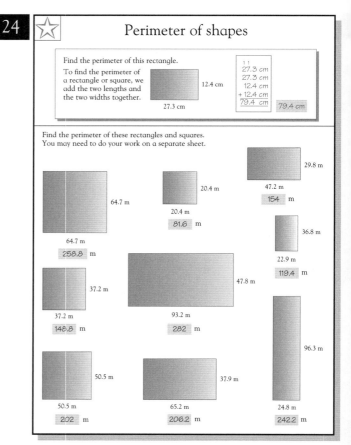

64.7 m / 64.7 m: 258.8 m

20.4 m / 20.4 m: 81.6 m

29.8 m / 47.2 m: 154 m

36.8 m / 22.9 m: 119.4 m

37.2 m / 37.2 m: 148.8 m

47.8 m / 93.2 m: 282 m

50.5 m / 50.5 m: 202 m

37.9 m / 65.2 m: 206.2 m

96.3 m / 24.8 m: 242.2 m

On this page and the next, the most likely problem will be confusion with the area work done previously. Remind children to add the four sides together to get the perimeter.

Decimal place value ⭐

Work out the answer to the problem.

2.385
What is the value of the digit 8?

2. Ones	3 Tenths	8 Hundredths	5 Thousandths	0 Ten-thousandths

2.3850
8 is in the hundredths place,
so, its value is 8 hundredths.

Name the place of the digit 8 in each of the problems.

0.387	3.87	4.82	8.11
hundredths	tenths	tenths	ones

Name the value of the highlighted digit.

6.5937	5.371	7.403	0.42
9 hundredths	3 tenths	7 ones	2 tenths

	6.24	3.611	1.062
Which number has a digit with the value 6 tenths?			3.611
Which number has a digit with the value 6 hundredths?			1.062
Which number has a digit with the value 6 ones?			6.24

How much greater is the second decimal than the first?

7.46 7.56	3.27 3.67	0.82 0.85
one tenth more	four tenths more	three hundredths more

Be sure that children understand that the place value of a digit is the place that it is in, while the value of the digit is the amount that it is worth in that place.

26

⭐ Speed problems

How long will it take a bike rider to travel 36 km at a constant speed of 9 kilometres per hour?

4 hours
9)36
Time = Distance ÷ Speed

If a car travelled 150 km at a constant speed in 5 hours, at what speed was it travelling?

30 km/h
5)150
Speed = Distance ÷ Time

If a bus travels for 5 hours at 40 km/h, how far does it travel?

5 × 40 = 200 km
Distance = Speed x Time

A car travels along a road at a steady speed of 60 km/h. How far will it travel in 6 hours?

60 × 6 = 360   360 km

A train covers a distance of 480 km in 8 hours. If it travels at a constant speed, how fast is it travelling?

$\frac{60}{8)480}$ 60 km/h

John walks at a steady speed of 3 km/h. How long will it take him to travel 24 kilometres?

$\frac{8}{3)24}$ 8 hours

A car travels at a constant speed of 65 km/h. How far will it have travelled in 4 hours?

65 × 4 = 260   260 km

Melanie completes a long distance run at an average speed of 6 km/h. If it takes her 3 hours, how far did she run?

6 × 3 = 18   18 km

Sarah cycles 30 km to her grandmother's house at a steady speed of 10 km/h. If she leaves home at 2:00 P.M., what time will she arrive?

$\frac{3}{10)30}$
2 + 3 = 5   5:00 P.M.

If children experience difficulties on this page, ask them what they need to find, i.e. speed, distance, or time, and refer to the formula necessary to do this. Encourage children to develop simple examples that will help them to remember the formulas.

27

Conversion table ⭐

This is part of a conversion table that shows how to change dollars to pesos when 10 Mexican pesos (10MN) equal $1.

Canadian Dollars	Mexican Pesos
1	10
2	20
3	30

How many pesos would you get for $2?   20MN

How much is 25MN worth in dollars? $2.50

	Canadian Dollars	Mexican Pesos
How many dollars would you get for 40MN? $4.00	1	10
How many dollars would you get for 85MN? $8.50	2	20
How much is 1MN worth? 10¢	3	30
Change $65 into pesos. 650MN	4	40
What is $3.50 in pesos? 35MN	5	50
Change 250MN into dollars. $25.00	6	60
How many pesos could you get for $0.40? 4MN	7	70
	8	80
	9	90
	10	100

The rate then changes to 8MN to the dollar. The conversion chart now looks like the one shown here.

	Canadian Dollars	Mexican Pesos
	1	8
How many pesos are worth $4? 32MN	2	16
How many dollars can you get for 56MN? $7.00	3	24
How many pesos are worth $9.50? 76MN	4	32
How many pesos can you get for $20? 160MN	5	40
How many dollars would you get for 120MN? $15.00	6	48
What is the value of 4MN? 50¢	7	56
	8	64
	9	72
	10	80

Most of the questions require reading off from a conversion chart. Errors may occur if the chart is not read across accurately. Children may need extra help for questions that involve amounts not on the chart. Check that the right chart is used for the second part.

⭐ Interpreting circle graphs

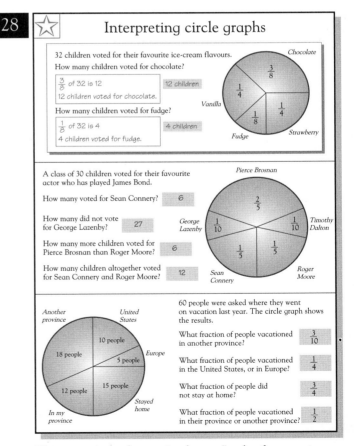

32 children voted for their favourite ice-cream flavours. How many children voted for chocolate?

$\frac{3}{8}$ of 32 is 12
12 children voted for chocolate.   12 children

How many children voted for fudge?

$\frac{1}{8}$ of 32 is 4
4 children voted for fudge.   4 children

A class of 30 children voted for their favourite actor who has played James Bond.

How many voted for Sean Connery?   6

How many did not vote for George Lazenby?   27

How many more children voted for Pierce Brosnan than Roger Moore?   6

How many children altogether voted for Sean Connery and Roger Moore?   12

60 people were asked where they went on vacation last year. The circle graph shows the results.

What fraction of people vacationed in another province? $\frac{3}{10}$

What fraction of people vacationed in the United States, or in Europe? $\frac{1}{4}$

What fraction of people did not stay at home? $\frac{3}{4}$

What fraction of people vacationed in their province or another province? $\frac{1}{2}$

This page introduces pie charts. In the first section children are required to find fractions of an amount. If unsure, remind the child to divide the total by the denominator and multiply by the numerator. The most likely errors will come from misreading the question.

Probability scale 0 to 1

Look at this probability line.
Impossible = 0
Poor chance = 0.25
Fair = 0.5
Good chance = 0.75
Certain = 1

Write each letter in the correct place on the probability line.
a. It will be daylight in New Orleans at midnight.
b. The sun will come up tomorrow.
c. If I toss a coin it will come down heads.

```
a               c               b
|───────────────↓───────────────↓
0      0.25     0.5     0.75     1
```

```
e       b       a       c       d
|───────|───────|───────|───────|
0      0.25     0.5     0.75     1
```

Write each letter in the correct place on the probability line.

a. If I cut a pack of cards I will get a red card.

b. If I cut a pack of cards I will get a diamond.

c. If I cut a pack of cards I will get a diamond, a spade, or a club.

d. If I cut a pack of cards I will get a diamond, a spade, a club, or a heart.

e. If I cut a pack of cards it will be a 15.

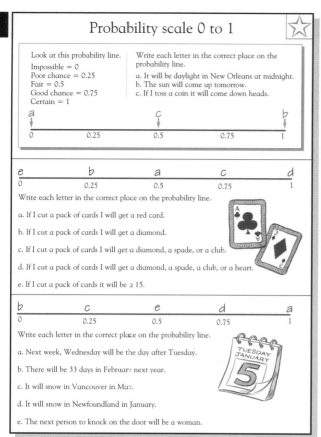

```
b       c       e       d       a
|───────|───────|───────|───────|
0      0.25     0.5     0.75     1
```

Write each letter in the correct place on the probability line.

a. Next week, Wednesday will be the day after Tuesday.

b. There will be 33 days in February next year.

c. It will snow in Vancouver in May.

d. It will snow in Newfoundland in January.

e. The next person to knock on the door will be a woman.

The first section assumes a knowledge of the suits of a pack of cards. If children are unfamiliar with cards, some discussion will be necessary. In the second section, the examples have been chosen to fall into the categories listed on the probability line.

30

Likely outcomes

Throw one coin 20 times. Keep a tally.

| H | ⫴⫴ ⦀⦀ |
| T | ⫴⫴ ⫴⫴ |

Put your results on a bar graph.

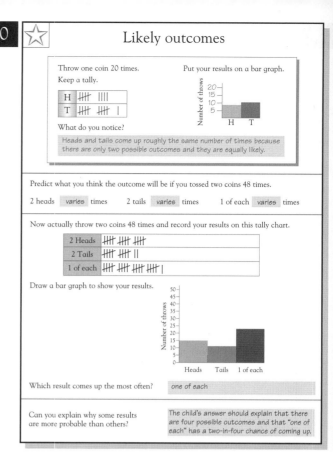

What do you notice?

Heads and tails come up roughly the same number of times because there are only two possible outcomes and they are equally likely.

Predict what you think the outcome will be if you tossed two coins 48 times.

2 heads [varies] times   2 tails [varies] times   1 of each [varies] times

Now actually throw two coins 48 times and record your results on this tally chart.

2 Heads	⫴⫴ ⫴⫴ ⫴⫴
2 Tails	⫴⫴ ⫴⫴ ⦀
1 of each	⫴⫴ ⫴⫴ ⫴⫴ ⫴⫴ ⦀

Draw a bar graph to show your results.

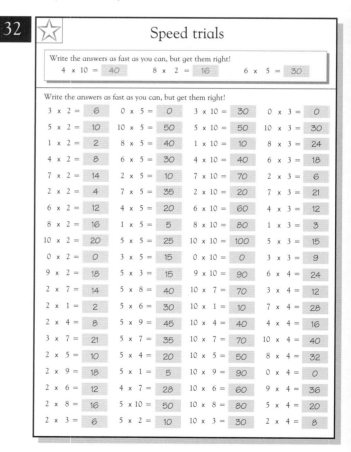

Which result comes up the most often?   one of each

Can you explain why some results are more probable than others?

The child's answer should explain that there are four possible outcomes and that "one of each" has a two-in-four chance of coming up.

Childrens' predictions in the first question may be considerably different from the result. Once the work is done, check that children use the experience to improve their understanding of likely outcomes. The tally chart may differ from the one shown here.

31

Naming quadrilaterals

Name this shape.

Rhombus

Name these shapes.

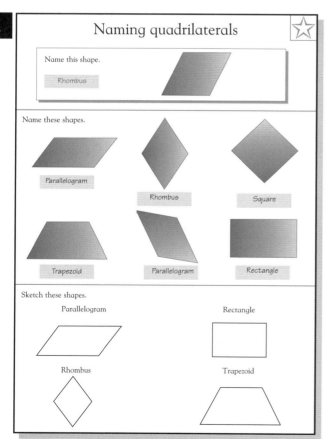

Parallelogram

Rhombus

Square

Trapezoid

Parallelogram

Rectangle

Sketch these shapes.

Parallelogram

Rectangle

Rhombus

Trapezoid

If children have problems identifying these shapes, it may be necessary to provide some more examples for identification practice.

Speed trials

Write the answers as fast as you can, but get them right!

4 x 10 = 40   8 x 2 = 16   6 x 5 = 30

Write the answers as fast as you can, but get them right!

3 x 2 = 6	0 x 5 = 0	3 x 10 = 30	0 x 3 = 0
5 x 2 = 10	10 x 5 = 50	5 x 10 = 50	10 x 3 = 30
1 x 2 = 2	8 x 5 = 40	1 x 10 = 10	8 x 3 = 24
4 x 2 = 8	6 x 5 = 30	4 x 10 = 40	6 x 3 = 18
7 x 2 = 14	2 x 5 = 10	7 x 10 = 70	2 x 3 = 6
2 x 2 = 4	7 x 5 = 35	2 x 10 = 20	7 x 3 = 21
6 x 2 = 12	4 x 5 = 20	6 x 10 = 60	4 x 3 = 12
8 x 2 = 16	1 x 5 = 5	8 x 10 = 80	1 x 3 = 3
10 x 2 = 20	5 x 5 = 25	10 x 10 = 100	5 x 3 = 15
0 x 2 = 0	3 x 5 = 15	0 x 10 = 0	3 x 3 = 9
9 x 2 = 18	5 x 3 = 15	9 x 10 = 90	6 x 4 = 24
2 x 7 = 14	5 x 8 = 40	10 x 7 = 70	3 x 4 = 12
2 x 1 = 2	5 x 6 = 30	10 x 1 = 10	7 x 4 = 28
2 x 4 = 8	5 x 9 = 45	10 x 4 = 40	4 x 4 = 16
3 x 7 = 21	5 x 7 = 35	10 x 7 = 70	10 x 4 = 40
2 x 5 = 10	5 x 4 = 20	10 x 5 = 50	8 x 4 = 32
2 x 9 = 18	5 x 1 = 5	10 x 9 = 90	0 x 4 = 0
2 x 6 = 12	4 x 7 = 28	10 x 6 = 60	9 x 4 = 36
2 x 8 = 16	5 x 10 = 50	10 x 8 = 80	5 x 4 = 20
2 x 3 = 6	5 x 2 = 10	10 x 3 = 30	2 x 4 = 8

All the 3s

You will need to know these:

1 x 3 = 3   2 x 3 = 6   3 x 3 = 9   4 x 3 = 12   5 x 3 = 15   10 x 3 = 30

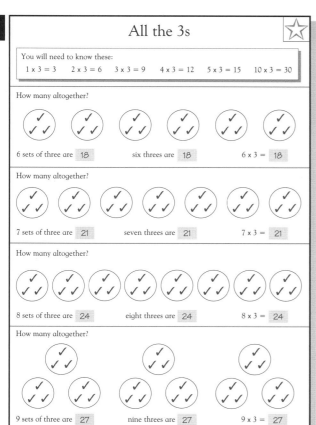

How many altogether?

6 sets of three are 18   six threes are 18   6 x 3 = 18

How many altogether?

7 sets of three are 21   seven threes are 21   7 x 3 = 21

How many altogether?

8 sets of three are 24   eight threes are 24   8 x 3 = 24

How many altogether?

9 sets of three are 27   nine threes are 27   9 x 3 = 27

34

All the 3s again

You should know all of the three times table by now.

1 x 3 = 3	2 x 3 = 6	3 x 3 = 9
6 x 3 = 18	7 x 3 = 21	8 x 3 = 24

4 x 3 = 12   5 x 3 = 15
9 x 3 = 27   10 x 3 = 30

Say these to yourself a few times.

Cover the three times table with a sheet of paper so you can't see the numbers.
Write the answers. Be as fast as you can, but get them right!

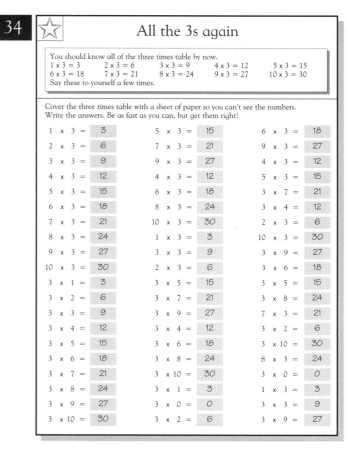

1 x 3 = 3	5 x 3 = 15	6 x 3 = 18
2 x 3 = 6	7 x 3 = 21	9 x 3 = 27
3 x 3 = 9	9 x 3 = 27	4 x 3 = 12
4 x 3 = 12	4 x 3 = 12	5 x 3 = 15
5 x 3 = 15	6 x 3 = 18	3 x 7 = 21
6 x 3 = 18	8 x 3 = 24	3 x 4 = 12
7 x 3 = 21	10 x 3 = 30	2 x 3 = 6
8 x 3 = 24	1 x 3 = 3	10 x 3 = 30
9 x 3 = 27	3 x 3 = 9	3 x 9 = 27
10 x 3 = 30	2 x 3 = 6	3 x 6 = 18
3 x 1 = 3	3 x 5 = 15	3 x 5 = 15
3 x 2 = 6	3 x 7 = 21	3 x 8 = 24
3 x 3 = 9	3 x 9 = 27	7 x 3 = 21
3 x 4 = 12	3 x 4 = 12	3 x 2 = 6
3 x 5 = 15	3 x 6 = 18	3 x 10 = 30
3 x 6 = 18	3 x 8 = 24	8 x 3 = 24
3 x 7 = 21	3 x 10 = 30	3 x 0 = 0
3 x 8 = 24	3 x 1 = 3	1 x 3 = 3
3 x 9 = 27	3 x 0 = 0	3 x 3 = 9
3 x 10 = 30	3 x 2 = 6	3 x 9 = 27

35

All the 4s

You should know these:

1 x 4 = 4   2 x 4 = 8   3 x 4 = 12   4 x 4 = 16   5 x 4 = 20   10 x 4 = 40

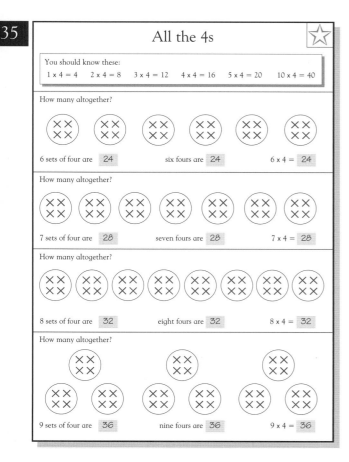

How many altogether?

6 sets of four are 24   six fours are 24   6 x 4 = 24

How many altogether?

7 sets of four are 28   seven fours are 28   7 x 4 = 28

How many altogether?

8 sets of four are 32   eight fours are 32   8 x 4 = 32

How many altogether?

9 sets of four are 36   nine fours are 36   9 x 4 = 36

All the 4s again

You should know all of the four times table by now.

1 x 4 = 4	2 x 4 = 8	3 x 4 = 12	4 x 4 = 16	5 x 4 = 20
6 x 4 = 24	7 x 4 = 28	8 x 4 = 32	9 x 4 = 36	10 x 4 = 40

Say these to yourself a few times.

Cover the four times table with a sheet of paper so you can't see the numbers.
Write the answers. Be as fast as you can, but get them right!

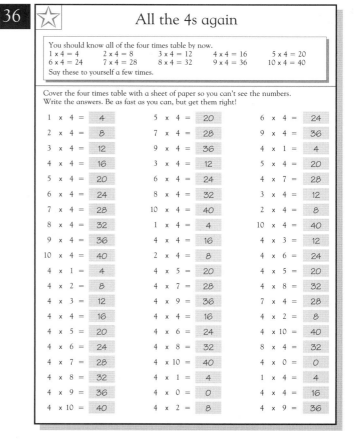

1 x 4 = 4	5 x 4 = 20	6 x 4 = 24
2 x 4 = 8	7 x 4 = 28	9 x 4 = 36
3 x 4 = 12	9 x 4 = 36	4 x 1 = 4
4 x 4 = 16	3 x 4 = 12	5 x 4 = 20
5 x 4 = 20	6 x 4 = 24	4 x 7 = 28
6 x 4 = 24	8 x 4 = 32	3 x 4 = 12
7 x 4 = 28	10 x 4 = 40	2 x 4 = 8
8 x 4 = 32	1 x 4 = 4	10 x 4 = 40
9 x 4 = 36	4 x 4 = 16	4 x 3 = 12
10 x 4 = 40	2 x 4 = 8	4 x 6 = 24
4 x 1 = 4	4 x 5 = 20	4 x 5 = 20
4 x 2 = 8	4 x 7 = 28	4 x 8 = 32
4 x 3 = 12	4 x 9 = 36	7 x 4 = 28
4 x 4 = 16	4 x 4 = 16	4 x 2 = 8
4 x 5 = 20	4 x 6 = 24	4 x 10 = 40
4 x 6 = 24	4 x 8 = 32	8 x 4 = 32
4 x 7 = 28	4 x 10 = 40	4 x 0 = 0
4 x 8 = 32	4 x 1 = 4	1 x 4 = 4
4 x 9 = 36	4 x 0 = 0	4 x 4 = 16
4 x 10 = 40	4 x 2 = 8	4 x 9 = 36

Speed trials

You should know all of the 1, 2, 3, 4, 5, and 10 times tables by now, but how quickly can you do them?
Ask someone to time you as you do this page.
Remember, you must be fast but also correct.

4 x 2 = 8	6 x 3 = 18	9 x 5 = 45
8 x 3 = 24	3 x 4 = 12	8 x 10 = 80
7 x 4 = 28	7 x 5 = 35	7 x 2 = 14
6 x 5 = 30	3 x 10 = 30	6 x 3 = 18
8 x 10 = 80	1 x 2 = 2	5 x 4 = 20
8 x 2 = 16	7 x 3 = 21	4 x 5 = 20
5 x 3 = 15	4 x 4 = 16	3 x 10 = 30
9 x 4 = 36	6 x 5 = 30	2 x 2 = 4
5 x 5 = 25	4 x 10 = 40	1 x 3 = 3
7 x 10 = 70	6 x 2 = 12	0 x 4 = 0
0 x 2 = 0	5 x 3 = 15	10 x 5 = 50
4 x 3 = 12	8 x 4 = 32	9 x 2 = 18
6 x 4 = 24	0 x 5 = 0	8 x 3 = 24
3 x 5 = 15	2 x 10 = 20	7 x 4 = 28
4 x 10 = 40	7 x 2 = 14	6 x 5 = 30
7 x 2 = 14	8 x 3 = 24	5 x 10 = 50
3 x 3 = 9	9 x 4 = 36	4 x 0 = 0
2 x 4 = 8	5 x 5 = 25	3 x 2 = 6
7 x 5 = 35	7 x 10 = 70	2 x 8 = 16
9 x 10 = 90	5 x 2 = 10	1 x 9 = 9

38

Some of the 6s

You should already know parts of the 6 times table because they are parts of the 1, 2, 3, 4, 5, and 10 times tables.
1 x 6 = 6   2 x 6 = 12   3 x 6 = 18
4 x 6 = 24   5 x 6 = 30   10 x 6 = 60
Find out if you can remember them quickly and correctly.

Cover the six times table with paper so you can't see the numbers.
Write the answers as quickly as you can.

What is three sixes?	18	What is ten sixes?	60
What is two sixes?	12	What is four sixes?	24
What is one six?	6	What is five sixes?	30

Write the answers as quickly as you can.

How many sixes make 12?	2	How many sixes make 6?	1
How many sixes make 30?	5	How many sixes make 18?	3
How many sixes make 24?	4	How many sixes make 60?	10

Write the answers as quickly as you can.

Multiply six by three.	18	Multiply six by ten.	60
Multiply six by two.	12	Multiply six by five.	30
Multiply six by one.	6	Multiply six by four.	24

Write the answers as quickly as you can.

4 x 6 = 24	2 x 6 = 12	10 x 6 = 60
5 x 6 = 30	1 x 6 = 6	3 x 6 = 18

Write the answers as quickly as you can.
A box contains six eggs. A man buys five boxes. How many eggs does he have? 30

A pack contains six sticks of gum.
How many sticks will there be in 10 packs? 60

39

The rest of the 6s

You need to learn these:
6 x 6 = 36   7 x 6 = 42   8 x 6 = 48   9 x 6 = 54

This work will help you remember the 6 times table.

Complete these sequences.

6   12   18   24   30   36   42   48   54   60

5 x 6 = 30   so   6 x 6 = 30 plus another 6 = 36

18   24   30   36   42   48   54   60

6 x 6 = 36   so   7 x 6 = 36 plus another 6 = 42

6   12   18   24   30   36   42   48   54   60

7 x 6 = 42   so   8 x 6 = 42 plus another 6 = 48

6   12   18   24   30   36   42   48   54   60

8 x 6 = 48   so   9 x 6 = 48 plus another 6 = 54

6   12   18   24   30   36   42   48   54   60

Test yourself on the rest of the 6 times table.
Cover the above part of the page with a sheet of paper.

What is six sixes?	36	What is seven sixes? 42
What is eight sixes?	48	What is nine sixes? 54

8 x 6 = 48   7 x 6 = 42   6 x 6 = 36   9 x 6 = 54

Practise the 6s

You should know all of the 6 times table now, but how quickly can you remember it?
Ask someone to time you as you do this page.
Remember, you must be fast but also correct.

1 x 6 = 6	2 x 6 = 12	7 x 6 = 42
2 x 6 = 12	4 x 6 = 24	3 x 6 = 18
3 x 6 = 18	6 x 6 = 36	9 x 6 = 54
4 x 6 = 24	8 x 6 = 48	6 x 4 = 24
5 x 6 = 30	10 x 6 = 60	1 x 6 = 6
6 x 6 = 36	1 x 6 = 6	6 x 2 = 12
7 x 6 = 42	3 x 6 = 18	6 x 8 = 48
8 x 6 = 48	5 x 6 = 30	0 x 6 = 0
9 x 6 = 54	7 x 6 = 42	6 x 3 = 18
10 x 6 = 60	9 x 6 = 54	5 x 6 = 30
6 x 1 = 6	6 x 3 = 18	6 x 7 = 42
6 x 2 = 12	6 x 5 = 30	2 x 6 = 12
6 x 3 = 18	6 x 7 = 42	6 x 9 = 54
6 x 4 = 24	6 x 9 = 54	4 x 6 = 24
6 x 5 = 30	6 x 2 = 12	8 x 6 = 48
6 x 6 = 36	6 x 4 = 24	10 x 6 = 60
6 x 7 = 42	6 x 6 = 36	6 x 5 = 30
6 x 8 = 48	6 x 8 = 48	6 x 0 = 0
6 x 9 = 54	6 x 10 = 60	6 x 1 = 6
6 x 10 = 60	6 x 0 = 0	6 x 6 = 36

Speed trials

You should know all of the 1, 2, 3, 4, 5, 6, and 10 times tables by now,
but how quickly can you remember them?
Ask someone to time you as you do this page.
Remember, you must be fast but also correct.

4 x 6 = 24	6 x 3 = 18	9 x 6 = 54
5 x 3 = 15	8 x 6 = 48	8 x 6 = 48
7 x 3 = 21	6 x 6 = 36	7 x 3 = 21
6 x 5 = 30	3 x 10 = 30	6 x 6 = 36
6 x 10 = 60	6 x 2 = 12	5 x 4 = 20
8 x 2 = 16	7 x 3 = 21	4 x 6 = 24
5 x 3 = 15	4 x 6 = 24	3 x 6 = 18
9 x 6 = 54	6 x 5 = 30	2 x 6 = 12
5 x 5 = 25	6 x 10 = 60	6 x 3 = 18
7 x 6 = 42	6 x 2 = 12	0 x 6 = 0
0 x 2 = 0	5 x 3 = 15	10 x 5 = 50
6 x 3 = 18	8 x 4 = 32	6 x 2 = 12
6 x 6 = 36	0 x 6 = 0	8 x 3 = 24
3 x 5 = 15	5 x 10 = 50	7 x 6 = 42
4 x 10 = 40	7 x 6 = 42	6 x 5 = 30
7 x 10 = 70	8 x 3 = 24	5 x 10 = 50
3 x 6 = 18	9 x 6 = 54	6 x 0 = 0
2 x 4 = 8	5 x 5 = 25	3 x 10 = 30
6 x 9 = 54	7 x 10 = 70	2 x 8 = 16
9 x 10 = 90	5 x 6 = 30	1 x 8 = 8

42

Some of the 7s

You should already know parts of the 7 times table because they are parts of the
1, 2, 3, 4, 5, 6 and 10 times tables.
1 x 7 = 7   2 x 7 = 14   3 x 7 = 21   4 x 7 = 28
5 x 7 = 35   6 x 7 = 42   10 x 7 = 70
Find out if you can remember them quickly and correctly.

Cover the seven times table with paper and write the answers to these questions as
quickly as you can.

What is three sevens?	21	What is ten sevens?	70
What is two sevens?	14	What is four sevens?	28
What is six sevens?	42	What is five sevens?	35

Write the answers as quickly as you can.

How many sevens make 14?	2	How many sevens make 42?	6
How many sevens make 35?	5	How many sevens make 21?	3
How many sevens make 28?	4	How many sevens make 70?	10

Write the answers as quickly as you can.

Multiply seven by three.	21	Multiply seven by ten.	70
Multiply seven by two.	14	Multiply seven by five.	35
Multiply seven by six.	42	Multiply seven by four.	28

Write the answers as quickly as you can.

4 x 7 = 28	2 x 7 = 14	10 x 7 = 70
5 x 7 = 35	1 x 7 = 7	3 x 7 = 21

Write the answers as quickly as you can.
A bag has seven candies. Ann buys five bags. How many candies does she have? 35

How many days are there in six weeks? 42

The rest of the 7s

You should now know all of the 1, 2, 3, 4, 5, 6, and 10 times tables.
You need to learn only these parts of the seven times table.
7 x 7 = 49   8 x 7 = 56   9 x 7 = 63

This work will help you remember the 7 times table.

Complete these sequences.

7   14   21   28   35   42   49   56   63   70

6 x 7 = 42   so   7 x 7 = 42 plus another 7 = 49

21   28   35   42   49   56   63   70

7 x 7 = 49   so   8 x 7 = 49 plus another 7 = 56

7   14   21   28   35   42   49   56   63   70

8 x 7 = 56   so   9 x 7 = 56 plus another 7 = 63

7   14   21   28   35   42   49   56   63   70

Test yourself on the rest of the 7 times table.
Cover the section above with a sheet of paper.

What is seven sevens?	49	What is eight sevens?	56
What is nine sevens?	63	What is ten sevens?	70

8 x 7 = 56   7 x 7 = 49   9 x 7 = 63   10 x 7 = 70

How many days are there in eight weeks? 56

A package contains seven pens.
How many pens will there be in nine packets? 63

How many sevens make 56? 8

Practise the 7s

You should know all of the 7 times table now, but how quickly can you remember it?
Ask someone to time you as you do this page.
Remember, you must be fast but also correct.

1 x 7 = 7	2 x 7 = 14	7 x 6 = 42
2 x 7 = 14	4 x 7 = 28	3 x 7 = 21
3 x 7 = 21	6 x 7 = 42	9 x 7 = 63
4 x 7 = 28	8 x 7 = 56	7 x 4 = 28
5 x 7 = 35	10 x 7 = 70	1 x 7 = 7
6 x 7 = 42	1 x 7 = 7	7 x 2 = 14
7 x 7 = 49	3 x 7 = 21	7 x 8 = 56
8 x 7 = 56	5 x 7 = 35	0 x 7 = 0
9 x 7 = 63	7 x 7 = 49	7 x 3 = 21
10 x 7 = 70	9 x 7 = 63	5 x 7 = 35
7 x 1 = 7	7 x 3 = 21	7 x 7 = 49
7 x 2 = 14	7 x 5 = 35	2 x 7 = 14
7 x 3 = 21	7 x 7 = 49	7 x 9 = 63
7 x 4 = 28	7 x 9 = 63	4 x 7 = 28
7 x 5 = 35	7 x 2 = 14	8 x 7 = 56
7 x 6 = 42	7 x 4 = 28	10 x 7 = 70
7 x 7 = 49	7 x 6 = 42	7 x 5 = 35
7 x 8 = 56	7 x 8 = 56	7 x 0 = 0
7 x 9 = 63	7 x 10 = 70	7 x 1 = 7
7 x 10 = 70	7 x 0 = 0	6 x 7 = 42

Speed trials ☆

You should know all of the 1, 2, 3, 4, 5, 6, 7, and 10 times tables by now, but how quickly can you remember them?
Ask someone to time you as you do this page.
Remember, you must be fast but also correct.

4 x 7 = 28	7 x 3 = 21	9 x 7 = 63
5 x 10 = 50	8 x 7 = 56	7 x 6 = 42
7 x 5 = 35	6 x 6 = 36	8 x 3 = 24
6 x 5 = 30	5 x 10 = 50	6 x 6 = 36
6 x 10 = 60	6 x 3 = 18	7 x 4 = 28
8 x 7 = 56	7 x 5 = 35	4 x 6 = 24
5 x 8 = 40	4 x 6 = 24	3 x 7 = 21
9 x 6 = 54	6 x 5 = 30	2 x 8 = 16
5 x 7 = 35	7 x 10 = 70	7 x 3 = 21
7 x 6 = 42	6 x 7 = 42	0 x 6 = 0
0 x 5 = 0	5 x 7 = 35	10 x 7 = 70
6 x 3 = 18	8 x 4 = 32	6 x 2 = 12
6 x 7 = 42	0 x 7 = 0	8 x 7 = 56
3 x 5 = 15	5 x 8 = 40	7 x 7 = 49
4 x 7 = 28	7 x 6 = 42	6 x 5 = 30
7 x 10 = 70	8 x 3 = 24	5 x 10 = 50
7 x 8 = 56	9 x 6 = 54	7 x 0 = 0
2 x 7 = 14	7 x 7 = 49	3 x 10 = 30
4 x 9 = 36	9 x 10 = 90	2 x 7 = 14
9 x 10 = 90	5 x 6 = 30	7 x 8 = 56

46

☆ Some of the 8s

You should already know some of the 8 times table because it is part of the 1, 2, 3, 4, 5, 6, 7, and 10 times tables.
1 x 8 = 8   2 x 8 = 16   3 x 8 = 24   4 x 8 = 32
5 x 8 = 40   6 x 8 = 48   7 x 8 = 56   10 x 8 = 80
Find out if you can remember them quickly and correctly.

Cover the 8 times table with paper so you can't see the numbers.
Write the answers as quickly as you can.

What is three eights? 24	What is ten eights? 80
What is two eights? 16	What is four eights? 32
What is six eights? 48	What is five eights? 40

Write the answers as quickly as you can.

How many eights equal 16? 2	How many eights equal 40? 5
How many eights equal 32? 4	How many eights equal 24? 3
How many eights equal 56? 7	How many eights equal 48? 6

Write the answers as quickly as you can.

Multiply eight by three. 24	Multiply eight by ten. 80
Multiply eight by two. 16	Multiply eight by five. 40
Multiply eight by six. 48	Multiply eight by four. 32

Write the answers as quickly as you can.

6 x 8 = 48	2 x 8 = 16	10 x 8 = 80
5 x 8 = 40	7 x 8 = 56	3 x 8 = 24

Write the answers as quickly as you can.
A pizza has eight slices. John buys six pizzas.
How many slices does he have? 48
Which number multiplied by 8 gives the answer 56? 7

The rest of the 8s ☆

You need to learn only these parts of the eight times table.
8 x 8 = 64   9 x 8 = 72

This work will help you remember the 8 times table.

Complete these sequences.

8   16   24   32   40   48   56   64   72   80

7 x 8 = 56   so   8 x 8 = 56 plus another 8 = 64

24   32   40   48   56   64   72   80

8 x 8 = 64   so   9 x 8 = 64 plus another 8 = 72

8   16   24   32   40   48   56   64   72   80

8   16   24   32   40   48   56   64   72   80

Test yourself on the rest of the 8 times table.
Cover the section above with a sheet of paper.

What is seven eights? 56	What is eight eights? 64
What is nine eights? 72	What is eight nines? 72

8 x 8 = 64   9 x 8 = 72   8 x 9 = 72   10 x 8 = 80

What number multiplied by 8 gives the answer 72? 9

A number multiplied by 8 gives the answer 80. What is the number? 10

David puts out building bricks in piles of 8.
How many bricks will there be in 10 piles? 80

What number multiplied by 5 gives the answer 40? 8

How many 8s make 72? 9

☆ Practise the 8s

You should know all of the 8 times table now, but how quickly can you remember it?
Ask someone to time you as you do this page.
Be fast but also correct.

1 x 8 = 8	2 x 8 = 16	8 x 6 = 48
2 x 8 = 16	4 x 8 = 32	3 x 8 = 24
3 x 8 = 24	6 x 8 = 48	9 x 8 = 72
4 x 8 = 32	8 x 8 = 64	8 x 4 = 32
5 x 8 = 40	10 x 8 = 80	1 x 8 = 8
6 x 8 = 48	1 x 8 = 8	8 x 2 = 16
7 x 8 = 56	3 x 8 = 24	7 x 8 = 56
8 x 8 = 64	5 x 8 = 40	0 x 8 = 0
9 x 8 = 72	7 x 8 = 56	8 x 3 = 24
10 x 8 = 80	9 x 8 = 72	5 x 8 = 40
8 x 1 = 8	8 x 3 = 24	8 x 8 = 64
8 x 2 = 16	8 x 5 = 40	2 x 8 = 16
8 x 3 = 24	8 x 8 = 64	8 x 9 = 72
8 x 4 = 32	8 x 9 = 72	4 x 8 = 32
8 x 5 = 40	8 x 2 = 16	8 x 6 = 48
8 x 6 = 48	8 x 4 = 32	10 x 8 = 80
8 x 7 = 56	8 x 6 = 48	8 x 5 = 40
8 x 8 = 64	8 x 8 = 64	8 x 0 = 0
8 x 9 = 72	8 x 10 = 80	8 x 1 = 8
8 x 10 = 80	8 x 0 = 0	6 x 8 = 48

Speed trials ⭐

You should know all of the 1, 2, 3, 4, 5, 6, 7, 8, and 10 times tables now,
but how quickly can you remember them?
Ask someone to time you as you do this page.
Be fast but also correct.

4 x 8 = 32	7 x 8 = 56	9 x 8 = 72
5 x 10 = 50	8 x 7 = 56	7 x 6 = 42
7 x 8 = 56	6 x 8 = 48	8 x 3 = 24
8 x 5 = 40	8 x 10 = 80	8 x 8 = 64
6 x 10 = 60	6 x 3 = 18	7 x 4 = 28
8 x 7 = 56	7 x 7 = 49	4 x 8 = 32
5 x 8 = 40	5 x 6 = 30	3 x 7 = 21
9 x 8 = 72	6 x 7 = 42	2 x 8 = 16
8 x 8 = 64	7 x 10 = 70	7 x 3 = 21
7 x 6 = 42	6 x 9 = 54	0 x 8 = 0
7 x 5 = 35	5 x 8 = 40	10 x 8 = 80
6 x 8 = 48	8 x 4 = 32	6 x 2 = 12
6 x 7 = 42	0 x 8 = 0	8 x 6 = 48
5 x 7 = 35	5 x 9 = 45	7 x 8 = 56
8 x 4 = 32	7 x 6 = 42	6 x 5 = 30
7 x 10 = 70	8 x 3 = 24	8 x 10 = 80
2 x 8 = 16	9 x 6 = 54	8 x 7 = 56
4 x 7 = 28	8 x 6 = 48	5 x 10 = 50
6 x 9 = 54	9 x 10 = 90	8 x 2 = 16
9 x 10 = 90	6 x 6 = 36	8 x 9 = 72

50

⭐ Some of the 9s

You should already know nearly all of the 9 times table because it is part of the
1, 2, 3, 4, 5, 6, 7, 8, and 10 times tables.
    1 x 9 = 9   2 x 9 = 18   3 x 9 = 27   4 x 9 = 36   5 x 9 = 45
    6 x 9 = 54   7 x 9 = 63   8 x 9 = 72   10 x 9 = 90
Find out if you can remember them quickly and correctly.

Cover the nine times table so you can't see the numbers.
Write the answers as quickly as you can.

What is three nines?	27	What is ten nines?	90
What is two nines?	18	What is four nines?	36
What is six nines?	54	What is five nines?	45
What is seven nines?	63	What is eight nines?	72

Write the answers as quickly as you can.

How many nines equal 18?	2	How many nines equal 54?	6
How many nines equal 90?	10	How many nines equal 27?	3
How many nines equal 72?	8	How many nines equal 36?	4
How many nines equal 45?	5	How many nines equal 63?	7

Write the answers as quickly as you can.

Multiply nine by seven.	63	Multiply nine by ten.	90
Multiply nine by two.	18	Multiply nine by five.	45
Multiply nine by six.	54	Multiply nine by four.	36
Multiply nine by three.	27	Multiply nine by eight.	72

Write the answers as quickly as you can.

6 x 9 = 54	2 x 9 = 18	10 x 9 = 90
5 x 9 = 45	3 x 9 = 27	8 x 9 = 72
0 x 9 = 0	7 x 9 = 63	4 x 9 = 36

51

The rest of the 9s ⭐

You need to learn only this part of the nine times table.
        9 x 9 = 81

This work will help you remember the 9 times table.
Complete these sequences.

| 9 | 18 | 27 | 36 | 45 | 54 | 63 | 72 | 81 | 90 |

8 x 9 = 72 so 9 x 9 = 72 plus another 9 = 81

| 27 | 36 | 45 | 54 | 63 | 72 | 81 | 90 |

| 9 | 18 | 27 | 36 | 45 | 54 | 63 | 72 | 81 | 90 |

| 9 | 18 | 27 | 36 | 45 | 54 | 63 | 72 | 81 | 90 |

Look for a pattern in the nine times table.

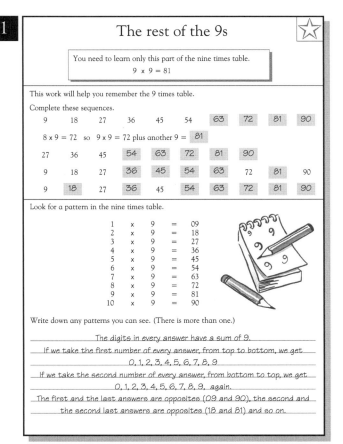

1	x	9	=	09
2	x	9	=	18
3	x	9	=	27
4	x	9	=	36
5	x	9	=	45
6	x	9	=	54
7	x	9	=	63
8	x	9	=	72
9	x	9	=	81
10	x	9	=	90

Write down any patterns you can see. (There is more than one.)

The digits in every answer have a sum of 9.
If we take the first number of every answer, from top to bottom, we get
0, 1, 2, 3, 4, 5, 6, 7, 8, 9
If we take the second number of every answer, from bottom to top, we get
0, 1, 2, 3, 4, 5, 6, 7, 8, 9, again.
The first and the last answers are opposites (09 and 90), the second and
the second last answers are opposites (18 and 81) and so on.

Encourage children to notice patterns. It does not
matter how they express these. One pattern is to
deduct 1 from the number being multiplied. This
gives the first digit of the answer. Then deduct this
first digit from 9 to get the second digit of the answer.

⭐ Practise the 9s

You should know all of the 9 times table now, but how quickly can you remember it?
Ask someone to time you as you do this page.
Be fast and correct.

1 x 9 = 9	2 x 9 = 18	9 x 6 = 54
2 x 9 = 18	4 x 9 = 36	3 x 9 = 27
3 x 9 = 27	6 x 9 = 54	9 x 9 = 81
4 x 9 = 36	9 x 7 = 63	9 x 4 = 36
5 x 9 = 45	10 x 9 = 90	1 x 9 = 9
6 x 9 = 54	1 x 9 = 9	9 x 2 = 18
7 x 9 = 63	3 x 9 = 27	7 x 9 = 63
8 x 9 = 72	5 x 9 = 45	0 x 9 = 0
9 x 9 = 81	7 x 9 = 63	9 x 3 = 27
10 x 9 = 90	9 x 9 = 81	5 x 9 = 45
9 x 1 = 9	9 x 3 = 27	9 x 9 = 81
9 x 2 = 18	9 x 5 = 45	2 x 9 = 18
9 x 3 = 27	0 x 9 = 0	8 x 9 = 72
9 x 4 = 36	9 x 1 = 9	4 x 9 = 36
9 x 5 = 45	9 x 2 = 18	9 x 7 = 63
9 x 6 = 54	9 x 4 = 36	10 x 9 = 90
9 x 7 = 63	9 x 6 = 54	9 x 5 = 45
9 x 8 = 72	9 x 8 = 72	9 x 0 = 0
9 x 9 = 81	9 x 10 = 90	9 x 1 = 9
9 x 10 = 90	9 x 0 = 0	6 x 9 = 54

Speed trials

You should know all of the times tables by now, but how quickly can you remember them?
Ask someone to time you as you do this page.
Be fast and correct.

6 x 8 = 48	4 x 8 = 32	8 x 10 = 80
9 x 10 = 90	9 x 8 = 72	7 x 9 = 63
5 x 8 = 40	6 x 6 = 36	8 x 5 = 40
7 x 5 = 35	8 x 9 = 72	8 x 7 = 56
6 x 4 = 24	6 x 4 = 24	7 x 4 = 28
8 x 8 = 64	7 x 3 = 21	4 x 9 = 36
5 x 10 = 50	5 x 9 = 45	6 x 7 = 42
9 x 8 = 72	6 x 8 = 48	4 x 6 = 24
8 x 3 = 24	7 x 7 = 49	7 x 8 = 56
7 x 7 = 49	6 x 9 = 54	6 x 9 = 54
9 x 5 = 45	7 x 8 = 56	10 x 8 = 80
4 x 8 = 32	8 x 4 = 32	6 x 5 = 30
6 x 7 = 42	0 x 9 = 0	8 x 8 = 64
2 x 9 = 18	10 x 10 = 100	7 x 6 = 42
8 x 4 = 32	7 x 6 = 42	6 x 8 = 48
7 x 10 = 70	8 x 7 = 56	9 x 10 = 90
2 x 8 = 16	9 x 6 = 54	8 x 4 = 32
4 x 7 = 28	8 x 6 = 48	7 x 10 = 70
6 x 9 = 54	9 x 9 = 81	5 x 8 = 40
9 x 9 = 81	6 x 7 = 42	8 x 9 = 72

54

Times tables for division

Knowing the times tables can also help with division problems.
Look at these examples.
3 x 6 = 18 which means that 18 ÷ 3 = 6 and that 18 ÷ 6 = 3
4 x 5 = 20 which means that 20 ÷ 4 = 5 and that 20 ÷ 5 = 4
9 x 3 = 27 which means that 27 ÷ 3 = 9 and that 27 ÷ 9 = 3

Use your knowledge of the times tables to work these division problems.

3 x 8 = 24 which means that 24 ÷ 3 = 8 and that 24 ÷ 8 = 3
4 x 7 = 28 which means that 28 ÷ 4 = 7 and that 28 ÷ 7 = 4
3 x 5 = 15 which means that 15 ÷ 3 = 5 and that 15 − 5 = 3
4 x 3 = 12 which means that 12 ÷ 3 = 4 and that 12 − 4= 3
3 x 10 = 30 which means that 30 ÷ 3 = 10 and that 30 ÷ 10 = 3
4 x 8 = 32 which means that 32 ÷ 4 = 8 and that 32 − 8 = 4
3 x 9 = 27 which means that 27 ÷ 3 = 9 and that 27 − 9 = 3
4 x 10 = 40 which means that 40 ÷ 4 = 10 and that 40 ÷ 10 = 4

These division problems help practise the 3 and 4 times tables.

20 ÷ 4 = 5	15 ÷ 3 = 5	16 ÷ 4 = 4
24 ÷ 4 = 6	27 ÷ 3 = 9	30 ÷ 3 = 10
12 ÷ 3 = 4	18 ÷ 3 = 6	28 ÷ 4 = 7
24 ÷ 3 = 8	32 ÷ 4 = 8	21 ÷ 3 = 7

How many fours in 36? 9	Divide 27 by three. 9
Divide 28 by 4. 7	How many threes in 21? 7
How many fives in 35? 7	Divide 40 by 5. 8
Divide 15 by 3. 5	How many eights in 48? 6

55

Times tables for division

This page will help you remember times tables by dividing by 2, 3, 4, 5, and 10.
20 ÷ 5 = 4   18 ÷ 3 = 6   60 ÷ 10 = 6

Complete the problems.

40 ÷ 10 = 4	14 ÷ 2 = 7	32 ÷ 4 = 8
25 ÷ 5 = 5	21 ÷ 3 = 7	16 ÷ 4 = 4
24 ÷ 4 = 6	28 ÷ 4 = 7	12 ÷ 2 = 6
45 ÷ 5 = 9	35 ÷ 5 = 7	12 ÷ 3 = 4
10 ÷ 2 = 5	40 ÷ 10 = 4	12 ÷ 4 = 3
20 ÷ 10 = 2	20 ÷ 2 = 10	20 ÷ 2 = 10
6 ÷ 2 = 3	18 ÷ 3 = 6	20 ÷ 4 = 5
24 ÷ 3 = 8	32 ÷ 4 = 8	20 ÷ 5 = 4
30 ÷ 5 = 6	40 ÷ 5 = 8	20 ÷ 10 = 2
30 ÷ 10 = 3	80 ÷ 10 = 8	18 ÷ 2 = 9
40 ÷ 5 = 8	6 ÷ 2 = 3	18 ÷ 3 = 6
21 ÷ 3 = 7	15 ÷ 3 = 5	15 ÷ 3 = 5
14 ÷ 2 = 7	24 ÷ 4 = 6	15 ÷ 5 = 3
27 ÷ 3 = 9	15 ÷ 5 = 3	24 ÷ 3 = 8
90 ÷ 10 = 9	10 ÷ 10 = 1	24 ÷ 4 = 6
15 ÷ 5 = 3	4 ÷ 2 = 2	50 ÷ 5 = 10
15 ÷ 3 = 5	9 ÷ 3 = 3	50 ÷ 10 = 5
20 ÷ 5 = 4	4 ÷ 4 = 1	30 ÷ 3 = 10
20 ÷ 4 = 5	10 ÷ 5 = 2	30 ÷ 5 = 6
16 ÷ 2 = 8	100 ÷ 10 = 10	30 ÷ 10 = 3

Times tables for division

This page will help you remember times tables by dividing by 2, 3, 4, 5, 6, and 10.
30 ÷ 6 = 5   12 ÷ 6 = 2   60 ÷ 10 = 6

Complete the problems.

18 ÷ 6 = 3	27 ÷ 3 = 9	48 ÷ 6 = 8
30 ÷ 10 = 3	18 ÷ 6 = 3	35 ÷ 5 = 7
14 ÷ 2 = 7	20 ÷ 2 = 10	36 ÷ 4 = 9
18 ÷ 3 = 6	24 ÷ 6 = 4	24 ÷ 3 = 8
20 ÷ 4 = 5	24 ÷ 3 = 8	20 ÷ 2 = 10
15 ÷ 5 = 3	24 ÷ 4 = 6	30 ÷ 6 = 5
36 ÷ 6 = 6	30 ÷ 10 = 3	25 ÷ 5 = 5
50 ÷ 10 = 5	18 ÷ 2 = 9	32 ÷ 4 = 8
8 ÷ 2 = 4	18 ÷ 3 = 6	27 ÷ 3 = 9
15 ÷ 3 = 5	36 ÷ 4 = 9	16 ÷ 2 = 8
16 ÷ 4 = 4	36 ÷ 6 = 6	42 ÷ 6 = 7
25 ÷ 5 = 5	40 ÷ 5 = 8	5 ÷ 5 = 1
6 ÷ 6 = 1	100 ÷ 10 = 10	4 ÷ 4 = 1
10 ÷ 10 = 1	16 ÷ 4 = 4	28 ÷ 4 = 7
42 ÷ 6 = 7	42 ÷ 6 = 7	14 ÷ 2 = 7
24 ÷ 4 = 6	48 ÷ 6 = 8	24 ÷ 6 = 4
54 ÷ 6 = 9	54 ÷ 6 = 9	18 ÷ 6 = 3
90 ÷ 10 = 9	60 ÷ 6 = 10	54 ÷ 6 = 9
30 ÷ 6 = 5	60 ÷ 10 = 6	60 ÷ 6 = 10
30 ÷ 5 = 6	30 ÷ 6 = 5	40 ÷ 5 = 8

Times tables for division

This page will help you remember times tables by dividing by 2, 3, 4, 5, 6, and 7.

14 ÷ 7 = 2   28 ÷ 7 = 4   70 ÷ 7 = 10

Complete the problems.

21 ÷ 7 = 3	18 ÷ 6 = 3	49 ÷ 7 = 7
35 ÷ 5 = 7	28 ÷ 7 = 4	35 ÷ 5 = 7
14 ÷ 2 = 7	24 ÷ 6 = 4	35 ÷ 7 = 5
18 ÷ 6 = 3	24 ÷ 4 = 6	24 ÷ 6 = 4
20 ÷ 5 = 4	24 ÷ 2 = 12	21 ÷ 3 = 7
15 ÷ 3 = 5	21 ÷ 7 = 3	70 ÷ 7 = 10
36 ÷ 4 = 9	42 ÷ 7 = 6	42 ÷ 7 = 6
56 ÷ 7 = 8	18 ÷ 3 = 6	32 ÷ 4 = 8
18 ÷ 2 = 9	49 ÷ 7 = 7	27 ÷ 3 = 9
15 ÷ 5 = 3	36 ÷ 4 = 9	16 ÷ 4 = 4
49 ÷ 7 = 7	36 ÷ 6 = 6	42 ÷ 6 = 7
25 ÷ 5 = 5	40 ÷ 5 = 8	45 ÷ 5 = 9
7 ÷ 7 = 1	70 ÷ 7 = 10	40 ÷ 4 = 10
63 ÷ 7 = 9	24 ÷ 3 = 8	24 ÷ 3 = 8
42 ÷ 7 = 6	42 ÷ 6 = 7	14 ÷ 7 = 2
24 ÷ 6 = 4	48 ÷ 6 = 8	24 ÷ 4 = 6
54 ÷ 6 = 9	54 ÷ 6 = 9	18 ÷ 3 = 6
28 ÷ 7 = 4	60 ÷ 6 = 10	56 ÷ 7 = 8
30 ÷ 6 = 5	63 ÷ 7 = 9	63 ÷ 7 = 9
35 ÷ 7 = 5	25 ÷ 5 = 5	48 ÷ 6 = 8

Times tables for division

This page will help you remember times tables by dividing by 2, 3, 4, 5, 6, 7, 8, and 9.

16 ÷ 8 = 2   35 ÷ 7 = 5   27 ÷ 9 = 3

Complete the problems.

42 ÷ 6 = 7	81 ÷ 9 = 9	56 ÷ 7 = 8
32 ÷ 8 = 4	56 ÷ 7 = 8	45 ÷ 5 = 9
14 ÷ 7 = 2	72 ÷ 9 = 8	35 ÷ 7 = 5
18 ÷ 9 = 2	24 ÷ 8 = 3	18 ÷ 9 = 2
63 ÷ 7 = 9	27 ÷ 9 = 3	21 ÷ 3 = 7
72 ÷ 9 = 8	72 ÷ 9 = 8	28 ÷ 7 = 4
72 ÷ 8 = 9	42 ÷ 6 = 7	64 ÷ 8 = 8
56 ÷ 7 = 8	27 ÷ 3 = 9	32 ÷ 8 = 4
18 ÷ 6 = 3	14 ÷ 7 = 2	27 ÷ 9 = 3
81 ÷ 9 = 9	36 ÷ 4 = 9	16 ÷ 8 = 2
63 ÷ 9 = 7	36 ÷ 6 = 6	42 ÷ 6 = 7
45 ÷ 5 = 9	48 ÷ 8 = 6	45 ÷ 9 = 5
54 ÷ 9 = 6	21 ÷ 7 = 3	40 ÷ 4 = 10
70 ÷ 7 = 10	24 ÷ 3 = 8	24 ÷ 8 = 3
42 ÷ 7 = 6	40 ÷ 8 = 5	63 ÷ 7 = 9
30 ÷ 5 = 6	45 ÷ 9 = 5	24 ÷ 6 = 4
54 ÷ 6 = 9	54 ÷ 6 = 9	18 ÷ 6 = 3
56 ÷ 8 = 7	42 ÷ 7 = 6	56 ÷ 8 = 7
30 ÷ 5 = 6	63 ÷ 9 = 7	63 ÷ 9 = 7
35 ÷ 7 = 5	50 ÷ 5 = 10	48 ÷ 8 = 6

Times tables practice grids

This is a times tables grid.

X	3	4	5
7	21	28	35
8	24	32	40

Complete each times tables grid.

X	1	3	5	7	9
2	2	6	10	14	18
3	3	9	15	21	27

X	4	6
6	24	36
7	28	42
8	32	48

X	6	7	8	9	10
3	18	21	24	27	30
4	24	28	32	36	40
5	30	35	40	45	50

X	10	7	8	4
3	30	21	24	12
5	50	35	40	20
7	70	49	56	28

X	6	2	4	7
5	30	10	20	35
10	60	20	40	70

X	8	7	9	6
9	72	63	81	54
7	56	49	63	42

Times tables practice grids

Here are more times tables grids.

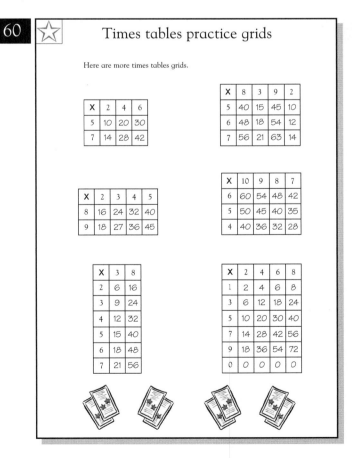

X	2	4	6
5	10	20	30
7	14	28	42

X	8	3	9	2
5	40	15	45	10
6	48	18	54	12
7	56	21	63	14

X	2	3	4	5
8	16	24	32	40
9	18	27	36	45

X	10	9	8	7
6	60	54	48	42
5	50	45	40	35
4	40	36	32	28

X	3	8
2	6	16
3	9	24
4	12	32
5	15	40
6	18	48
7	21	56

X	2	4	6	8
1	2	4	6	8
3	6	12	18	24
5	10	20	30	40
7	14	28	42	56
9	18	36	54	72
0	0	0	0	0

Times tables practice grids

Here are some other times tables grids.

X	8	9
7	56	63
8	64	72

X	9	8	7	6	5	4
9	81	72	63	54	45	36
8	72	64	56	48	40	32
7	63	56	49	42	35	28

X	2	5	9
4	8	20	36
7	14	35	63
8	16	40	72

X	2	3	4	5	7
4	8	12	16	20	28
6	12	18	24	30	42
8	16	24	32	40	56

X	3	5	7
2	6	10	14
8	24	40	56
6	18	30	42
0	0	0	0
4	12	20	28
7	21	35	49

X	8	7	9	6
7	56	49	63	42
9	72	63	81	54
0	0	0	0	0
10	80	70	90	60
8	64	56	72	48
6	48	42	54	36

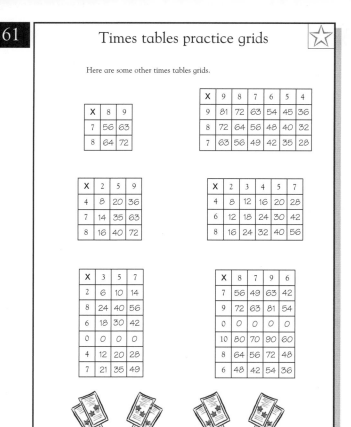
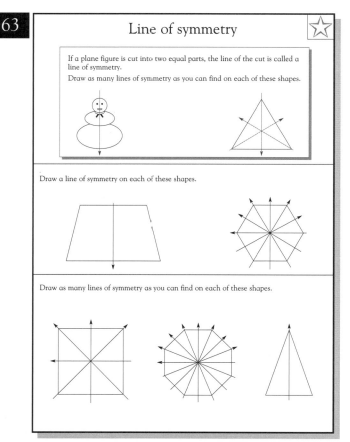

Speed trials

Try this final test.

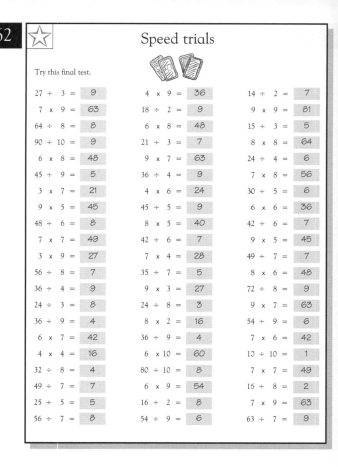

27 ÷ 3 = 9	4 x 9 = 36	14 ÷ 2 = 7
7 x 9 = 63	18 ÷ 2 = 9	9 x 9 = 81
64 ÷ 8 = 8	6 x 8 = 48	15 ÷ 3 = 5
90 ÷ 10 = 9	21 ÷ 3 = 7	8 x 8 = 64
6 x 8 = 48	9 x 7 = 63	24 ÷ 4 = 6
45 ÷ 9 = 5	36 ÷ 4 = 9	7 x 8 = 56
3 x 7 = 21	4 x 6 = 24	30 ÷ 5 = 6
9 x 5 = 45	45 ÷ 5 = 9	6 x 6 = 36
48 ÷ 6 = 8	8 x 5 = 40	42 ÷ 6 = 7
7 x 7 = 49	42 ÷ 6 = 7	9 x 5 = 45
3 x 9 = 27	7 x 4 = 28	49 ÷ 7 = 7
56 ÷ 8 = 7	35 ÷ 7 = 5	8 x 6 = 48
36 ÷ 4 = 9	9 x 3 = 27	72 ÷ 8 = 9
24 ÷ 3 = 8	24 ÷ 8 = 3	9 x 7 = 63
36 ÷ 9 = 4	8 x 2 = 16	54 ÷ 9 = 6
6 x 7 = 42	36 ÷ 9 = 4	7 x 6 = 42
4 x 4 = 16	6 x 10 = 60	10 ÷ 10 = 1
32 ÷ 8 = 4	80 ÷ 10 = 8	7 x 7 = 49
49 ÷ 7 = 7	6 x 9 = 54	15 ÷ 8 = 2
25 ÷ 5 = 5	16 ÷ 2 = 8	7 x 9 = 63
56 ÷ 7 = 8	54 ÷ 9 = 6	63 ÷ 7 = 9

Line of symmetry

If a plane figure is cut into two equal parts, the line of the cut is called a line of symmetry.
Draw as many lines of symmetry as you can find on each of these shapes.

Draw a line of symmetry on each of these shapes.

Draw as many lines of symmetry as you can find on each of these shapes.

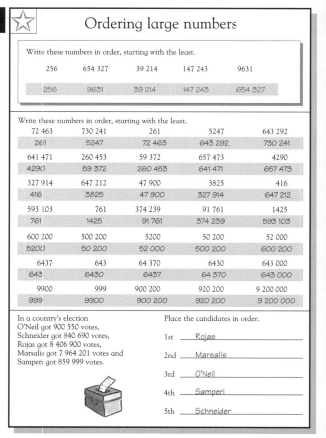

If children find it difficult to see where a line of symmetry falls, talk about where the shape could be folded so that both parts overlap exactly.

Ordering large numbers

Write these numbers in order, starting with the least.

256	654 327	39 214	147 243	9631
256	9631	39 214	147 243	654 327

Write these numbers in order, starting with the least.

72 463	730 241	261	5247	643 292
261	5247	72 463	643 292	730 241
641 471	260 453	59 372	657 473	4290
4290	59 372	260 453	641 471	657 473
327 914	647 212	47 900	3825	416
416	3825	47 900	327 914	647 212
593 103	761	374 239	91 761	1425
761	1425	91 761	374 239	593 103
600 200	500 200	5200	50 200	52 000
5200	50 200	52 000	500 200	600 200
6437	643	64 370	6430	643 000
643	6430	6437	64 370	643 000
9900	999	900 200	920 200	9 200 000
999	9900	900 200	920 200	9 200 000

In a country's election O'Neil got 900 550 votes, Schneider got 840 690 votes, Rojas got 8 406 900 votes, Marsalis got 7 964 201 votes and Samperi got 859 999 votes.

Place the candidates in order.

1st ___Rojas___

2nd ___Marsalis___

3rd ___O'Neil___

4th ___Samperi___

5th ___Schneider___

If children are weak on place value, help them identify the significant digits when sorting a group of numbers. Take care when the same digits are used but with different place values.

Rounding whole numbers

Write these numbers to the nearest hundred.

529 `500`   1687 `1700`

If the place to the right of the place we are rounding is 5, round to the number above.

652 `700`

Round to the nearest hundred.

873	`900`	295	`300`	7348	`7300`	3561	`3600`
16 537	`16 500`	4855	`4900`	569	`600`	1200	`1200`
22 851	`22 900`	227	`200`	782	`800`	452	`500`

Round to the nearest ten-thousand.

23 478	`20 000`	418 700	`420 000`	58 397	`60 000`	351 899	`350 000`
109 544	`110 000`	31 059	`30 000`	67 414	`70 000`	33 500	`30 000`
89 388	`90 000`	801 821	`800 000`	134 800	`130 000`	45 010	`50 000`

Round to the nearest ten.

87	`90`	397	`400`	52	`50`	65	`70`
1392	`1390`	15	`20`	12 489	`12 490`	2861	`2860`
75	`80`	715	`720`	34	`30`	18 149	`18 150`

Round to the nearest thousand.

3284	`3000`	112 810	`113 000`	10 518	`11 000`	83 477	`83 000`
8499	`8000`	225 500	`226 000`	4500	`5000`	6112	`6000`
1059	`1000`	93 606	`94 000`	6752	`7000`	2550	`3000`

If children are confused about where to round, help them underline the rounding place and circle the digit to its right– that is the digit to compare to 5.

66

Choosing units of measure

Circle the units that are the closest estimate.
The amount of orange juice in a full glass.

6 millilitres   (350 millilitres)   2 litres

Circle the units that are the closest estimate.

The mass of a box of cereal	(750 grams)	3 kilograms	2 tonnes
The length of a football field	20 centimetres	(100 metres)	1 kilometre
The area of a rug	20 sq centimetres	(30 sq metres)	1 sq kilometre
The amount of cough medicine in a bottle	(120 millilitres)	6 litres	1 litre
The distance from home plate to first base	120 centimetres	(30 metres)	6 metres
The mass of a package of sugar	2 grams	(10 kilograms)	1/2 tonne
The length of an airport runway	(2 kilometres)	50 metres	500 centimetres
The amount of water in a full pail	8 millilitres	2 millilitres	(3 litres)
The area of a place mat	(200 sq centimetres)	6 sq metres	1 sq kilometre

Children need mental benchmarks for each of the units in order to choose the best unit of measure. Suggest examples, such as the mass of a few raisins for grams and the mass of a pair of shoes for a kilogram.

67

Comparing fractions

Which is greater, $\frac{2}{3}$ or $\frac{3}{4}$? $\boxed{\frac{3}{4}}$

The common denominator of 3 and 4 is 12.

So $\frac{2}{3} = \frac{8}{12}$ and $\frac{3}{4} = \frac{9}{12}$

$\frac{3}{4}$ is greater.

Which is greater?

$\frac{1}{4}$ or $\frac{1}{3}$ $\boxed{\frac{1}{3}}$	$\frac{5}{6}$ or $\frac{7}{9}$ $\boxed{\frac{5}{6}}$	$\frac{1}{2}$ or $\frac{5}{8}$ $\boxed{\frac{5}{8}}$	$\frac{4}{9}$ or $\frac{1}{3}$ $\boxed{\frac{4}{9}}$
$\frac{2}{5}$ or $\frac{3}{8}$ $\boxed{\frac{2}{5}}$	$\frac{7}{10}$ or $\frac{8}{9}$ $\boxed{\frac{8}{9}}$	$\frac{8}{10}$ or $\frac{7}{8}$ $\boxed{\frac{7}{8}}$	$\frac{7}{12}$ or $\frac{2}{3}$ $\boxed{\frac{2}{3}}$
$\frac{2}{3}$ or $\frac{5}{8}$ $\boxed{\frac{2}{3}}$	$\frac{4}{11}$ or $\frac{1}{3}$ $\boxed{\frac{1}{3}}$	$\frac{3}{5}$ or $\frac{2}{3}$ $\boxed{\frac{2}{3}}$	$\frac{3}{8}$ or $\frac{1}{4}$ $\boxed{\frac{3}{8}}$

Which two fractions in each row are equal?

$\frac{1}{4}$	$\frac{4}{8}$	$\frac{4}{12}$	$\frac{3}{12}$	$\frac{7}{8}$	$\frac{5}{8}$	$\boxed{\frac{1}{4} \text{ and } \frac{3}{12}}$
$\frac{5}{8}$	$\frac{6}{9}$	$\frac{7}{10}$	$\frac{8}{12}$	$\frac{1}{2}$	$\frac{3}{4}$	$\boxed{\frac{6}{9} \text{ and } \frac{8}{12}}$
$\frac{7}{12}$	$\frac{6}{14}$	$\frac{7}{14}$	$\frac{3}{8}$	$\frac{4}{8}$	$\frac{9}{7}$	$\boxed{\frac{7}{14} \text{ and } \frac{4}{8}}$
$\frac{3}{8}$	$\frac{3}{9}$	$\frac{2}{6}$	$\frac{4}{7}$	$\frac{9}{10}$	$\frac{6}{7}$	$\boxed{\frac{3}{9} \text{ and } \frac{2}{6}}$
$\frac{3}{10}$	$\frac{5}{15}$	$\frac{2}{10}$	$\frac{3}{15}$	$\frac{4}{10}$	$\frac{7}{15}$	$\boxed{\frac{2}{10} \text{ and } \frac{3}{15}}$

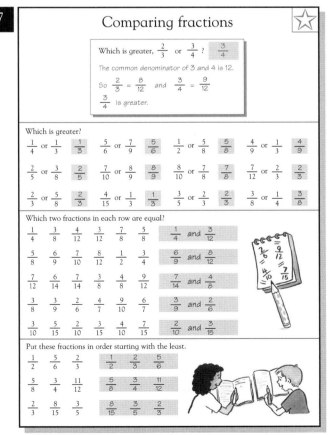

Put these fractions in order starting with the least.

$\frac{1}{2}$ $\frac{5}{6}$ $\frac{2}{3}$	$\boxed{\frac{1}{2} \ \ \frac{2}{3} \ \ \frac{5}{6}}$
$\frac{5}{8}$ $\frac{3}{4}$ $\frac{11}{12}$	$\boxed{\frac{5}{8} \ \ \frac{3}{4} \ \ \frac{11}{12}}$
$\frac{2}{3}$ $\frac{8}{15}$ $\frac{3}{5}$	$\boxed{\frac{8}{15} \ \ \frac{3}{5} \ \ \frac{2}{3}}$

Difficulty in finding a common denominator indicates a weakness in times tables knowledge. Children need to convert all the fractions in the later questions into a common form before answering the question. Be careful that they do not try to guess the answer.

Converting fractions to decimals

Convert these fractions to decimals.

$\frac{3}{10} = \boxed{0.3}$

(because the three goes in the tenths column)

$\frac{7}{100} = \boxed{0.07}$

(because the seven goes in the hundredths column)

Convert these fractions to decimals.

$\frac{6}{10} = \boxed{0.6}$	$\frac{9}{100} = \boxed{0.09}$	$\frac{4}{100} = \boxed{0.04}$	$\frac{6}{100} = \boxed{0.06}$
$\frac{4}{10} = \boxed{0.4}$	$\frac{2}{10} = \boxed{0.2}$	$\frac{1}{10} = \boxed{0.1}$	$\frac{7}{100} = \boxed{0.07}$
$\frac{8}{100} = \boxed{0.08}$	$\frac{5}{10} = \boxed{0.5}$	$\frac{7}{10} = \boxed{0.7}$	$\frac{8}{10} = \boxed{0.8}$
$\frac{2}{100} = \boxed{0.02}$	$\frac{5}{100} = \boxed{0.05}$	$\frac{1}{100} = \boxed{0.01}$	$\frac{3}{10} = \boxed{0.3}$

Convert $\frac{1}{4}$ to a decimal.

To do this we have to divide the bottom number into the top.

When we run out of numbers we put in the decimal point and enough zeros to finish the sum. Be careful to keep the decimal point in your answer above the decimal point in the sum.

```
      0.25
  4)1.00
      8
      20
      20
       0
```

Convert these fractions to decimals.

$\frac{1}{2} = \boxed{0.5}$	$\frac{3}{4} = \boxed{0.75}$	$\frac{2}{5} = \boxed{0.4}$	$\frac{1}{5} = \boxed{0.2}$
$\frac{4}{5} = \boxed{0.8}$	$\frac{3}{8} = \boxed{0.375}$	$\frac{3}{5} = \boxed{0.6}$	$\frac{1}{4} = \boxed{0.25}$

Difficulty in the first section highlights weakness in understanding place value to the first two decimal places. It may be necessary to reinforce understanding of 10ths and 100ths in decimals.

Adding fractions ☆

Work out the answer to the problem.

$\frac{1}{5} + \frac{3}{5} = \frac{4}{5}$ $\frac{4}{9} + \frac{2}{9} = \frac{\cancel{6}}{\cancel{9}_3} = \frac{2}{3}$

Remember to reduce to simplest form if you need to.

Work out the answer to each sum. Reduce to simplest form if you need to.

$\frac{2}{7} + \frac{3}{7} = \frac{5}{7}$ $\frac{2}{9} + \frac{5}{9} = \frac{7}{9}$ $\frac{1}{3} + \frac{1}{3} = \frac{2}{3}$

$\frac{3}{10} + \frac{4}{10} = \frac{7}{10}$ $\frac{1}{8} + \frac{2}{8} = \frac{3}{8}$ $\frac{2}{9} + \frac{3}{9} = \frac{5}{9}$

$\frac{2}{5} + \frac{1}{5} = \frac{3}{5}$ $\frac{1}{7} + \frac{5}{7} = \frac{6}{7}$ $\frac{4}{9} + \frac{1}{9} = \frac{5}{9}$

$\frac{3}{20} + \frac{4}{20} = \frac{7}{20}$ $\frac{3}{100} + \frac{8}{100} = \frac{11}{100}$ $\frac{7}{10} + \frac{2}{10} = \frac{9}{10}$

$\frac{1}{6} + \frac{2}{6} = \frac{3}{6} = \frac{1}{2}$ $\frac{31}{100} + \frac{19}{100} = \frac{50}{100} = \frac{1}{2}$ $\frac{11}{20} + \frac{4}{20} = \frac{15}{20} = \frac{3}{4}$

$\frac{3}{10} + \frac{3}{10} = \frac{6}{10} = \frac{3}{5}$ $\frac{1}{12} + \frac{5}{12} = \frac{6}{12} = \frac{1}{2}$ $\frac{2}{6} + \frac{2}{6} = \frac{4}{6} = \frac{2}{3}$

$\frac{3}{8} + \frac{3}{8} = \frac{6}{8} = \frac{3}{4}$ $\frac{3}{8} + \frac{1}{8} = \frac{4}{8} = \frac{1}{2}$ $\frac{5}{12} + \frac{3}{12} = \frac{8}{12} = \frac{2}{3}$

$\frac{1}{4} + \frac{1}{4} = \frac{2}{4} = \frac{1}{2}$ $\frac{3}{20} + \frac{2}{20} = \frac{5}{20} = \frac{1}{4}$ $\frac{2}{6} + \frac{2}{6} = \frac{4}{6} = \frac{2}{3}$

$\frac{2}{7} + \frac{4}{7} = \frac{6}{7}$ $\frac{2}{9} + \frac{2}{9} = \frac{4}{9}$ $\frac{13}{20} + \frac{5}{20} = \frac{18}{20} = \frac{9}{10}$

$\frac{81}{100} + \frac{9}{100} = \frac{90}{100} = \frac{9}{10}$ $\frac{7}{20} + \frac{6}{20} = \frac{13}{20}$ $\frac{3}{8} + \frac{2}{8} = \frac{5}{8}$

$\frac{6}{10} + \frac{2}{10} = \frac{8}{10} = \frac{4}{5}$ $\frac{29}{100} + \frac{46}{100} = \frac{75}{100} = \frac{3}{4}$ $\frac{73}{100} + \frac{17}{100} = \frac{90}{100} = \frac{9}{10}$

Difficulty in reducing a sum to a simpler form points to a weakness in finding the greatest common factor of the numerator and denominator. Children can reduce the answer in stages, first looking at whether 2 is a common factor, then 3, and so on.

70

☆ Subtracting fractions

Write the answer to each problem.

$\frac{4}{5} - \frac{2}{5} = \frac{2}{5}$ $\frac{8}{9} - \frac{5}{9} = \frac{\cancel{3}}{\cancel{9}_3} = \frac{1}{3}$

Reduce to simplest form if you need to.

Write the answer to each problem. Reduce to simplest form if you need to.

$\frac{3}{5} - \frac{1}{5} = \frac{2}{5}$ $\frac{6}{7} - \frac{3}{7} = \frac{3}{7}$ $\frac{9}{10} - \frac{6}{10} = \frac{3}{10}$

$\frac{7}{10} - \frac{4}{10} = \frac{3}{10}$ $\frac{5}{9} - \frac{4}{9} = \frac{1}{9}$ $\frac{2}{3} - \frac{1}{3} = \frac{1}{3}$

$\frac{7}{8} - \frac{3}{8} = \frac{4}{8} = \frac{1}{2}$ $\frac{14}{20} - \frac{10}{20} = \frac{4}{20} = \frac{1}{5}$ $\frac{5}{6} - \frac{1}{6} = \frac{4}{6} = \frac{2}{3}$

$\frac{11}{12} - \frac{5}{12} = \frac{6}{12} = \frac{1}{2}$ $\frac{17}{20} - \frac{12}{20} = \frac{5}{20} = \frac{1}{4}$ $\frac{9}{12} - \frac{3}{12} = \frac{6}{12} = \frac{1}{2}$

$\frac{8}{10} - \frac{6}{10} = \frac{2}{10} = \frac{1}{5}$ $\frac{12}{12} - \frac{2}{12} = \frac{10}{12} = \frac{5}{6}$ $\frac{9}{10} - \frac{3}{10} = \frac{6}{10} = \frac{3}{5}$

$\frac{8}{9} - \frac{2}{9} = \frac{6}{9} = \frac{2}{3}$ $\frac{7}{8} - \frac{1}{8} = \frac{6}{8} = \frac{3}{4}$ $\frac{9}{12} - \frac{5}{12} = \frac{4}{12} = \frac{1}{3}$

$\frac{3}{4} - \frac{2}{4} = \frac{1}{4}$ $\frac{6}{8} - \frac{3}{8} = \frac{3}{8}$ $\frac{18}{20} - \frac{8}{20} = \frac{10}{20} = \frac{1}{2}$

$\frac{4}{6} - \frac{2}{6} = \frac{2}{6} = \frac{1}{3}$ $\frac{5}{12} - \frac{4}{12} = \frac{1}{12}$ $\frac{3}{8} - \frac{2}{8} = \frac{1}{8}$

$\frac{5}{7} - \frac{1}{7} = \frac{4}{7}$ $\frac{5}{16} - \frac{1}{16} = \frac{4}{16} = \frac{1}{4}$ $\frac{90}{100} - \frac{80}{100} = \frac{10}{100} = \frac{1}{10}$

See the notes on page 69.

71

Adding fractions ☆

Write the answer to each problem.

$\frac{3}{8} + \frac{5}{8} = \frac{8}{8} = 1$ $\frac{3}{4} + \frac{3}{4} = \frac{\cancel{6}}{\cancel{4}_2} = \frac{3}{2} = 1\frac{1}{2}$

Write the answer to each problem.

$\frac{7}{10} + \frac{6}{10} = \frac{13}{10} = 1\frac{3}{10}$ $\frac{6}{7} + \frac{5}{7} = \frac{11}{7} = 1\frac{4}{7}$ $\frac{2}{3} + \frac{2}{3} = \frac{4}{3} = 1\frac{1}{3}$

$\frac{5}{10} + \frac{6}{10} = \frac{11}{10} = 1\frac{1}{10}$ $\frac{8}{13} + \frac{5}{13} = \frac{13}{13} = 1$ $\frac{7}{8} + \frac{4}{8} = \frac{11}{8} = 1\frac{3}{8}$

$\frac{7}{8} + \frac{5}{8} = \frac{12}{8} = \frac{3}{2} = 1\frac{1}{2}$ $\frac{2}{5} + \frac{3}{5} = \frac{5}{5} = 1$ $\frac{5}{8} + \frac{5}{8} = \frac{10}{8} = \frac{5}{4} = 1\frac{1}{4}$

$\frac{10}{20} + \frac{15}{20} = \frac{25}{20} = \frac{5}{4} = 1\frac{1}{4}$ $\frac{2}{3} + \frac{1}{3} = \frac{3}{3} = 1$ $\frac{5}{6} + \frac{5}{6} = \frac{10}{6} = \frac{5}{3} = 1\frac{2}{3}$

$\frac{5}{6} + \frac{3}{6} = \frac{8}{6} = \frac{4}{3} = 1\frac{1}{3}$ $\frac{6}{12} + \frac{7}{12} = \frac{13}{12} = 1\frac{1}{12}$ $\frac{8}{10} + \frac{6}{10} = \frac{14}{10} = \frac{7}{5} = 1\frac{2}{5}$

$\frac{12}{20} + \frac{10}{20} = \frac{22}{20} = \frac{11}{10} = 1\frac{1}{10}$ $\frac{3}{10} + \frac{7}{10} = \frac{10}{10} = 1$ $\frac{75}{100} + \frac{75}{100} = \frac{150}{100} = \frac{3}{2} = 1\frac{1}{2}$

$\frac{10}{20} + \frac{16}{20} = \frac{26}{20} = \frac{13}{10} = 1\frac{3}{10}$ $\frac{4}{5} + \frac{4}{5} = \frac{8}{5} = 1\frac{3}{5}$ $\frac{11}{21} + \frac{17}{21} = \frac{28}{21} = \frac{4}{3} = 1\frac{1}{3}$

If children leave the answer as a fraction or do not reduce it, they are completing only one of the two steps to finding the simplest form. Have them write the answer as a mixed number first, and then reduce the fraction part.

☆ Adding fractions

Write the answer to each problem.

$\frac{2}{3} + \frac{1}{6} = \frac{4}{6} + \frac{1}{6} = \frac{5}{6}$ $\frac{3}{4} + \frac{5}{6} = \frac{9}{12} + \frac{10}{12} = \frac{19}{12} = 1\frac{7}{12}$

Work out the answer to each problem. Rename as a mixed number if you need to.

$\frac{2}{5} + \frac{7}{10} = \frac{4}{10} + \frac{7}{10} = \frac{11}{10} = 1\frac{1}{10}$ $\frac{3}{4} + \frac{7}{10} = \frac{15}{20} + \frac{14}{20} = \frac{29}{20} = 1\frac{9}{20}$

$\frac{1}{4} + \frac{5}{6} = \frac{3}{12} + \frac{10}{12} = \frac{13}{12} = 1\frac{1}{12}$ $\frac{3}{4} + \frac{7}{8} = \frac{6}{8} + \frac{7}{8} = \frac{13}{8} = 1\frac{5}{8}$

$\frac{2}{3} + \frac{1}{4} = \frac{8}{12} + \frac{3}{12} = \frac{11}{12}$ $\frac{5}{6} + \frac{11}{12} = \frac{10}{12} + \frac{11}{12} = \frac{21}{12} = 1\frac{3}{4}$

$\frac{5}{7} + \frac{3}{14} = \frac{10}{14} + \frac{3}{14} = \frac{13}{14}$ $\frac{5}{8} + \frac{7}{10} = \frac{25}{40} + \frac{28}{40} = \frac{53}{40} = 1\frac{13}{40}$

$\frac{3}{4} + \frac{3}{5} = \frac{15}{20} + \frac{12}{20} = \frac{27}{20} = 1\frac{7}{20}$ $\frac{1}{2} + \frac{5}{9} = \frac{9}{18} + \frac{10}{18} = \frac{19}{18} = 1\frac{1}{18}$

$\frac{2}{3} + \frac{7}{9} = \frac{6}{9} + \frac{7}{9} = \frac{13}{9} = 1\frac{4}{9}$ $\frac{1}{3} + \frac{7}{8} = \frac{8}{24} + \frac{21}{24} = \frac{29}{24} = 1\frac{5}{24}$

$\frac{3}{8} + \frac{1}{6} = \frac{9}{24} + \frac{4}{24} = \frac{13}{24}$ $\frac{2}{3} + \frac{4}{5} = \frac{10}{15} + \frac{12}{15} = \frac{22}{15} = 1\frac{7}{15}$

$\frac{4}{5} + \frac{5}{6} = \frac{24}{30} + \frac{25}{30} = \frac{49}{30} = 1\frac{19}{30}$ $\frac{2}{3} + \frac{3}{10} = \frac{20}{30} + \frac{9}{30} = \frac{29}{30}$

Difficulty in finding a common denominator indicates a weakness in finding the least common multiple of two numbers. Children can always find a common denominator by multiplying the given denominators.

73

Subtracting fractions ☆

Work out the answer to the problems.

$$\frac{7}{9} - \frac{1}{3} = \frac{7}{9} - \frac{3}{9} = \frac{4}{9} \qquad \frac{7}{10} - \frac{3}{8} = \frac{28}{40} - \frac{15}{40} = \frac{13}{40}$$

Work out the answer to each problem. Reduce to the simplest form if you need to.

$$\frac{5}{8} - \frac{1}{2} = \frac{5}{8} - \frac{4}{8} = \frac{1}{8} \qquad \frac{5}{6} - \frac{1}{4} = \frac{10}{12} - \frac{3}{12} = \frac{7}{12}$$

$$\frac{9}{10} - \frac{3}{8} = \frac{36}{40} - \frac{15}{40} = \frac{21}{40} \qquad \frac{9}{10} - \frac{5}{8} = \frac{36}{40} - \frac{25}{40} = \frac{11}{40}$$

$$\frac{6}{7} - \frac{2}{5} = \frac{30}{35} - \frac{14}{35} = \frac{16}{35} \qquad \frac{11}{12} - \frac{1}{6} = \frac{11}{12} - \frac{2}{12} = \frac{9}{12} = \frac{3}{4}$$

$$\frac{7}{12} - \frac{1}{6} = \frac{7}{12} - \frac{2}{12} = \frac{5}{12} \qquad \frac{7}{10} - \frac{1}{4} = \frac{28}{40} - \frac{10}{40} = \frac{18}{40} = \frac{9}{20}$$

$$\frac{5}{9} - \frac{1}{3} = \frac{5}{9} - \frac{3}{9} = \frac{2}{9} \qquad \frac{7}{9} - \frac{1}{4} = \frac{28}{36} - \frac{9}{36} = \frac{19}{36}$$

$$\frac{7}{16} - \frac{1}{8} = \frac{7}{16} - \frac{2}{16} = \frac{5}{16} \qquad \frac{3}{7} - \frac{1}{5} = \frac{15}{35} - \frac{7}{35} = \frac{8}{35}$$

$$\frac{3}{8} - \frac{1}{6} = \frac{9}{24} - \frac{4}{24} = \frac{5}{24} \qquad \frac{3}{5} - \frac{1}{4} = \frac{12}{20} - \frac{5}{20} = \frac{7}{20}$$

$$\frac{2}{3} - \frac{1}{2} = \frac{4}{6} - \frac{3}{6} = \frac{1}{6} \qquad \frac{4}{5} - \frac{1}{4} = \frac{16}{20} - \frac{5}{20} = \frac{11}{20}$$

See the notes on page 72.

74

☆ Adding mixed numbers

Work out the answer to each problem.

$$8\frac{10}{30} + 1\frac{3}{30} = 9\frac{13}{30} = 9\frac{13}{30} \qquad 3\frac{1}{4} + 1\frac{1}{6} = 3\frac{3}{12} + 1\frac{1}{12} = 4\frac{5}{12}$$

Work out the answer to each problem.

$$2\frac{1}{8} + 3\frac{3}{8} = 5\frac{4}{8} = 5\frac{1}{2} \qquad 3\frac{5}{6} + 1\frac{1}{8} = 3\frac{20}{24} + 1\frac{3}{24} = 4\frac{23}{24}$$

$$3\frac{3}{4} + 2\frac{1}{16} = 3\frac{12}{16} + 2\frac{1}{16} = 5\frac{13}{16} \qquad 1\frac{2}{3} + 3\frac{2}{7} = 1\frac{14}{21} + 3\frac{6}{21} = 4\frac{20}{21}$$

$$4\frac{1}{4} + 2\frac{1}{6} = 4\frac{3}{12} + 2\frac{2}{12} = 6\frac{5}{12} \qquad 6\frac{1}{6} + 3\frac{2}{9} = 6\frac{3}{18} + 3\frac{4}{18} = 9\frac{7}{18}$$

$$7\frac{5}{6} + 2\frac{1}{10} = 7\frac{25}{30} + 2\frac{3}{30} = 9\frac{28}{30} = 9\frac{14}{15} \qquad 1\frac{7}{12} + 4\frac{1}{12} = 5\frac{8}{12} = 5\frac{2}{3}$$

$$5\frac{1}{4} + 3\frac{2}{5} = 5\frac{4}{20} + 3\frac{8}{20} = 8\frac{12}{20} = 8\frac{3}{5} \qquad 3\frac{3}{8} + 1\frac{1}{4} = 3\frac{3}{8} + 1\frac{2}{8} = 4\frac{5}{8}$$

$$6\frac{1}{4} + 2\frac{1}{4} = 8\frac{2}{4} = 8\frac{1}{2} \qquad 6\frac{2}{3} + 3\frac{1}{10} = 6\frac{20}{30} + 3\frac{3}{30} = 9\frac{23}{30}$$

$$7\frac{1}{3} + 1\frac{2}{9} = 7\frac{3}{9} + 1\frac{2}{9} = 8\frac{5}{9} \qquad 2\frac{2}{5} + 1\frac{3}{10} = 2\frac{4}{10} + 1\frac{3}{10} = 3\frac{7}{10}$$

A common error is forgetting to recopy the whole number when renaming the mixed numbers. Children can recopy both whole numbers first, then rename the two fractions.

75

Subtracting mixed numbers ☆

Work out the answer to the problems.

$$2\frac{7}{8} - 1\frac{5}{8} = 1\frac{2}{8} = 1\frac{1}{4} \qquad 9\frac{9}{10} - 6\frac{5}{8} = 9\frac{36}{40} - 6\frac{25}{40} = 3\frac{11}{40}$$

Work out the answer to each problem.

$$7\frac{3}{8} - 3\frac{1}{8} = 4\frac{2}{8} = 4\frac{1}{4} \qquad 2\frac{14}{15} - 1\frac{4}{9} = 2\frac{42}{45} - 1\frac{20}{45} = 1\frac{22}{45}$$

$$2\frac{2}{3} - 1\frac{1}{6} = 2\frac{4}{6} - 1\frac{1}{6} = 1\frac{3}{6} = 1\frac{1}{2} \qquad 6\frac{4}{5} - 2\frac{1}{2} = 6\frac{8}{10} - 2\frac{5}{10} = 4\frac{3}{10}$$

$$5\frac{11}{20} - 2\frac{1}{8} = 5\frac{22}{40} - 2\frac{5}{40} = 3\frac{17}{40} \qquad 8\frac{11}{12} - 5\frac{5}{12} = 3\frac{6}{12} = 3\frac{1}{2}$$

$$9\frac{7}{9} - 3\frac{4}{6} = 9\frac{14}{18} - 3\frac{12}{18} = 6\frac{2}{18} = 6\frac{1}{9} \qquad 4\frac{7}{8} - 2\frac{1}{4} = 4\frac{7}{8} - 2\frac{2}{8} = 2\frac{5}{8}$$

$$8\frac{2}{5} - 4\frac{1}{4} = 8\frac{8}{20} - 4\frac{5}{20} = 4\frac{3}{20} \qquad 4\frac{5}{6} - 3\frac{1}{4} = 4\frac{10}{12} - 3\frac{3}{12} = 1\frac{7}{12}$$

$$4\frac{2}{3} - 1\frac{2}{3} = 3\frac{0}{3} = 3 \qquad 9\frac{8}{9} - 3\frac{3}{4} = 9\frac{32}{36} - 3\frac{27}{36} = 6\frac{5}{36}$$

$$3\frac{8}{15} - 2\frac{2}{5} = 3\frac{8}{15} - 2\frac{6}{15} = 1\frac{2}{15} \qquad 2\frac{7}{9} - 1\frac{1}{5} = 2\frac{35}{45} - 1\frac{9}{45} = 1\frac{26}{45}$$

See the notes on page 74.

☆ Adding mixed numbers and fractions

Work out the answer to the problems.

$$4\frac{3}{4} + \frac{3}{4} = 4\frac{6}{4} = 5\frac{2}{4} = 5\frac{1}{2} \qquad 3\frac{1}{2} + \frac{2}{3} = 3\frac{3}{6} + \frac{4}{6} = 3\frac{7}{6} = 4\frac{1}{6}$$

Work out the answer to each problem.

$$6\frac{2}{3} + \frac{2}{3} = 6\frac{4}{3} = 7\frac{1}{3} \qquad 4\frac{1}{4} + \frac{7}{8} = 4\frac{2}{8} + \frac{7}{8} = 4\frac{9}{8} = 5\frac{1}{8}$$

$$4\frac{5}{8} + \frac{7}{8} = 4\frac{12}{8} = 5\frac{1}{2} \qquad 3\frac{7}{10} + \frac{1}{2} = 3\frac{7}{10} + \frac{5}{10} = 3\frac{12}{10} = 4\frac{1}{5}$$

$$2\frac{3}{7} + \frac{8}{7} = 2\frac{11}{7} = 3\frac{4}{7} \qquad 1\frac{1}{2} + \frac{3}{4} = 1\frac{2}{4} + \frac{3}{4} = 1\frac{5}{4} = 2\frac{1}{4}$$

$$3\frac{5}{6} + \frac{2}{3} = 3\frac{5}{6} + \frac{4}{6} = 3\frac{9}{6} = 4\frac{1}{2} \qquad 5\frac{3}{4} + \frac{4}{5} = 5\frac{15}{20} + \frac{16}{20} = 5\frac{31}{20} = 6\frac{11}{20}$$

$$3\frac{7}{8} + \frac{1}{4} = 3\frac{7}{8} + \frac{2}{8} = 3\frac{9}{8} = 4\frac{1}{8} \qquad 3\frac{6}{7} + \frac{3}{4} = 3\frac{24}{28} + \frac{21}{28} = 3\frac{45}{28} = 4\frac{17}{28}$$

$$7\frac{7}{8} + \frac{1}{4} = 7\frac{7}{8} + \frac{2}{8} = 7\frac{9}{8} = 8\frac{1}{8} \qquad 4\frac{2}{3} + \frac{5}{8} = 4\frac{16}{24} + \frac{15}{24} = 4\frac{31}{24} = 5\frac{7}{24}$$

$$1\frac{9}{10} + \frac{2}{5} = 1\frac{9}{10} + \frac{4}{10} = 1\frac{13}{10} = 2\frac{3}{10} \qquad 8\frac{5}{6} + \frac{3}{5} = 8\frac{25}{30} + \frac{18}{30} = 8\frac{43}{30} = 9\frac{13}{30}$$

The most difficult step is renaming the answer as a proper mixed number. If children have trouble, get them to first rename the fractional part as a mixed number, and then add the 1 from this mixed number to the other whole number part.

Simple use of parentheses ☆

Work out these problems.
(4 + 6) – (2 + 1) = [10 – 3 = 7]
(2 x 5) + (10 – 4) = [10 + 6 = 16]
Remember to work out the parentheses first.

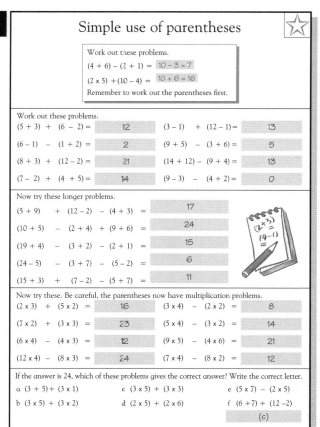

Work out these problems.
(5 + 3) + (6 – 2) = 12   (3 – 1) + (12 – 1) = 13
(6 – 1) – (1 + 2) = 2   (9 + 5) – (3 + 6) = 5
(8 + 3) + (12 – 2) = 21   (14 + 12) – (9 + 4) = 13
(7 – 2) + (4 + 5) = 14   (9 – 3) – (4 + 2) = 0

Now try these longer problems.
(5 + 9) + (12 – 2) – (4 + 3) = 17
(10 + 5) – (2 + 4) + (9 + 6) = 24
(19 + 4) – (3 + 2) – (2 + 1) = 15
(24 – 5) – (3 + 7) – (5 – 2) = 6
(15 + 3) + (7 – 2) – (5 + 7) = 11

Now try these. Be careful, the parentheses now have multiplication problems.
(2 x 3) + (5 x 2) = 16   (3 x 4) – (2 x 2) = 8
(7 x 2) + (3 x 3) = 23   (5 x 4) – (3 x 2) = 14
(6 x 4) – (4 x 3) = 12   (9 x 5) – (4 x 6) = 21
(12 x 4) – (8 x 3) = 24   (7 x 4) – (8 x 2) = 12

If the answer is 24, which of these problems gives the correct answer? Write the correct letter.
a (3 + 5) + (3 x 1)   c (3 x 5) + (3 x 3)   e (5 x 7) – (2 x 5)
b (3 x 5) + (3 x 2)   d (2 x 5) + (2 x 6)   f (6 +7) + (12 –2)
(c)

Errors on this page will most likely be the result of choosing the wrong order of operation. Remind children that they must work out the brackets first, before they add or subtract the results. Concentration and careful reading should prevent any problems.

78

☆ Simple use of parentheses

Work out these problems.
(3 + 2) x (4 + 1) = [5 x 5 = 25]
(10 x 5) ÷ (10 – 5) = [50 ÷ 5 = 10]
Remember to work out the parentheses first.

Work out these problems.
(7 + 3) x (8 – 4) = 40   (5 – 2) x (8 – 1) = 21
(9 + 5) ÷ (1 + 6) = 2   (14 – 6) x (4 + 3) = 56
(14 + 4) ÷ (12 – 6) = 3   (9 + 21) ÷ (8 – 5) = 10
(11 – 5) x (7 + 5) = 72   (8 + 20) ÷ (12 – 10) = 14
(6 + 9) ÷ (8 – 3) = 3   (14 – 3) x (6 + 1) = 77
(10 + 10) ÷ (2 + 3) = 4   (9 + 3) x (2 + 4) = 72

Now try these.
(4 x 3) ÷ (1 x 2) = 6   (5 x 4) ÷ (2 x 2) = 5
(8 x 5) ÷ (4 x 1) = 10   (6 x 4) ÷ (3 x 4) = 2
(2 x 4) x (2 x 3) = 48   (3 x 5) x (1 x 2) = 30
(8 x 4) ÷ (2 x 2) = 8   (6 x 4) ÷ (4 x 2) = 3

If the answer is 30, which of these problems gives the correct answer?
a (3 x 5) x (2 x 2)   d (20 ÷ 2) x (12 ÷ 3)
b (4 x 5) x (5 x 2)   e (5 x 12) ÷ (2 x 5)
c (12 x 5) ÷ (8 ÷ 4)   f (9 x 5) ÷ (10 ÷ 2)   c
If the answer is 8, which of these problems gives the correct answer?
a (16 ÷ 2) ÷ (2 x 1)   d (24 ÷ 6) x (8 ÷ 4)
b (9 ÷ 3) x (3 x 2)   e (8 ÷ 4) x (8 ÷ 1)
c (12 x 4) ÷ (6 x 2)   f (16 ÷ 4) x (20 ÷ 4)   d

This page continues the work of the previous page, but the brackets are multiplied or divided. It may be necessary to remind children to read carefully, as several operations take place in each equation.

Simple use of parentheses ☆

Work out these problems.
(5 + 3) + (9 – 2) = [8 + 7 = 15]
(5 + 2) – (4 – 1) = [7 – 3 = 4]
(4 + 2) x (3 + 1) = [6 x 4 = 24]
(3 x 5) ÷ (9 – 6) = [15 ÷ 3 = 5]
Remember to work out the parentheses first.

Work out these problems.
(5 + 4) + (7 – 3) = 13   (9 – 2) + (6 + 4) = 17
(7 + 3) – (9 – 7) = 8   (15 – 5) + (2 + 3) = 15
(11 x 2) – (3 x 2) = 16   (15 ÷ 3) + (9 x 2) = 23
(12 x 2) – (3 x 3) = 15   (6 ÷ 2) + (8 x 2) = 19
(9 x 3) – (7 x 3) = 6   (15 ÷ 5) + (3 x 4) = 15
(20 ÷ 5) – (8 ÷ 2) = 0   (5 x 10) – (12 x 4) = 2

Now try these.
(4 + 8) ÷ (3 x 2) = 2   (6 x 4) ÷ (3 x 2) = 4
(9 + 5) ÷ (2 x 1) = 7   (7 x 4) ÷ (3 + 4) = 4
(3 + 6) x (3 x 3) = 81   (5 x 5) ÷ (10 ÷ 2) = 5
(24 ÷ 2) x (3 x 2) = 72   (8 x 6) ÷ (2 x 12) = 2

Write down the letters of all the problems that make 25.
a (2 x 5) x (3 x 2)   d (40 ÷ 2) + (10 ÷ 2)
b (5 x 5) + (7 – 2)   e (10 x 5) – (5 x 5)
c (6 x 5) – (10 ÷ 2)   f (10 x 10) ÷ (10 – 6)   c, d, e, f
Write down the letters of all the problems that make 20.
a (10 ÷ 2) x (4 ÷ 4)   d (20 ÷ 4) x (8 ÷ 2)
b (7 x 3) – (3 ÷ 3)   e (10 ÷ 2) + (20 ÷ 2)
c (8 x 4) – (6 x 2)   f (14 ÷ 2) + (2 x 7)   b, c

This page reinforces all the elements of the previous two pages. Again, the most likely cause of error will be lack of concentration.

☆ Multiplying decimals

Work out these problems.

¹4.6	⁴3.9	³8.4
x 3	x 5	x 8
13.8	19.5	67.2

Work out these problems.

4.7 x 3	9.1 x 3	5.8 x 3	1.7 x 2	5.1 x 2
14.1	27.3	17.4	3.4	10.2
7.4 x 2	3.6 x 4	6.5 x 4	4.2 x 2	3.8 x 2
14.8	14.4	26.0	8.4	7.6
4.2 x 4	4.7 x 4	1.8 x 5	3.4 x 5	3.7 x 5
16.8	18.8	9.0	17.0	18.5
2.5 x 5	2.4 x 6	5.3 x 7	7.2 x 8	5.1 x 9
12.5	14.4	37.1	57.6	45.9
7.9 x 9	8.6 x 9	8.8 x 8	7.5 x 8	9.9 x 6
71.1	77.4	70.4	60.0	59.4
6.8 x 7	5.7 x 6	6.9 x 7	7.5 x 9	8.4 x 9
47.6	34.2	48.3	67.5	75.6
7.3 x 8	2.8 x 7	3.8 x 8	7.7 x 7	9.4 x 9
58.4	19.6	30.4	53.9	84.6

Ensure that children work from right to left. Problems will highlight gaps in their knowledge of times tables. Remind them that the number they are multiplying has one decimal place, so their answer must have one decimal place also, and this can be put in at the end.

Multiplying decimals

Work out these problems.

1 1	3 1	4 2
37.5	26.2	65.3
x 2	x 5	x 9
75.0	131.0	587.7

Work out these problems.

53.3	93.2	51.4	34.6	35.2
x 2	x 2	x 2	x 3	x 3
106.6	186.4	102.8	103.8	105.6

46.5	25.8	16.4	47.1	37.4
x 4	x 4	x 3	x 5	x 5
186.0	103.2	49.2	235.5	187.0

12.4	46.3	17.5	36.5	72.4
x 5	x 5	x 6	x 6	x 7
62.0	231.5	105.0	219.0	506.8

37.5	20.3	73.4	92.6	47.9
x 7	x 7	x 7	x 6	x 6
262.5	142.1	513.8	555.6	287.4

53.9	75.6	28.8	79.4	99.9
x 8	x 8	x 8	x 8	x 9
431.2	604.8	230.4	635.2	899.1

37.9	14.8	35.4	46.8	27.2
x 9	x 9	x 9	x 8	x 7
341.1	133.2	318.6	374.4	190.4

39.5	84.2	68.5	73.2	47.6
x 6	x 9	x 8	x 9	x 6
237.0	757.8	548.0	658.8	285.6

This page further revises decimal multiplication, using larger numbers.

82

Real-life problems

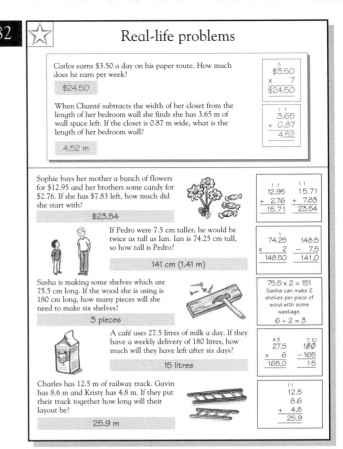

Carlos earns $3.50 a day on his paper route. How much does he earn per week?

$24.50

$$\begin{array}{r} 3 \\ \$3.50 \\ \times \quad 7 \\ \hline \$24.50 \end{array}$$

When Chanté subtracts the width of her closet from the length of her bedroom wall she finds she has 3.65 m of wall space left. If the closet is 0.87 m wide, what is the length of her bedroom wall?

4.52 m

$$\begin{array}{r} 1 1 \\ 3.65 \\ + 0.87 \\ \hline 4.52 \end{array}$$

Sophie buys her mother a bunch of flowers for $12.95 and her brothers some candy for $2.76. If she has $7.83 left, how much did she start with?

$23.54

$$\begin{array}{r} 1 1 \quad 1 1 \\ 12.95 \quad 15.71 \\ + 2.76 \quad + 7.83 \\ \hline 15.71 \quad 23.54 \end{array}$$

If Pedro were 7.5 cm taller, he would be twice as tall as Ian. Ian is 74.25 cm tall, so how tall is Pedro?

141 cm (1.41 m)

$$\begin{array}{r} 74.25 \quad 148.5 \\ \times \quad 2 \quad - 7.5 \\ \hline 148.50 \quad 141.0 \end{array}$$

Sasha is making some shelves which are 75.5 cm long. If the wood she is using is 180 cm long, how many pieces will she need to make six shelves?

3 pieces

75.5 x 2 = 151
Sasha can make 2 shelves per piece of wood with some wastage.
6 ÷ 2 = 3

A café uses 27.5 litres of milk a day. If they have a weekly delivery of 180 litres, how much will they have left after six days?

15 litres

$$\begin{array}{r} 4 3 \quad 7 10 \\ 27.5 \quad 1\cancel{8}0 \\ \times \quad 6 \quad - 165 \\ \hline 165.0 \quad 15 \end{array}$$

Charles has 12.5 m of railway track. Gavin has 8.6 m and Kristy has 4.8 m. If they put their track together how long will their layout be?

25.9 m

$$\begin{array}{r} 1 1 \\ 12.5 \\ 8.6 \\ + 4.8 \\ \hline 25.9 \end{array}$$

This page provides an opportunity to apply math skills to real-life problems. Children will need to choose the operation carefully. Some questions require more than one operation.

83

Real-life problems

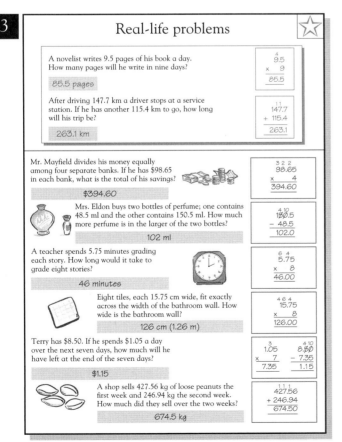

A novelist writes 9.5 pages of his book a day. How many pages will he write in nine days?

85.5 pages

$$\begin{array}{r} 4 \\ 9.5 \\ \times \quad 9 \\ \hline 85.5 \end{array}$$

After driving 147.7 km a driver stops at a service station. If he has another 115.4 km to go, how long will his trip be?

263.1 km

$$\begin{array}{r} 1 1 \\ 147.7 \\ + 115.4 \\ \hline 263.1 \end{array}$$

Mr. Mayfield divides his money equally among four separate banks. If he has $98.65 in each bank, what is the total of his savings?

$394.60

$$\begin{array}{r} 3 2 2 \\ 98.65 \\ \times \quad 4 \\ \hline 394.60 \end{array}$$

Mrs. Eldon buys two bottles of perfume; one contains 48.5 ml and the other 150.5 ml. How much more perfume is in the larger of the two bottles?

102 ml

$$\begin{array}{r} 4 10 \\ 15\cancel{0}.5 \\ - 48.5 \\ \hline 102.0 \end{array}$$

A teacher spends 5.75 minutes grading each story. How long would it take to grade eight stories?

46 minutes

$$\begin{array}{r} 6 4 \\ 5.75 \\ \times \quad 8 \\ \hline 46.00 \end{array}$$

Eight tiles, each 15.75 cm wide, fit exactly across the width of the bathroom wall. How wide is the bathroom wall?

126 cm (1.26 m)

$$\begin{array}{r} 4 6 4 \\ 15.75 \\ \times \quad 8 \\ \hline 126.00 \end{array}$$

Terry has $8.50. If he spends $1.05 a day over the next seven days, how much will he have left at the end of the seven days?

$1.15

$$\begin{array}{r} 3 \\ 1.05 \quad 8.\cancel{5}0 \\ \times \quad 7 \quad - 7.35 \\ \hline 7.35 \quad 1.15 \end{array}$$

A shop sells 427.56 kg of loose peanuts the first week and 246.94 kg the second week. How much did they sell over the two weeks?

674.5 kg

$$\begin{array}{r} 1 1 1 \\ 427.56 \\ + 246.94 \\ \hline 674.50 \end{array}$$

This page also revises various operations applied to real-life situations.

Real-life problems

In a class of 30 children, 6 children are painting. What percent of children are painting?

$\frac{6}{30}$ of the children are painting and to change a fraction to a percent we multiply by 100.

20%

$$\frac{\cancel{6}}{\cancel{30}} \times 100 = 20$$

40% of a class is made up of girls. If there are 12 girls, how many children are in the class?

If 12 girls are 40% of the class, we divide 12 by 40 to find 1%. Then we multiply by 100 to find 100%.

30 children

$$\frac{\cancel{12}}{\cancel{40}} \times 100 = 30$$

A shop has 60 books by a new author. If the shop sells 45 books, what percent does it sell?

75%

$$\frac{45}{\cancel{60}} \times 100 = 75$$

A school disco sells 65% of its tickets. If it had 120 tickets to start with, how many has it sold?

78 tickets

$$\frac{120}{100} \times 65 = 78$$

200 people go on a school trip. If 14% are adults, how many children go on the trip?

172 children

$$100 - 14 = 86\%$$
$$\frac{200}{100} \times 86 = 172$$

A shop sells 150 T-shirts but 12 are returned because they are faulty. What percent of the T-shirts was faulty?

8%

$$\frac{12}{150} \times 100 = 8$$

A group of 120 children are asked their favourite colours.

15% like red. How many children like red? 18

$$\frac{120}{100} \times 15 = 18$$

20% like green. How many children like green? 24

$$\frac{120}{100} \times 20 = 24$$

30% like yellow. How many children like yellow? 36

$$\frac{120}{100} \times 30 = 36$$

35% like blue. How many children like blue? 42

$$\frac{120}{100} \times 35 = 42$$

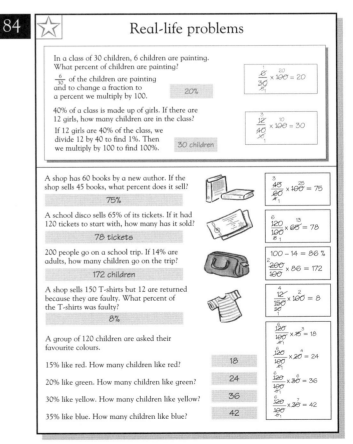

In questions 1 and 4, children should see that the answer can be expressed as a fraction, which can then be converted to a percentage by multiplying by 100.

Conversions: length

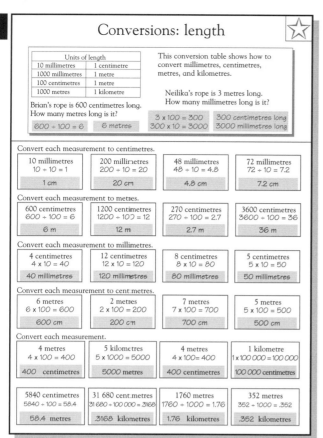

Units of length	
10 millimetres	1 centimetre
1000 millimetres	1 metre
100 centimetres	1 metre
1000 metres	1 kilometre

This conversion table shows how to convert millimetres, centimetres, metres, and kilometres.

Neilika's rope is 3 metres long. How many millimetres long is it?

Brian's rope is 600 centimetres long. How many metres long is it?

600 ÷ 100 = 6   6 metres

3 x 100 = 300   300 centimetres long
300 x 10 = 3000   3000 millimetres long

Convert each measurement to centimetres.

10 millimetres 10 ÷ 10 = 1	200 millimetres 200 ÷ 10 = 20	48 millimetres 48 ÷ 10 = 4.8	72 millimetres 72 ÷ 10 = 7.2
1 cm	20 cm	4.8 cm	7.2 cm

Convert each measurement to metres.

600 centimetres 600 ÷ 100 = 6	1200 centimetres 1200 ÷ 100 = 12	270 centimetres 270 ÷ 100 = 2.7	3600 centimetres 3600 ÷ 100 = 36
6 m	12 m	2.7 m	36 m

Convert each measurement to millimetres.

4 centimetres 4 x 10 = 40	12 centimetres 12 x 10 = 120	8 centimetres 8 x 10 = 80	5 centimetres 5 x 10 = 50
40 millimetres	120 millimetres	80 millimetres	50 millimetres

Convert each measurement to centimetres.

6 metres 6 x 100 = 600	2 metres 2 x 100 = 200	7 metres 7 x 100 = 700	5 metres 5 x 100 = 500
600 cm	200 cm	700 cm	500 cm

Convert each measurement.

4 metres 4 x 100 = 400	5 kilometres 5 x 1000 = 5000	4 metres 4 x 100 = 400	1 kilometre 1 x 100 000 = 100 000
400 centimetres	5000 metres	400 centimetres	100 000 centimetres

5840 centimetres 5840 ÷ 100 = 58.4	31 680 centimetres 31 680 ÷ 100 000 = .3168	1760 metres 1760 ÷ 1000 = 1.76	352 metres 352 ÷ 1000 = .352
58.4 metres	.3168 kilometres	1.76 kilometres	.352 kilometres

If children are confused whether to multiply or divide, have them think about whether the new unit is a longer or a shorter unit. If the unit is longer, there will be fewer of them, so division will be the appropriate operation to use.

86

Conversions: capacity

Units of capacity	
1000 millilitres	1 litre

This conversion table shows how to convert millilitres and litres.

Katya's thermos holds 8 litres. How many millilitres does it hold?

8 x 1000 = 8000   8000 millilitres

Hannah's thermos holds 60 000 millilitres. How many litres does it hold?

60 000 ÷ 1000 = 60   60 litres

Convert each measurement to litres.

32 000 millilitres 32 000 ÷ 1000 = 32	16 000 millilitres 16 000 ÷ 1000 = 16	9600 millilitres 9600 ÷ 1000 = 9.6	8000 millilitres 8000 ÷ 1000 = 8
32 litres	16 litres	9.6 litres	8 litres

Convert each measurement to millilitres.

6 litres 6 x 1000 = 6000	12 litres 12 x 1000 = 12 000	36 litres 36 x 1000 = 36 000	50 litres 50 x 1000 = 50 000
6000 ml	12 000 ml	36 000 ml	50 000 ml

4 litres 4 x 1000 = 4000	12 litres 12 x 1000 = 12 000	30 litres 30 x 1000 = 30 000	16 litres 16 x 1000 = 16 000
4000 ml	12 000 ml	30 000 ml	16 000 ml

Convert each measurement to litres.

14 000 millilitres 14 000 ÷ 1000 = 14	32 000 millilitres 32 000 ÷ 1000 = 32	100 000 millilitres 100 000 ÷ 1000 = 100	20 000 millilitres 20 000 ÷ 1000 = 20
14 litres	32 litres	100 litres	20 litres

Convert each measurement.

3000 millilitres 3000 ÷ 1000 = 3	5 litres 5 x 1000 = 5000	36 000 millilitres 36 000 ÷ 1000 = 36	72 litres 72 x 1000 = 72 000
3 litres	5000 millilitres	36 litres	72 000 millilitres

1 litre 1 x 1000 = 1000	24 000 millilitres 24 000 ÷ 1000 = 24	7 litres 7 x 1000 = 7000	11 000 millilitres 11 000 ÷ 1000 = 11
1000 millilitres	24 litres	7000 millilitres	11 litres

See the notes for page 85.

87

Fraction of a number

Work out to find the fraction of the number. Write the answer in the box.

$\frac{1}{6}$ of 42
$\frac{1}{6}$ x 42 = $\frac{42}{6}$ = 7
1 x 7 = 7
So, $\frac{1}{6}$ of 42 = 7

$\frac{3}{5}$ of 35
$\frac{1}{5}$ x 35 = $\frac{35}{5}$ = 7
3 x 7 = 21
So, $\frac{3}{5}$ of 35 = 21

$\frac{1}{4}$ of 100 = $\frac{100}{4}$ = 25

$\frac{1}{3}$ of 69 = $\frac{69}{3}$ = 23

Work out to find the fraction of the number. Write the answer in the box.

$\frac{1}{8}$ of 72	9	$\frac{1}{5}$ of 250	50	$\frac{1}{2}$ of 38	19
$\frac{1}{9}$ of 54	6	$\frac{1}{2}$ of 84	42	$\frac{1}{6}$ of 72	12
$\frac{1}{4}$ of 52	13	$\frac{1}{7}$ of 140	20	$\frac{1}{3}$ of 36	12
$\frac{1}{5}$ of 175	35	$\frac{1}{8}$ of 64	8	$\frac{1}{4}$ of 100	25
$\frac{1}{6}$ of 300	50	$\frac{1}{9}$ of 81	9	$\frac{1}{2}$ of 114	57
$\frac{1}{10}$ of 100	10	$\frac{1}{5}$ of 55	11	$\frac{1}{7}$ of 140	20
$\frac{3}{4}$ of 100	75	$\frac{2}{3}$ of 75	50	$\frac{4}{7}$ of 42	24
$\frac{2}{5}$ of 25	10	$\frac{5}{8}$ of 40	25	$\frac{2}{3}$ of 27	18
$\frac{5}{9}$ of 36	20	$\frac{2}{3}$ of 225	150	$\frac{5}{6}$ of 120	100
$\frac{3}{4}$ of 56	42	$\frac{5}{7}$ of 133	95	$\frac{2}{3}$ of 180	120
$\frac{4}{5}$ of 100	80	$\frac{2}{10}$ of 100	20	$\frac{3}{8}$ of 64	24
$\frac{2}{3}$ of 210	140	$\frac{4}{9}$ of 90	40	$\frac{7}{8}$ of 72	63

If children have difficulty with the first step, have them use long division to find the quotient.

Showing decimals

Write the decimals on the number line.

0.4, 0.5, 0.6, 0.8, 0.9, 0.25, 0.45, 0.63

Write the decimals on the number line.

0.56, 0.2, 0.87, 0.45, 0.98, 0.6, 0.1

Write the decimals on the number line.

1.41, 1.8, 1.3, 1.98, 1.68, 1.2

Write these decimals on the number line.

2.5, 3.75, 2.25, 3.1, 3.68, 4.2

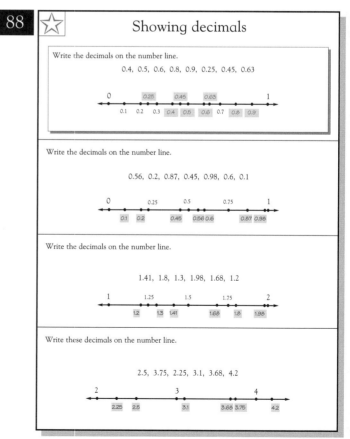

If children are confused about where to place the decimals to hundredths, have them first fill in all of the tenths on the number line. Then ask which of those tenths the decimals to hundredths fall between.

89

Area of right-angled triangles ★

Find the area of this right-angled triangle.

Because the area of this triangle is half the area of the rectangle shown, we can find the area of the rectangle and then divide it by two to find the area of the triangle.
So the area = (8 cm x 4 cm) ÷ 2
= 32 cm² ÷ 2 = 16 cm²

4 cm

8 cm

Area = 16 cm²

Find the area of these right-angled triangles.

5 cm
12 cm
30 cm²

3 cm
10 cm
15 cm²

9 cm
2 cm
9 cm²

4 cm
14 cm
28 cm²

5 cm
6 cm
15 cm²

6 cm
8 cm
24 cm²

6 cm
12 cm
36 cm²

20 cm
30 cm²

3 cm
7 cm
4 cm
14 cm²

The operation of multiplying the sides together and dividing by two should offer no serious difficulty to children, but make sure they are really clear about why they are doing this.

90

★ Speed problems

How long would it take to travel 120 km at 8 km/h?
(Time = Distance ÷ Speed)

15 hours

15
8)120

If a bus takes 3 hours to travel 150 km, how fast is it going?
(Speed = Distance ÷ Time)

50 km/h

50
3)150

If a car travels at 60 km/h for 2 hours, how far has it gone?
(Distance = Speed × Time)

120 km

60
× 2
120

If a man walks for 6 kilometres at a steady speed of 3 km/h, how long will it take him?

2 hours

$\frac{6}{3} = 2$

A truck driver travels 120 km in 3 hours. If he drove at a steady speed, how fast was he going?

40 km/h

40
3)120

A car travels at a steady speed of 40 km/h. How far will it travel in 4 hours?

160 km

40
× 4
160

Shane walks 10 km at 4 km/h. Damien walks 12 km at 5 km/h. Which of them will take the longest?

Shane

Shane 4)10 2½
Damien 5)12 2⅖
2½ > 2⅖

Courtney drives for 30 minutes at 50 km/h and for 1 hour at 40 km/h. How far has he travelled altogether?

65 km

30 min = ½ h
25
2)50
25 + 40 = 65

A racing car travels 340 km in 120 minutes. What speed is it travelling at?

170 km/h

120 min = 2 h
170
2)340

If children experience difficulty on this page, ask them what they need to find – speed, distance or time – and refer them to the necessary formula. Encourage them to develop simple examples that will help them to remember the formulas.

91

Conversion tables ★

Draw a table to convert dollars to cents.

$	cents
1	100
2	200
3	300

Complete the conversion chart below.

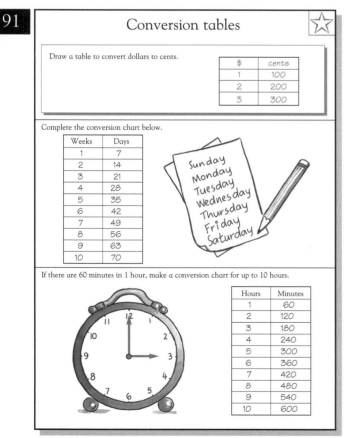

Weeks	Days
1	7
2	14
3	21
4	28
5	35
6	42
7	49
8	56
9	63
10	70

Sunday
Monday
Tuesday
Wednesday
Thursday
Friday
Saturday

If there are 60 minutes in 1 hour, make a conversion chart for up to 10 hours.

Hours	Minutes
1	60
2	120
3	180
4	240
5	300
6	360
7	420
8	480
9	540
10	600

Children will grasp that they are dealing with multiples of 7 and later, 60. Any problems will be due to weaknesses in tables or from missing out numbers as they work down the chart. Encourage care and concentration.

★ Reading bar graphs

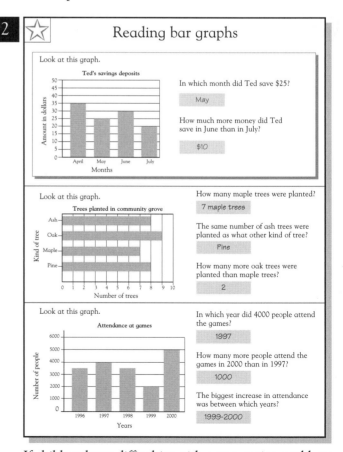

Look at this graph.

Ted's savings deposits

In which month did Ted save $25?

May

How much more money did Ted save in June than in July?

$10

Look at this graph.

Trees planted in community grove

How many maple trees were planted?

7 maple trees

The same number of ash trees were planted as what other kind of tree?

Pine

How many more oak trees were planted than maple trees?

2

Look at this graph.

Attendance at games

In which year did 4000 people attend the games?

1997

How many more people attend the games in 2000 than in 1997?

1000

The biggest increase in attendance was between which years?

1999-2000

If children have difficulties with computation problems, have them write down each of the numbers they read off the graph before computing with them.

Expanded form

What is the value of 3 in 2308?	300
Write 32 084 in expanded form.	30 000 + 2000 + 80 + 4

What is the value of 6 in these numbers?

26	6	162	60	36 904	6000
12 612	600	6130	6000	567 902	60 000
13 036	6	9764	60	17 632	600

What is the value of 4 in these numbers?

14 300	4000	942	40	8764	4
10 408	400	1043	40	45 987	40 000
6045	40	804 001	4000	694	4

Circle the numbers that have a 7 with the value of seventy thousand.

457 682   67 924   (870 234)   (372 987)

(171 345)   767 707   (79 835)   16 757

Write the numbers in expanded form.

34 897	30 000 + 4000 + 800 + 90 + 7
508 061	500 000 + 8000 + 60 + 1
50 810	50 000 + 800 + 10
8945	8000 + 900 + 40 + 5
60 098	60 000 + 90 + 8

Some children are confused about how to represent the zeros in a number. Be sure they know to skip those terms when they write the expanded form.

94

Cubes of small numbers

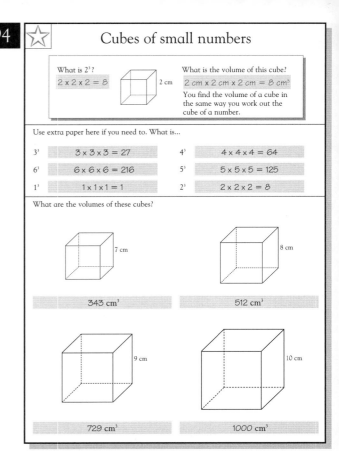

What is 2^3? $2 \times 2 \times 2 = 8$

What is the volume of this cube? $2\ cm \times 2\ cm \times 2\ cm = 8\ cm^3$ 2 cm
You find the volume of a cube in the same way you work out the cube of a number.

Use extra paper here if you need to. What is...

3^3	$3 \times 3 \times 3 = 27$	4^3	$4 \times 4 \times 4 = 64$
6^3	$6 \times 6 \times 6 = 216$	5^3	$5 \times 5 \times 5 = 125$
1^3	$1 \times 1 \times 1 = 1$	2^3	$2 \times 2 \times 2 = 8$

What are the volumes of these cubes?

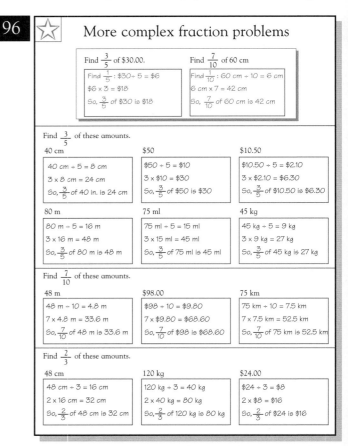

7 cm — 343 cm^3

8 cm — 512 cm^3

9 cm — 729 cm^3

10 cm — 1000 cm^3

The most common mistake children make is confusing three cubed with three times three, especially when they are working quickly through the examples. It is necessary to reinforce the concept of cubing a number. Children may need some paper for their working out.

95

Multiplying fractions

Write the product.

$\frac{3}{8} \times \frac{4}{7} = \frac{3}{14}$ $\frac{1}{5} \times \frac{3}{10} = \frac{3}{2} = 1\frac{1}{2}$

Write the product.

$\frac{1}{4} \times \frac{1}{4} = \frac{1}{16}$ $\frac{3}{10} \times \frac{2}{6} = \frac{1}{10}$ $6 \times \frac{3}{4} = \frac{9}{2} = 4\frac{1}{2}$

$8 \times \frac{1}{4} = 2$ $\frac{2}{5} \times \frac{5}{7} = \frac{2}{7}$ $\frac{2}{5} \times \frac{5}{6} = \frac{1}{3}$

$\frac{2}{5} \times \frac{2}{3} = \frac{4}{15}$ $4 \times \frac{3}{16} = \frac{3}{4}$ $\frac{3}{8} \times 10 = \frac{15}{4} = 3\frac{3}{4}$

$\frac{1}{3} \times 15 = 5$ $\frac{5}{9} \times \frac{1}{5} = \frac{1}{9}$ $\frac{3}{4} \times \frac{4}{9} = \frac{1}{3}$

$\frac{1}{4} \times \frac{2}{7} = \frac{1}{14}$ $\frac{2}{9} \times \frac{3}{4} = \frac{1}{6}$ $12 \times \frac{3}{10} = \frac{18}{5} = 3\frac{3}{5}$

$\frac{2}{3} \times \frac{1}{3} = \frac{2}{9}$ $\frac{1}{12} \times 2 = \frac{1}{6}$ $\frac{3}{4} \times \frac{1}{4} = \frac{3}{16}$

$\frac{5}{6} \times 8 = \frac{20}{3} = 6\frac{2}{3}$ $7 \times \frac{1}{8} = \frac{7}{8}$ $\frac{1}{6} \times \frac{5}{6} = \frac{5}{36}$

$\frac{1}{2} \times 25 = \frac{25}{2} = 12\frac{1}{2}$ $\frac{7}{10} \times \frac{5}{7} = \frac{1}{2}$ $4 \times \frac{3}{4} = 3$

Some children are confused about how to multiply a fraction by a whole number. Remind them that any whole number is also a fraction with 1 as the denominator.

More complex fraction problems

Find $\frac{3}{5}$ of $30.00.

Find $\frac{1}{5}$: $30 ÷ 5 = $6
$6 × 3 = $18
So, $\frac{3}{5}$ of $30 is $18

Find $\frac{7}{10}$ of 60 cm.

Find $\frac{1}{10}$: 60 cm ÷ 10 = 6 cm
6 cm × 7 = 42 cm
So, $\frac{7}{10}$ of 60 cm is 42 cm

Find $\frac{3}{5}$ of these amounts.

40 cm	$50	$10.50
40 cm ÷ 5 = 8 cm	$50 ÷ 5 = $10	$10.50 ÷ 5 = $2.10
3 × 8 cm = 24 cm	3 × $10 = $30	3 × $2.10 = $6.30
So, $\frac{3}{5}$ of 40 in. is 24 cm	So, $\frac{3}{5}$ of $50 is $30	So, $\frac{3}{5}$ of $10.50 is $6.30

80 m	75 ml	45 kg
80 m ÷ 5 = 16 m	75 ml ÷ 5 = 15 ml	45 kg ÷ 5 = 9 kg
3 × 16 m = 48 m	3 × 15 ml = 45 ml	3 × 9 kg = 27 kg
So, $\frac{3}{5}$ of 80 m is 48 m	So, $\frac{3}{5}$ of 75 ml is 45 ml	So, $\frac{3}{5}$ of 45 kg is 27 kg

Find $\frac{7}{10}$ of these amounts.

48 m	$98.00	75 km
48 m ÷ 10 = 4.8 m	$98 ÷ 10 = $9.80	75 km ÷ 10 = 7.5 km
7 × 4.8 m = 33.6 m	7 × $9.80 = $68.60	7 × 7.5 km = 52.5 km
So, $\frac{7}{10}$ of 48 m is 33.6 m	So, $\frac{7}{10}$ of $98 is $68.60	So, $\frac{7}{10}$ of 75 km is 52.5 km

Find $\frac{2}{3}$ of these amounts.

48 cm	120 kg	$24.00
48 cm ÷ 3 = 16 cm	120 kg ÷ 3 = 40 kg	$24 ÷ 3 = $8
2 × 16 cm = 32 cm	2 × 40 kg = 80 kg	2 × $8 = $16
So, $\frac{2}{3}$ of 48 cm is 32 cm	So, $\frac{2}{3}$ of 120 kg is 80 kg	So, $\frac{2}{3}$ of $24 is $16

Ensure that children are dividing the amount by the denominator and multiplying the result by the numerator. You could explain that we divide by the bottom to find one part and multiply by the top to find the number of parts we want.

Finding percentages ★

Find 30% of 140. $\frac{14\cancel{0}}{10\cancel{0}} \times 3\cancel{0} = 42$ (Divide by 100 to find 1% and then multiply by 30 to find 30%.)

Find 12% of 75. $\frac{\cancel{75}^{3}}{\cancel{100}_{4}} \times \cancel{12}^{3} = 9$ (Divide by 100 to find 1% and then multiply by 12 to find 12%.)

Find 30% of these numbers.

620 $\frac{620}{100} \times 30 = 186$ 240 $\frac{240}{100} \times 30 = 72$

80 $\frac{80}{100} \times 30 = 24$ 160 $\frac{160}{100} \times 30 = 48$

Find 60% of these numbers.

60 $\frac{60}{100} \times 60 = 36$ 100 $\frac{100}{100} \times 60 = 60$

160 $\frac{160}{100} \times 60 = 96$ 580 $\frac{580}{100} \times 60 = 348$

Find 45% of these numbers.

80 g $\frac{80}{100} \times 45 = 36\,g$ 40 cm $\frac{40}{100} \times 45 = 18\,cm$

240 ml $\frac{240}{100} \times 45 = 108\,ml$ 600 km $\frac{600}{100} \times 45 = 270\,km$

Find 12% of these numbers.

$150 $\frac{150}{100} \times 12 = \$18$ $600 $\frac{600}{100} \times 12 = \$72$

125 m $\frac{125}{100} \times 12 = 15\,m$ 775 m $\frac{775}{100} \times 12 = 93\,m$

The most common error when finding percentages is to reverse the operation, i.e. to divide by the percentage required and multiply by 100. Explain again that if the whole is 100% we divide the number by 100 to find 1% and then multiply by the percentage we want.

★ Addition

Work out the answer to each problem.

```
  1 1              1 3 1
   634            1472
  4812              96
+ 1428            8391
_____          + 564
  6874          _____
                10 523
```

Remember to regroup if you need to.

Find each sum.

```
 5 831      3 724      9 994       524
 8 375      9 942      7 358      7034
+  219     +  623     +  471     +  95
_____     _____     _____     _____
14 425     14 289     17 823      7653
```

```
 7 341      9 328      7159        208
   299        347        39       4943
+ 5 143    + 8 222    +  748     +  55
_____     _____     _____     _____
12 783     17 897      7946       5206
```

Find each sum.

```
 8 594      7 362      3041       7 641
   629        843       571         93
 9 878      4 732      5210       8 521
+   96     +   53     +  71      +  843
_____     _____     _____     _____
19 197     12 990      8893      17 098
```

```
 8 795      6 043        27        146
   659          4       153       3714
 3 212        147      8612         26
+  961     + 8 948     + 127     + 5003
_____     _____     _____     _____
13 627     15 142      8919       8889
```

This page should be fairly straightforward, but errors may creep in as the lists get longer towards the end. Errors will most likely be mistakes in adding the longer lists, adding across place value, or a failure to carry.

More addition ★

Work out the answer to each problem.

```
 1 1  1          1 2 1
23 714          11 541
 9 024            861
+  348          29 652
_____          +   5
33 086          _____
                42 059
```

Remember to regroup if you need to.

Find each sum.

```
17 203     29 521     65 214     25 046
   112      6 211        973         15
+ 5 608    +   58     + 1 291    +  263
_____     _____     _____     _____
22 923     35 790     67 478     25 324
```

```
 6 958     73 009     11 536     87 019
    71          3         48        127
+16 911    +  581     + 2 435    + 5 652
_____     _____     _____     _____
23 940     73 593     14 019     92 798
```

Find each sum.

```
79 622     64 599      6 940     72 148
 8 011        122        936        999
47 391      6 375     58 274      7 481
+    7     +   91     +   36     + 21 685
_____     _____     _____     _____
135 031    71 187     66 186     102 313
```

```
58 975     36 403          8         23
   858         73     22 849     99 951
 8 423        712        502        358
+   27     + 6 229    + 4 034    + 6 231
_____     _____     _____     _____
68 283     43 417     27 393     106 563
```

Any problems on this page will be similar to those encountered on the previous page. As the numbers get larger, errors are more likely to occur.

★ Dividing by ones

$477 \div 2$ can be written in two ways:

$238\frac{1}{2}$ or $238\;r\;1$
$2\overline{)477}$ $2\overline{)477}$

Work out the answers to these problems. Use fraction remainders.

```
 239 1/2       215 3/4      115 4/5      122 6/7
  239           215          115          122
2)479         4)863        5)579        7)860
  4             8            5            7
  7             6            7            16
  6             4            5            14
  19            23           29           20
  18            20           25           14
  1            3            4            6
```

```
 87 1/2        55 2/3       50 7/9       97 2/3
  87            55           50           97
2)175         3)167        9)457        3)293
  16            15           45           27
  15            17           7            23
  14            15                        21
  1            2                          2
```

Work out the answers to these problems. Use unit remainders.

```
 352 r 1       127 r 2      82 r 2       131 r 4
  352           127          82           131
2)705         5)637        4)330        7)921
  6             5            32           7
  10            13           10           22
  10            10           8            21
  5             37           2            11
  4             35                        7
  1            2                         4
```

Children may think that the two types of division represent different procedures. Point out that the only difference is in how to write the remainder.

Dividing by ones

361 ÷ 2 can be written in two ways:

$180\frac{1}{2}$ or   180 r 1

2) 361   2) 361

Work out the answers to these problems. Use fraction remainders.

80	70	$43\frac{5}{8}$	$60\frac{7}{9}$
80	70	43	60
4)320	7)490	8)349	9)547
320	490	32	54
0	0	29	7
		24	
		5	

$403\frac{1}{2}$	$218\frac{1}{2}$	$471\frac{1}{2}$	$120\frac{1}{3}$
403	218	471	12
2)807	2)437	2)943	3)361
806	42	80	360
1	17	1 4	1
	16	1 4	
	1	3	
		2	
		1	

Work out the answers to these problems. Use unit remainders.

$83\ r\ 2$	90	101	$91\ r\ 2$
83	90	101	91
5)417	9)810	3)303	4)366
40	810	303	36
17	0	0	6
15			4
2			2

Children may have trouble deciding where to place digits in the quotient. Have them place the digit directly above the number being subtracted in that step.

Dividing

589 ÷ 5 can be written in two ways:

$117\frac{4}{5}$ or   117 r 4

5)589   5)589

Work out the answers to these problems. Use fractions remainders.

$54\frac{3}{8}$	$39\frac{8}{9}$	$64\frac{4}{7}$	$113\frac{1}{7}$
54	39	64	11
8)435	9)359	7)452	7)792
40	27	42	7
35	89	32	09
32	81	28	7
3	8	4	22
			21
			1

$117\frac{1}{8}$	$114\frac{1}{7}$	$32\frac{1}{9}$	$142\frac{1}{3}$
117	114	32	142
8)937	7)799	9)289	6)854
8	7	27	60
13	09	19	25
8	7	18	24
57	29	1	14
56	28		12
1	1		2

Work out the answers to these problems. Use unit remainders.

$72\ r\ 5$	$136\ r\ 1$	119	$68\ r\ 3$
72	136	119	68
9)653	4)545	8)952	6)411
63	4	8	36
23	14	15	51
18	12	8	48
5	25	72	3
	24	72	
	1	0	

See the notes for page 101.

Everyday problems

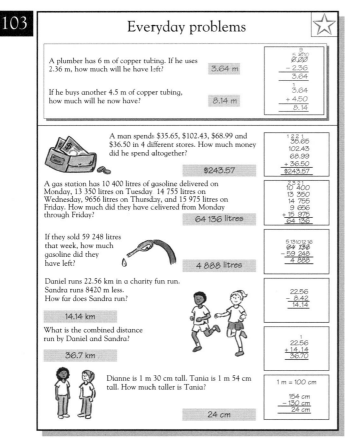

A plumber has 6 m of copper tubing. If he uses 2.36 m, how much will he have left?   **3.64 m**

```
     9
  5 9 10
  6.00
- 2.36
  3.64
```

If he buys another 4.5 m of copper tubing, how much will he now have?   **8.14 m**

```
    1
  3.64
+ 4.50
  8.14
```

A man spends $35.65, $102.43, $68.99 and $36.50 in 4 different stores. How much money did he spend altogether?   **$243.57**

```
  1 2 2 1
  35.65
 102.43
  68.99
+ 36.50
$243.57
```

A gas station has 10 400 litres of gasoline delivered on Monday, 13 350 litres on Tuesday 14 755 litres on Wednesday, 9656 litres on Thursday, and 15 975 litres on Friday. How much did they have delivered from Monday through Friday?   **64 136 litres**

```
   2 3 2 1
  10 400
  13 350
  14 755
   9 656
+ 15 975
  64 136
```

If they sold 59 248 litres that week, how much gasoline did they have left?   **4 888 litres**

```
  5 13 10 12 16
  64 136
- 59 248
   4 888
```

Daniel runs 22.56 km in a charity fun run. Sandra runs 8420 m less. How far does Sandra run?   **14.14 km**

```
  22.56
-  8.42
  14.14
```

What is the combined distance run by Daniel and Sandra?   **36.7 km**

```
     1
  22.56
+ 14.14
  36.70
```

Dianne is 1 m 30 cm tall. Tania is 1 m 54 cm tall. How much taller is Tania?   **24 cm**

```
1 m = 100 cm

  154 cm
- 130 cm
   24 cm
```

Children will apply subtraction and addition skills to real-life problems. If they are unsure about which operation to use, discuss whether the answer will be larger (addition) or smaller (subtraction). Take care when units of measurement need to be converted.

Real-life problems

A man walks 18.34 km on Saturday and 16.57 km on Sunday. How far did he walk that weekend?   **34.91 km**

```
  1  1
  18.34
+ 16.57
  34.91
```

How much farther did he walk on Saturday?   **1.77 km**

```
    7 12 14
  18.34
- 16.57
   1.77
```

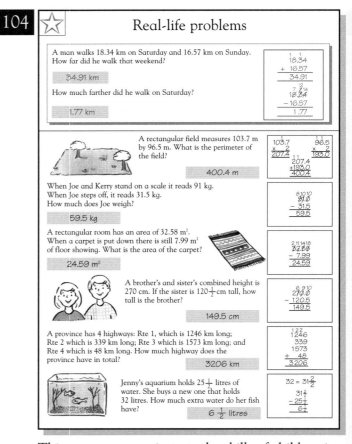

A rectangular field measures 103.7 m by 96.5 m. What is the perimeter of the field?   **400.4 m**

```
  103.7     96.5
  x   2     x   2
  207.4    193.0

  207.4
+ 193.0
  400.4
```

When Joe and Kerry stand on a scale it reads 91 kg. When Joe steps off, it reads 31.5 kg. How much does Joe weigh?   **59.5 kg**

```
  8 10 10
  91.0
- 31.5
  59.5
```

A rectangular room has an area of 32.58 m². When a carpet is put down there is still 7.99 m² of floor showing. What is the area of the carpet?   **24.59 m²**

```
  2 11 14 18
  32.58
-  7.99
  24.59
```

A brother's and sister's combined height is 270 cm. If the sister is $120\frac{1}{2}$ cm tall, how tall is the brother?   **149.5 cm**

```
   6 9 10
  270.0
- 120.5
  149.5
```

A province has 4 highways: Rte 1, which is 1246 km long; Rte 2 which is 339 km long; Rte 3 which is 1573 km long; and Rte 4 which is 48 km long. How much highway does the province have in total?   **3206 km**

```
   1 2 2
  1246
   339
  1573
+   48
  3206
```

Jenny's aquarium holds $25\frac{1}{2}$ litres of water. She buys a new one that holds 32 litres. How much extra water do her fish have?   **$6\frac{1}{2}$ litres**

```
  32 = 31 1/2...
  31 1/2
- 25 1/2
   6 1/2
```

This page once again tests the skills of children in real-life problems. In the first question, make sure that they are finding the perimeter and not the area.

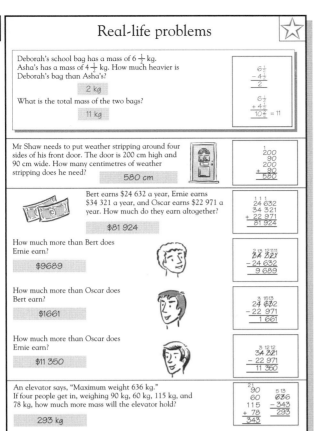

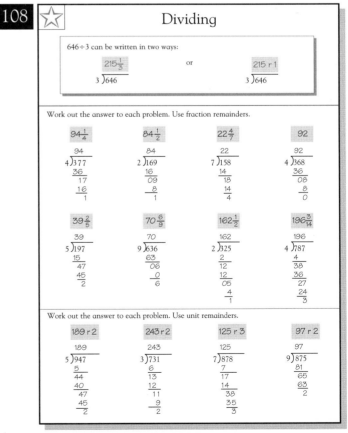

105 — Real-life problems ⭐

Deborah's school bag has a mass of $6\frac{1}{2}$ kg.
Asha's has a mass of $4\frac{1}{2}$ kg. How much heavier is
Deborah's bag than Asha's?

2 kg

$$\begin{array}{r} 6\frac{1}{2} \\ -4\frac{1}{2} \\ \hline 2 \end{array}$$

What is the total mass of the two bags?

11 kg

$$\begin{array}{r} 6\frac{1}{2} \\ +4\frac{1}{2} \\ \hline 10\frac{2}{2}=11 \end{array}$$

Mr Shaw needs to put weather stripping around four
sides of his front door. The door is 200 cm high and
90 cm wide. How many centimetres of weather
stripping does he need?   **580 cm**

$$\begin{array}{r} 200 \\ 200 \\ 90 \\ +\ 90 \\ \hline 580 \end{array}$$

Bert earns $24 632 a year, Ernie earns
$34 321 a year, and Oscar earns $22 971 a
year. How much do they earn altogether?

$81 924

$$\begin{array}{r} {\scriptstyle 1\ 1\ 1} \\ 24\ 632 \\ 34\ 321 \\ +\ 22\ 971 \\ \hline 81\ 924 \end{array}$$

How much more than Bert does
Ernie earn?

$9689

$$\begin{array}{r} {\scriptstyle 2\ 13\ 12\,11\,11} \\ \not{3}\not{4}\ \not{3}\not{2}\not{1} \\ -\ 24\ 632 \\ \hline 9\ 689 \end{array}$$

How much more than Oscar does
Bert earn?

$1661

$$\begin{array}{r} {\scriptstyle 3\ 15\,13} \\ 24\ \not{6}\not{3}\not{2} \\ -\ 22\ 971 \\ \hline 1\ 661 \end{array}$$

How much more than Oscar does
Ernie earn?

$11 350

$$\begin{array}{r} {\scriptstyle 3\ 12\,12} \\ \not{3}\not{4}\ \not{3}21 \\ -\ 22\ 971 \\ \hline 11\ 350 \end{array}$$

An elevator says, "Maximum weight 636 kg."
If four people get in, weighing 90 kg, 60 kg, 115 kg, and
78 kg, how much more mass will the elevator hold?

293 kg

$$\begin{array}{r} {\scriptstyle 2\,1} \\ 90 \\ 60 \\ 115 \\ +\ 78 \\ \hline 343 \end{array} \qquad \begin{array}{r} {\scriptstyle 5\ 13} \\ \not{6}\not{3}6 \\ -\ 343 \\ \hline 293 \end{array}$$

See the notes for page 104.

106 — ⭐ Multiplication by 2-digit numbers

Work out the answer to each problem.

$$\begin{array}{r} 27 \\ \times\ 76 \\ \hline 162 \\ 1890 \\ \hline 2052 \end{array} \qquad \begin{array}{r} 34 \\ \times\ 58 \\ \hline 272 \\ 1700 \\ \hline 1972 \end{array}$$

Work out the answer to each problem.

$$\begin{array}{r} 26 \\ \times\ 84 \\ \hline 104 \\ 2080 \\ \hline 2184 \end{array} \quad \begin{array}{r} 95 \\ \times\ 65 \\ \hline 475 \\ 5700 \\ \hline 6175 \end{array} \quad \begin{array}{r} 32 \\ \times\ 39 \\ \hline 288 \\ 960 \\ \hline 1248 \end{array} \quad \begin{array}{r} 78 \\ \times\ 49 \\ \hline 702 \\ 3120 \\ \hline 3822 \end{array}$$

$$\begin{array}{r} 97 \\ \times\ 46 \\ \hline 582 \\ 3880 \\ \hline 4462 \end{array} \quad \begin{array}{r} 94 \\ \times\ 37 \\ \hline 658 \\ 2820 \\ \hline 3478 \end{array} \quad \begin{array}{r} 32 \\ \times\ 64 \\ \hline 128 \\ 1920 \\ \hline 2048 \end{array} \quad \begin{array}{r} 47 \\ \times\ 75 \\ \hline 235 \\ 3290 \\ \hline 3525 \end{array}$$

$$\begin{array}{r} 28 \\ \times\ 95 \\ \hline 140 \\ 2520 \\ \hline 2660 \end{array} \quad \begin{array}{r} 47 \\ \times\ 62 \\ \hline 94 \\ 2820 \\ \hline 2914 \end{array} \quad \begin{array}{r} 36 \\ \times\ 87 \\ \hline 252 \\ 2880 \\ \hline 3132 \end{array} \quad \begin{array}{r} 45 \\ \times\ 33 \\ \hline 135 \\ 1350 \\ \hline 1485 \end{array}$$

$$\begin{array}{r} 46 \\ \times\ 85 \\ \hline 230 \\ 3680 \\ \hline 3910 \end{array} \quad \begin{array}{r} 29 \\ \times\ 72 \\ \hline 58 \\ 2030 \\ \hline 2088 \end{array} \quad \begin{array}{r} 85 \\ \times\ 29 \\ \hline 765 \\ 1700 \\ \hline 2465 \end{array} \quad \begin{array}{r} 63 \\ \times\ 84 \\ \hline 252 \\ 5040 \\ \hline 5292 \end{array}$$

Explain that multiplying by 84 means multiplying by
80, then by 4, and then adding the answers together.
Multiplying by 10 (or 80) means adding a zero and
multiplying by 1 (or 8). Multiplying by the tens digit
first, saves having to remember to put the zero later.

107 — Division by ones ⭐

$47 \div 2$ can be written in two ways:

$$\begin{array}{r} 23 \\ 2\overline{)47} \\ 4 \\ \hline 7 \\ 6 \\ \hline 1 \end{array} \quad 23\frac{1}{2} \qquad \text{or} \qquad \begin{array}{r} 23 \\ 2\overline{)47} \\ 4 \\ \hline 7 \\ 6 \\ \hline 1 \end{array} \quad 23\ r\ 1$$

Write the quotients for these problems with fraction remainders.

$8\frac{1}{2}$
$$\begin{array}{r} 8 \\ 2\overline{)17} \\ 16 \\ \hline 1 \end{array}$$

$4\frac{3}{4}$
$$\begin{array}{r} 4 \\ 4\overline{)19} \\ 16 \\ \hline 3 \end{array}$$

$5\frac{1}{3}$
$$\begin{array}{r} 5 \\ 3\overline{)16} \\ 15 \\ \hline 1 \end{array}$$

$9\frac{1}{4}$
$$\begin{array}{r} 9 \\ 4\overline{)37} \\ 36 \\ \hline 1 \end{array}$$

$9\frac{2}{3}$
$$\begin{array}{r} 9 \\ 3\overline{)29} \\ 27 \\ \hline 2 \end{array}$$

$22\frac{1}{2}$
$$\begin{array}{r} 22 \\ 2\overline{)45} \\ 4 \\ \hline 5 \\ 4 \\ \hline 1 \end{array}$$

$17\frac{2}{5}$
$$\begin{array}{r} 17 \\ 5\overline{)87} \\ 5 \\ \hline 37 \\ 35 \\ \hline 2 \end{array}$$

$9\frac{4}{5}$
$$\begin{array}{r} 9 \\ 5\overline{)49} \\ 45 \\ \hline 4 \end{array}$$

Write the quotients for these problems with unit remainders.

36 r 1
$$\begin{array}{r} 36 \\ 2\overline{)73} \\ 6 \\ \hline 13 \\ 12 \\ \hline 1 \end{array}$$

42 r 1
$$\begin{array}{r} 42 \\ 2\overline{)85} \\ 4 \\ \hline 5 \\ 4 \\ \hline 1 \end{array}$$

19 r 1
$$\begin{array}{r} 19 \\ 2\overline{)39} \\ 2 \\ \hline 19 \\ 18 \\ \hline 1 \end{array}$$

14 r 3
$$\begin{array}{r} 14 \\ 4\overline{)59} \\ 4 \\ \hline 19 \\ 16 \\ \hline 3 \end{array}$$

17 r 3
$$\begin{array}{r} 17 \\ 4\overline{)71} \\ 4 \\ \hline 31 \\ 28 \\ \hline 3 \end{array}$$

20 r 3
$$\begin{array}{r} 20 \\ 4\overline{)83} \\ 8 \\ \hline 3 \\ 0 \\ \hline 3 \end{array}$$

5 r 4
$$\begin{array}{r} 5 \\ 5\overline{)29} \\ 25 \\ \hline 4 \end{array}$$

9 r 2
$$\begin{array}{r} 9 \\ 5\overline{)47} \\ 45 \\ \hline 2 \end{array}$$

By now children will be comfortable with remainders.
In the second section, they have to place a decimal
point after the number being divided and add one or
two zeros. Encourage them to use the last section as
practice for the operation they found most difficult.

108 — ⭐ Dividing

$646 \div 3$ can be written in two ways:

$$215\frac{1}{3} \qquad \text{or} \qquad 215\ r\ 1$$
$$3\overline{)646}$$

Work out the answer to each problem. Use fraction remainders.

$94\frac{1}{4}$
$$\begin{array}{r} 94 \\ 4\overline{)377} \\ 36 \\ \hline 17 \\ 16 \\ \hline 1 \end{array}$$

$84\frac{1}{2}$
$$\begin{array}{r} 84 \\ 2\overline{)169} \\ 16 \\ \hline 09 \\ 8 \\ \hline 1 \end{array}$$

$22\frac{4}{7}$
$$\begin{array}{r} 22 \\ 7\overline{)158} \\ 14 \\ \hline 18 \\ 14 \\ \hline 4 \end{array}$$

92
$$\begin{array}{r} 92 \\ 4\overline{)368} \\ 36 \\ \hline 08 \\ 8 \\ \hline 0 \end{array}$$

$39\frac{2}{5}$
$$\begin{array}{r} 39 \\ 5\overline{)197} \\ 15 \\ \hline 47 \\ 45 \\ \hline 2 \end{array}$$

$70\frac{6}{9}$
$$\begin{array}{r} 70 \\ 9\overline{)636} \\ 63 \\ \hline 06 \\ 0 \\ \hline 6 \end{array}$$

$162\frac{1}{2}$
$$\begin{array}{r} 162 \\ 2\overline{)325} \\ 2 \\ \hline 12 \\ 12 \\ \hline 05 \\ 4 \\ \hline 1 \end{array}$$

$196\frac{3}{14}$
$$\begin{array}{r} 196 \\ 4\overline{)787} \\ 4 \\ \hline 38 \\ 36 \\ \hline 27 \\ 24 \\ \hline 3 \end{array}$$

Work out the answer to each problem. Use unit remainders.

189 r 2
$$\begin{array}{r} 189 \\ 5\overline{)947} \\ 5 \\ \hline 44 \\ 40 \\ \hline 47 \\ 45 \\ \hline 2 \end{array}$$

243 r 2
$$\begin{array}{r} 243 \\ 3\overline{)731} \\ 6 \\ \hline 13 \\ 12 \\ \hline 11 \\ 9 \\ \hline 2 \end{array}$$

125 r 3
$$\begin{array}{r} 125 \\ 7\overline{)878} \\ 7 \\ \hline 17 \\ 14 \\ \hline 38 \\ 35 \\ \hline 3 \end{array}$$

97 r 2
$$\begin{array}{r} 97 \\ 9\overline{)875} \\ 81 \\ \hline 65 \\ 63 \\ \hline 2 \end{array}$$

See the notes on page 101.

Division of 3-digit decimal numbers ☆

Work out these division sums.

```
   0.89              0.74
3)2.67            4)2.96
  24                28
  27                16
  27                16
   0                 0
```
0.89   0.74

Work out these division problems

```
   1.47        1.83        1.53        1.62
2)2.94      4)7.32      4)6.12      2)3.24
  2           4           4           2
  9          33          21          12
  8          32          20          12
 14          12          12          04
 14          12          12           4
  0           0           0           0
```
1.47   1.83   1.53   1.62

```
   4.99        3.24        1.56        1.87
2)9.98      3)9.72      4)6.24      4)7.48
  8           9           4           4
 19          07          22          34
 18           6          20          32
 18          12          24          28
 18          12          24          28
  0           0           0           0
```
4.99   3.24   1.56   1.87

```
   0.56        0.74        0.75        0.87
4)2.24      3)2.22      3)2.25      3)2.61
 20          21          21          24
 24          12          15          21
 24          12          15          21
  0           0           0           0
```
0.56   0.74   0.75   0.87

On this page, the decimal point has been incorporated into the middle of the number being divided. After the previous two pages, carrying across the decimal point should be familiar to children. No additional zeros need to be added on in this section.

☆ Division of 3-digit decimal numbers

Work out these division problems.

```
   1.99              1.61
5)9.95            6)9.66
  5                 6
  49                36
  45                36
  45                 6
  45                 6
   0                 0
```
1.99   1.61

Work out these division problems.

```
   1.63        1.85        1.27        1.52
5)8.15      5)9.25      5)6.35      6)9.12
  5           5           5           6
 31          42          13          31
 30          40          10          30
 15          25          35          12
 15          25          35          12
  0           0           0           0
```
1.63   1.85   1.27   1.52

```
   0.36        1.26        0.69        0.74
6)2.16      7)8.82      7)4.83      8)5.92
 18           7          42          56
 36          18          63          32
 36          14          63          32
  0          42           0           0
             42
              0
```
0.36   1.26   0.69   0.74

```
   1.09        0.91        0.63        1.06
8)8.72      9)8.19      9)5.67      6)6.36
 8           81          54           6
 72           9          27          36
 72           9          27          36
  0           0           0           0
```
1.09   0.91   0.63   1.06

The comments on the previous page also apply to this one, but as the dividing numbers are larger any weakness in multiplication facts for 6, 7, 8, and 9 times tables will show up.

Real-life problems ☆

A builder uses 1600 kg of sand a day. How much will he use in 5 days?
```
  3
  1600
x    5
  8000
```
8000 kg

If he uses 9500 kg the next week, how much more has he used than the week before?
```
  9500
- 8000
  1500
```
1500 kg

An electrician uses 184 m of cable while working on four houses. If he uses the same amount on each house, how much does he use on one house?
```
  46
4)184
  16
  24
  24
   0
```
46 m

A family looks at vacations in two different resorts. The first one costs $846.95. The second costs $932. How much will the family save if they choose the cheaper resort?
```
  932.00
- 846.95
   85.05
```
$85.05

Doris has 5 sections of fence, each 96 cm wide. If she puts them together, how much of her yard can she fence off?
```
   3
   96
x   5
  480
```
480 cm

Shula goes on a sponsored walk and collects $15.95 from her mother, $8.36 from her uncle, $4.65 from her brother, and $2.75 from her aunt. How much does she collect altogether?
```
  15.95
   8.36
   4.65
+  2.75
  31.71
```
$31.71

A taxi company has 9 cars. If each car holds 40.4 litres of gasoline, how many litres will it take to fill all of the cars?
```
    3
   40.4
x     9
  363.6
```
363.6 litres

This page provides an opportunity to apply the skills practiced. Children will need to select the operation necessary. If they are unsure about which operation to use, discuss whether the answer will be larger or smaller, which narrows down the options.

☆ Rounding money

Round to the nearest dollar.
$3.95 rounds to $4
$2.25 rounds to $2

Round to the nearest ten dollars.
$15.50 rounds to $20
$14.40 rounds to $10

Round to the nearest dollar.
$2.60 rounds to $3 $8.49 rounds to $8 $3.39 rounds to $3
$9.55 rounds to $10 $1.75 rounds to $2 $4.30 rounds to $4
$7.15 rounds to $7 $6.95 rounds to $7 $2.53 rounds to $3

Round to the nearest ten dollars.
$37.34 rounds to $40 $21.75 rounds to $20 $85.03 rounds to $90
$71.99 rounds to $70 $66.89 rounds to $70 $52.99 rounds to $50
$55.31 rounds to $60 $12.79 rounds to $10 $15.00 rounds to $20

Round to the nearest hundred dollars.
$307.12 rounds to $300 $175.50 rounds to $200 $115.99 rounds to $100
$860.55 rounds to $900 $417.13 rounds to $400 $650.15 rounds to $700
$739.10 rounds to $700 $249.66 rounds to $200 $367.50 rounds to $400

If children have difficulty, have them decide which are the two nearest hundred dollars, and which is closest to the number.

Estimating sums of money

Round to the leading digit. Estimate the sum.

$3.26 → $3
+ $4.82 → + $5
is about $8

$68.53 → $70
+ $34.60 → + $30
is about $100

Round to the leading digit. Estimate the sum.

$52.61 → $50
+ $27.95 → + $30
is about $80

$19.20 → $20
+ $22.13 → + $20
is about $40

$70.75 → $70
+ $12.49 → + $10
is about $80

$701.34 → $700
+ $100.80 → + $100
is about $800

$339.50 → $300
+ $422.13 → + $400
is about $700

$160.07 → $200
+ $230.89 → + $200
is about $400

$25.61 → $30
+ $72.51 → + $70
is about $100

$61.39 → $60
+ $19.50 → + $20
is about $80

$18.32 → $20
+ $13.90 → + $10
is about $30

$587.35 → $600
+ $251.89 → + $300
is about $900

$109.98 → $100
+ $210.09 → + $200
is about $300

$470.02 → $500
+ $203.17 → + $200
is about $700

Round to the leading digit. Estimate the sum.

$75.95 + $17.95 → $100

$41.67 + $20.35 → $60

$49.19 + $38.70 → $90

$784.65 + $101.05 → $900

$516.50 + $290.69 → $800

$58.78 + $33.25 → $90

$82.90 + $11.79 → $90

$90.09 + $14.50 → $100

In section 2, children need to estimate by rounding mentally. If they have trouble, have them write the rounded numbers above the originals first, and then add them.

Estimating differences of money

Round the numbers to the leading digit. Estimate the differences.

$8.75 → $9
− $5.10 → − $5
is about $4

$61.47 → $60
− $35.64 → − $40
is about $20

Round the numbers to the leading digit. Estimate the differences.

$17.90 → $20
− $12.30 → − $10
is about $10

$6.40 → $6
− $3.75 → − $4
is about $2

$87.45 → $90
− $54.99 → − $50
is about $40

$34.90 → $30
− $12.60 → − $10
is about $20

$8.68 → $9
− $4.39 → − $4
is about $5

$363.24 → $400
− $127.66 → − $100
is about $300

$78.75 → $80
− $24.99 → − $20
is about $60

$64.21 → $60
− $28.56 → − $30
is about $30

$723.34 → $700
− $487.12 → − $500
is about $200

Round the numbers to the leading digit. Estimate the differences.

$8.12 − $1.35
→ $8 − $1 = $7

$49.63 − $27.85
→ $50 − $30 = $20

$7.50 − $3.15
→ $8 − $3 = $5

$85.15 − $42.99
→ $90 − $40 = $50

$5.85 − $4.75
→ $6 − $5 = $1

$634.60 − $267.25
→ $600 − $300 = $300

$37.35 − $16.99
→ $40 − $20 = $20

$842.17 − $169.54
→ $800 − $200 = $600

$56.95 − $20.58
→ $60 − $20 = $40

$628.37 − $252.11
→ $600 − $300 = $300

See the comments on page 113.

Estimating sums and differences

Round the numbers to the leading digit. Estimate the sum or difference.

3576 → 4000
+ 1307 → + 1000
is about 5000

198 248 → 200 000
− 116 431 → − 100 000
is about 100 000

Round the numbers to the leading digit. Estimate the sum or difference.

685 → 700
+ 489 → + 500
is about 1200

21 481 → 20 000
− 12 500 → − 10 000
is about 10 000

7834 → 8 000
+ 3106 → + 3 000
is about 11 000

682 778 → 700 000
+ 130 001 → + 100 000
is about 800 000

58 499 → 60 000
− 22 135 → − 20 000
is about 40 000

902 276 → 900 000
− 615 999 → − 600 000
is about 300 000

46 801 → 50 000
+ 34 700 → + 30 000
is about 80 000

9734 → 10 000
− 8306 → − 8 000
is about 2 000

65 606 → 70 000
+ 85 943 → + 90 000
is about 160 000

5218 → 5000
− 3673 → − 4000
is about 1000

745 → 700
+ 451 → + 500
is about 1200

337 297 → 300 000
− 168 931 → − 200 000
is about 100 000

Write < or > for each problem.

329 + 495 > 800

11 569 − 6146 < 6000

563 − 317 < 300

8193 − 6668 > 1000

41 924 − 12 445 < 50 000

634 577 + 192 556 > 800 000

18 885 + 12 691 > 30 000

713 096 − 321 667 < 400 000

In section 2, children need to think about their estimates more carefully if the estimate is very close to the number on the right side of the equation. Have them look at the numbers in the next place to the right to adjust their estimates up or down.

Estimating products

Round to the leading digit. Estimate the product.

3456 x 6
3000 x 6 = 18 000

73 x 46
70 x 50 = 3500

Round to the leading digit. Estimate the sum.

1908 x 8
2000 x 8 = 16 000

5 x 6099
5 x 6000 = 30 000

7 x 1108
7 x 1000 = 7000

5239 x 9
5000 x 9 = 45 000

81 x 32
80 x 30 = 2400

19 x 62
20 x 60 = 1200

39 x 44
40 x 40 = 1600

94 x 12
90 x 10 = 900

Estimate the product.

6 x 7243	42 000	4785 x 4	20 000	3 x 8924	27 000
2785 x 5	15 000	6298 x 4	24 000	7 x 7105	49 000
8 x 2870	24 000	4176 x 7	28 000	5 x 4803	25 000
6777 x 9	63 000	6 x 8022	48 000	3785 x 4	16 000
42 x 51	2000	54 x 28	1500	23 x 75	1600
16 x 32	600	47 x 54	2500	59 x 52	3000
17 x 74	1400	33 x 22	600	81 x 18	1600
31 x 91	2700	38 x 87	3600	46 x 77	4000

Have children try to estimate the answer mentally. If they have trouble, have them write the rounded numbers first.

Estimating quotients

Round to compatible numbers. Estimate the quotient.

$3156 \div 6$
$3000 \div 6 =$ 500

$2159 \div 5$
$2500 \div 5 =$ 500

Round to compatible numbers. Estimate the quotient.

$1934 \div 8$
$1600 \div 8 = 200$

$4066 \div 5$
$4000 \div 5 = 800$

$1108 \div 4$
$1200 \div 4 = 300$

$5657 \div 9$
$5400 \div 9 = 600$

$3998 \div 6$
$4200 \div 6 = 700$

$5525 \div 7$
$5600 \div 7 = 800$

$1701 \div 3$
$1500 \div 3 = 500$

$1304 \div 2$
$1200 \div 2 = 600$

Estimate the quotient.

$4798 \div 7$ 700	$8205 \div 9$ 900	$5022 \div 5$ 1000
$3785 \div 4$ 900	$5528 \div 6$ 900	$2375 \div 8$ 300
$1632 \div 3$ 500	$4251 \div 4$ 1000	$4754 \div 9$ 500
$7352 \div 8$ 900	$1774 \div 2$ 900	$3322 \div 7$ 500
$3591 \div 6$ 600	$2887 \div 5$ 600	$5746 \div 2$ 3000
$3703 \div 3$ 1200	$2392 \div 6$ 400	$6621 \div 8$ 800

Children should round the dividend to a nearby number that can easily be divided by the divisor. Compatible numbers are ones that are just multiples of the divisor. Knowledge of basic division facts should allow these estimations to be done mentally.

Rounding mixed numbers

Round to the closest whole number.

$2\frac{5}{6}$

$\frac{5}{6}$ is more than $\frac{1}{2}$,
so, $2\frac{5}{6}$ rounds up to 3.

$3\frac{2}{5}$

$\frac{2}{5}$ is less than $\frac{1}{2}$,
so, $3\frac{2}{5}$ rounds down to 3.

Circle the fractions that are more than $\frac{1}{2}$.

$\frac{3}{7}$ $\frac{2}{9}$ ⓺$\frac{6}{7}$ ⓥ$\frac{5}{9}$ $\frac{3}{8}$ $\frac{1}{7}$ ⓥ$\frac{2}{3}$ ⓥ$\frac{4}{7}$

⓿$\frac{7}{10}$ $\frac{2}{5}$ $\frac{1}{3}$ ⓥ$\frac{5}{6}$ ⓥ$\frac{3}{4}$ $\frac{2}{9}$ ⓥ$\frac{5}{8}$ ⓥ$\frac{3}{5}$

Circle the fractions that are less than $\frac{1}{2}$.

⓵$\frac{1}{8}$ ⓥ$\frac{3}{9}$ $\frac{4}{5}$ ⓥ$\frac{2}{7}$ $\frac{3}{5}$ ⓥ$\frac{2}{5}$ ⓥ$\frac{7}{10}$ ⓥ$\frac{2}{9}$

$\frac{3}{4}$ ⓥ$\frac{1}{3}$ ⓥ$\frac{4}{9}$ ⓥ$\frac{3}{10}$ $\frac{5}{6}$ ⓥ$\frac{1}{4}$ ⓥ$\frac{3}{7}$ $\frac{5}{9}$

Round to the closest whole number.

$4\frac{3}{8}$ 4	$2\frac{6}{7}$ 3	$5\frac{3}{4}$ 6	$3\frac{2}{9}$ 3
$2\frac{5}{6}$ 3	$1\frac{7}{8}$ 2	$2\frac{2}{5}$ 2	$5\frac{1}{7}$ 5
$3\frac{1}{6}$ 3	$5\frac{3}{8}$ 5	$3\frac{3}{5}$ 4	$7\frac{8}{13}$ 8
$6\frac{3}{5}$ 7	$1\frac{1}{4}$ 1	$4\frac{5}{6}$ 5	$9\frac{3}{4}$ 10
$5\frac{2}{3}$ 6	$3\frac{3}{7}$ 3	$1\frac{6}{7}$ 2	$6\frac{3}{4}$ 7

If children have trouble rounding, explain that if the numerator is less than half as big as the denominator, the fraction is less than one-half.

Calculate the mean

What is the mean of 6 and 10? $(6+10) \div 2 = 8$

David is 9, Asha is 10, and Daniel is 5. What is their mean age? $(9 + 10 + 5) \div 3 = 8$ years

Calculate the mean of these amounts.

9 and 5	7	6 and 8	7
5 and 7	6	11 and 7	9
8 and 12	10	13 and 15	14
19 and 21	20	40 and 60	50

Calculate the mean of these amounts.

5, 7, and 3	5	11, 9, and 7	9
14, 10, and 6	10	12, 8, and 4	8
7, 3, 5, and 9	6	$1, $1.50, $2.50, and $3	$2
16¢, 9¢, 12¢, and 3¢	10¢	5 g, 7 g, 8 g, and 8 g	7 g

Calculate these answers.

The mean of two numbers is 7. If one of the numbers is 6, what is the other number?   8

The mean of three numbers is 4. If two of the numbers are 4 and 5, what is the third number?   3

The mean of four numbers is 12. If three of the numbers are 9, 15, and 8, what is the fourth number?   16

Two children record their last five spelling-test scores.

Gayle	17	18	16	14	15
Sally	19	20	12	13	11

Which child has the best mean score?   Gayle

The average of a number list is known as the 'mean'. Children should add the list and divide by the amount of numbers. In part 3, explain that if the mean is 7, the total must have been 14, so if they take away the number given they will find the number required.

Mean, median, and mode

Sian throws a dice 7 times. Here are her results:
4, 2, 1, 2, 4, 2, 6
What is the mean? $(4 + 2 + 1 + 2 + 4 + 2 + 6) \div 7 = 3$

What is the median? Put the numbers in order of size and find the middle number, example, 1, 2, 2, 2, 4, 4, 6.

The median is 2.

What is the mode?   The most common result, which is 2.

A school soccer team scores the following number of goals in their first 9 matches:
2, 2, 1, 3, 2, 1, 2, 4, 1

What is the mean score?   2

What is the median score?   2

Write down the mode for their results.   2

The ages of the local hockey players are:
17, 15, 16, 19, 17, 19, 22, 17, 18, 21, 17

What is the mean of their ages?   18

What is their median age?   17

Write down the mode for their ages.   17

The results of Susan's last 11 spelling tests were:
15, 12, 15, 17, 11, 16, 19, 11, 3, 11, 13

What is the mean of her scores?   13

What is her median score?   13

Write down the mode for her scores.   11

The work on this page leads on from previous work on the mean, but also expands it to the median and the mode. The biggest problem children may have is remembering which is which. Encourage them to develop a system that works for them.

Line graphs

Look at this graph.

Luis's Bike Trip

How many kilometres did Luis ride during the first hour of his trip?
6 kilometres

How many hours did Luis's trip take?
6 hours

How far did he travel in all?
20 kilometres

Luis stopped for lunch for one hour. What time did he stop?
11 A.M.

Did Luis cover more distance between 12 and 1 or between 1 and 2?
between 12 and 1

Between which two hours did Luis travel 4 kilometres?
between 10 and 11

During which hours did Luis ride the fastest?
between 9 and 10 and between 12 and 1

Did Luis travel farther before or after his lunch break?
he travelled the same distance: 10 kilometres

How much longer did it take Luis to ride 10 kilometres after lunch?
1 hour longer

Children may have trouble deciding how far Luis travelled between two times. Have them find the distance at the starting and ending times, and then subtract to get the answer.

Coordinates

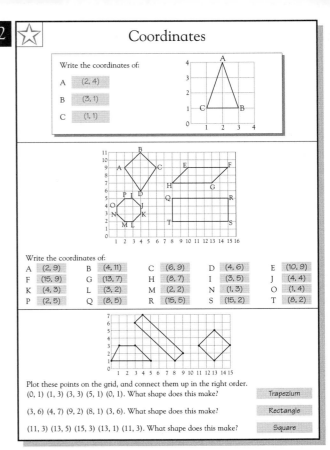

Write the coordinates of:

A (2, 4)
B (3, 1)
C (1, 1)

Write the coordinates of:

A (2, 9)	B (4, 11)	C (6, 9)	D (4, 6)	E (10, 9)
F (15, 9)	G (13, 7)	H (8, 7)	I (3, 5)	J (4, 4)
K (4, 3)	L (3, 2)	M (2, 2)	N (1, 3)	O (1, 4)
P (2, 5)	Q (8, 5)	R (15, 5)	S (15, 2)	T (8, 2)

Plot these points on the grid, and connect them up in the right order.
(0, 1) (1, 3) (3, 3) (5, 1) (0, 1). What shape does this make?
Trapezium

(3, 6) (4, 7) (9, 2) (8, 1) (3, 6). What shape does this make?
Rectangle

(11, 3) (13, 5) (15, 3) (13, 1) (11, 3). What shape does this make?
Square

Children should remember to read off the horizontal coordinate first. In the second section, it is important that they join the coordinates in the order in which they are written, to produce the shape intended.

Drawing angles

Acute angles are between 0° and 90°.   Obtuse angles are between 90° and 180°.

When you get to 180° you have a straight line.

Use a protractor to draw these angles. Remember to mark the angle you have drawn.

150°

135°

45°

110°

10°

20°

To do the work on this page and the next, children require a 360° protractor. Check that they read the protractor from the right direction. Remind children to mark the angles. This is important to avoid confusion when drawing reflex angles.

Reading and writing numbers

264 346 in words is Two hundred sixty-four thousand three hundred forty-six

One million three hundred twelve thousand five hundred two is 1 312 502

Write each of these numbers in words.

326 208 — Three hundred twenty-six thousand two hundred eight

704 543 — Seven hundred four thousand five hundred forty-three

240 701 — Two hundred forty thousand seven hundred one

278 520 — Two hundred seventy-eight thousand five hundred twenty

Write each of these in numbers.

Five hundred seventeen thousand forty-two — 517 042

Six hundred ninety-four thousand seven hundred eleven — 694 711

Eight hundred nine thousand two hundred three — 809 203

Nine hundred thousand four hundred four — 900 404

Write each of these numbers in words.

9 307 012 — Nine million three hundred seven thousand twelve

5 042 390 — Five million forty-two thousand three hundred ninety

9 908 434 — Nine million nine hundred eight thousand four hundred thirty-four

8 400 642 — Eight million four hundred thousand six hundred forty-two

Write each of these in numbers.

Eight million two hundred fifty-one — 8 000 251

Two million forty thousand four hundred four — 2 040 404

Seven million three hundred two thousand one hundred one — 7 302 101

Two million five hundred forty-one thousand five — 2 541 005

Children may use zeros incorrectly in numbers. In word form, zeros are omitted, but children should take care to include them when writing numbers in standard form.

Multiplying and dividing by 10

Write the answer in the box.
26 x 10 = 260
40 ÷ 10 = 4

Write the answer in the box.
76 x 10 = 760   43 x 10 = 430   93 x 10 = 930
66 x 10 = 660   13 x 10 = 130   47 x 10 = 470
147 x 10 = 1470   936 x 10 = 9360   284 x 10 = 2840
364 x 10 = 3640   821 x 10 = 8210   473 x 10 = 4730

Write the answer in the box.
30 ÷ 10 = 3   20 ÷ 10 = 2   70 ÷ 10 = 7
60 ÷ 10 = 6   50 ÷ 10 = 5   580 ÷ 10 = 58
310 ÷ 10 = 31   270 ÷ 10 = 27   100 ÷ 10 = 10
540 ÷ 10 = 54   890 ÷ 10 = 89   710 ÷ 10 = 71

Write the number that has been multiplied by 10.
37 x 10 = 370   64 x 10 = 640   74 x 10 = 740
81 x 10 = 810   10 x 10 = 100   83 x 10 = 830
714 x 10 = 7140   307 x 10 = 3070   529 x 10 = 5290
264 x 10 = 2640   829 x 10 = 8290   648 x 10 = 6480

Write the number that has been divided by 10.
30 ÷ 10 = 3   20 ÷ 10 = 2   90 ÷ 10 = 9
420 ÷ 10 = 42   930 ÷ 10 = 93   740 ÷ 10 = 74
570 ÷ 10 = 57   380 ÷ 10 = 38   860 ÷ 10 = 86

Children should realize that multiplying a whole number by 10 means writing a zero at the end. To divide a multiple of ten by 10, simply take the final zero off the number. In the two final sections, the inverse operation is used for solving the problems.

Identifying patterns

Continue each pattern.
Steps of 9:   5 14 23 32 41 50
Steps of 14: 20 34 48 62 76 90

Continue each pattern.

21	38	55	72	89	106	123	140
13	37	61	85	109	133	157	181
7	25	43	61	79	97	115	133
32	48	64	80	96	112	128	144
12	31	50	69	88	107	126	145
32	54	76	98	120	142	164	186
24	64	104	144	184	224	264	304
4	34	64	94	124	154	184	214
36	126	216	306	396	486	576	666
12	72	132	192	252	312	372	432
25	45	65	85	105	125	145	165
22	72	122	172	222	272	322	372
25	100	175	250	325	400	475	550
60	165	270	375	480	585	690	795
8	107	206	305	404	503	602	701
10	61	112	163	214	265	316	367
26	127	228	329	430	531	632	733
48	100	152	204	256	308	360	412

Children should determine what number to add to the first number to make the second number, and check to make sure that adding the same number turns the second number into the third. They can then continue the pattern.

Recognizing multiples of 6, 7, and 8

Circle the multiples of 6.
8 (12) 15 (18) 20 (24)

Circle the multiples of 6.
8   22   14   (18)   (36)   40
16   38   44   25   (30)   (60)
(6)   21   19   (54)   56   (24)
(12)   (48)   10   20   35   26
(42)   39   23   28   (36)   32

Circle the multiples of 7.
(7)   17   24   59   (42)   55
15   20   (21)   46   12   (70)
(14)   27   69   36   47   (49)
65   19   57   (28)   38   (63)
33   34   (35)   37   60   (56)

Circle the multiples of 8.
(40)   26   15   25   38   (56)
26   (8)   73   41   (64)   12
75   58   62   (24)   31   (72)
12   (80)   (32)   46   38   78
(16)   42   66   28   (48)   68

Circle the number that is a multiple of 6 and 7.
18   54   (42)   21   28   63

Circle the numbers that are multiples of 6 and 8.
16   (24)   36   (48)   54   42

Circle the number that is a multiple of 7 and 8.
24   32   40   28   42   (56)

Success on this page will basically depend on a knowledge of multiplication tables. Where children experience difficulties, multiplication table practice should be encouraged.

Factors of numbers from 1 to 30

The factors of 10 are   1   2   5   10
Circle the factors of 4.   (1) (2)   3   (4)

Write all the factors of each number.
The factors of 26 are   1, 2, 13, 26
The factors of 30 are   1, 2, 3, 5, 6, 10, 15, 30
The factors of 9 are   1, 3, 9
The factors of 12 are   1, 2, 3, 4, 6, 12
The factors of 15 are   1, 3, 5, 15
The factors of 22 are   1, 2, 11, 22
The factors of 20 are   1, 2, 4, 5, 10, 20
The factors of 21 are   1, 3, 7, 21
The factors of 24 are   1, 2, 3, 4, 6, 8, 12, 24

Circle all the factors of each number.
Which numbers are factors of 14?   (1)(2) 3 5 (7) 9 12 (14)
Which numbers are factors of 13?   (1) 2 3 4 5 6 7 8 9 10 11 (13)
Which numbers are factors of 7?   (1) 2 3 4 5 6 (7)
Which numbers are factors of 11?   (1) 2 3 4 5 6 7 8 9 10 (11)
Which numbers are factors of 6?   (1)(2)(3) 4 5 (6)
Which numbers are factors of 8?   (1)(2) 3 (4) 5 6 7 (8)
Which numbers are factors of 17?   (1) 2 5 7 12 14 16 (17)
Which numbers are factors of 18?   (1)(2)(3) 4 5 (6) 8 (9) 10 12 (18)

Some numbers only have factors of 1 and themselves. They are called prime numbers. Write down all the prime numbers that are less than 30 in the box.

2, 3, 5, 7, 11, 13, 17, 19, 23, 29

Encourage a systematic approach such as starting at 1 and working forward to the number that is half of the number in question. Children often forget that 1 and the number itself are factors of a given number. You may need to point out that 1 is not a prime number.

Recognizing equivalent fractions ⭐

Make each pair of fractions equal by writing a number in the box.

$$\frac{1}{2} = \frac{2}{4} \qquad \frac{1}{3} = \frac{2}{6}$$

Make each pair of fractions equal by writing a number in the box.

$$\frac{1}{2} = \frac{5}{10} \qquad \frac{3}{4} = \frac{6}{8} \qquad \frac{1}{3} = \frac{3}{9}$$

$$\frac{2}{3} = \frac{8}{12} \qquad \frac{6}{12} = \frac{3}{6} \qquad \frac{4}{8} = \frac{1}{2}$$

$$\frac{1}{5} = \frac{2}{10} \qquad \frac{4}{12} = \frac{2}{6} \qquad \frac{3}{5} = \frac{6}{10}$$

$$\frac{1}{4} = \frac{2}{8} \qquad \frac{6}{18} = \frac{1}{3} \qquad \frac{3}{12} = \frac{1}{4}$$

$$\frac{3}{9} = \frac{1}{3} \qquad \frac{4}{10} = \frac{2}{5} \qquad \frac{3}{4} = \frac{9}{12}$$

$$\frac{4}{16} = \frac{1}{4} \qquad \frac{15}{20} = \frac{3}{4} \qquad \frac{6}{12} = \frac{1}{2}$$

$$\frac{3}{5} = \frac{6}{10} \qquad \frac{3}{6} = \frac{1}{2} \qquad \frac{9}{12} = \frac{3}{4}$$

Make each row of fractions equal by writing a number in each box.

$$\frac{1}{2} = \frac{2}{4} = \frac{3}{6} = \frac{4}{8} = \frac{5}{10} = \frac{6}{12}$$

$$\frac{1}{4} = \frac{2}{8} = \frac{3}{12} = \frac{4}{16} = \frac{5}{20} = \frac{6}{24}$$

$$\frac{3}{4} = \frac{6}{8} = \frac{9}{12} = \frac{12}{16} = \frac{15}{20} = \frac{18}{24}$$

$$\frac{1}{3} = \frac{2}{6} = \frac{3}{9} = \frac{4}{12} = \frac{5}{15} = \frac{12}{36}$$

$$\frac{1}{5} = \frac{2}{10} = \frac{3}{15} = \frac{4}{20} = \frac{5}{25} = \frac{6}{30}$$

$$\frac{2}{3} = \frac{4}{6} = \frac{6}{9} = \frac{8}{12} = \frac{10}{15} = \frac{14}{21}$$

If children have problems with this page, point out that fractions remain the same as long as you multiply both the numerator and denominator by the same number, or divide the numerator and denominator by the same number.

⭐ Rounding decimals

Round each decimal to the nearest whole number.

3.4	3
5.7	6
4.5	5

If the whole number has 5 after it, round it to the whole number above.

Round each decimal to the nearest whole number.

6.2	6	2.5	3	1.5	2	3.8	4
5.5	6	2.8	3	3.2	3	8.5	9
5.4	5	7.9	8	3.7	4	2.3	2
1.1	1	8.6	9	8.3	8	9.2	9
4.7	5	6.3	6	7.3	7	8.7	9

Round each decimal to the nearest whole number.

14.4	14	42.3	42	74.1	74	59.7	60
29.9	30	32.6	33	63.5	64	96.4	96
18.2	18	37.5	38	39.6	40	76.3	76
40.1	40	28.7	29	26.9	27	12.5	13
29.5	30	38.5	39	87.2	87	41.6	42

Round each decimal to the nearest whole number.

137.6	138	423.5	424	426.2	426	111.8	112
641.6	642	333.5	334	805.2	805	246.8	247
119.5	120	799.6	800	562.3	562	410.2	410
682.4	682	759.6	760	531.5	532	829.9	830
743.4	743	831.1	831	276.7	277	649.3	649

If children experience difficulties, you might want to use a number line showing tenths. Errors often occur when a number with 9 in the ones column is rounded up. Children also often neglect to alter the tens digit in a number such as 19.7.

Real-life problems ⭐

Write the answer in the box.

Yasmin has $4.60 and she is given another $1.20. How much money does she have?

$5.80

$$\begin{array}{r} \$4.60 \\ + \$1.20 \\ \hline \$5.80 \end{array}$$

David has 120 marbles. He divides them equally among his 5 friends. How many marbles does each get?   24

$$\begin{array}{r} 24 \\ 5)\overline{120} \\ 10 \\ \hline 20 \\ 20 \\ \hline 0 \end{array}$$

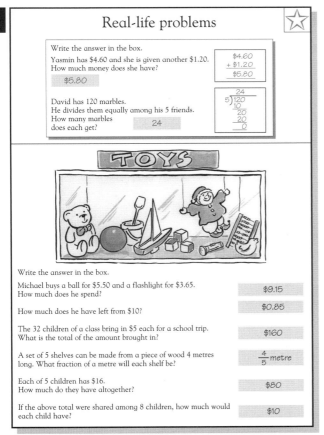

Write the answer in the box.

Michael buys a ball for $5.50 and a flashlight for $3.65. How much does he spend? $9.15

How much does he have left from $10? $0.85

The 32 children of a class bring in $5 each for a school trip. What is the total of the amount brought in? $160

A set of 5 shelves can be made from a piece of wood 4 metres long. What fraction of a metre will each shelf be? $\frac{4}{5}$ metre

Each of 5 children has $16. How much do they have altogether? $80

If the above total were shared among 8 children, how much would each child have? $10

This page tests children's ability to choose the operation required to solve real-life problems, mostly involving money. Discussing whether the answer will be larger or smaller than the question will help children decide on their choice of operation.

⭐ Real-life problems

Find the answer to each problem.

A box is 16 cm wide. How wide will 6 boxes side by side be?   96 cm

$$\begin{array}{r} 3 \\ 16 \text{ cm} \\ \times 6 \\ \hline 96 \text{ cm} \end{array}$$

Josh is 1.20 m tall. His sister is 1.55 m tall. How much taller than Josh is his sister?   0.35 m

$$\begin{array}{r} 1.55 \text{ m} \\ - 1.20 \text{ m} \\ \hline 0.35 \text{ m} \end{array}$$

Find the answer to each problem.

A can contains 56 g of lemonade mix. If 12 g are used, how much is left?   44 g

$$\begin{array}{r} 56 \text{ g} \\ - 12 \text{ g} \\ \hline 44 \text{ g} \end{array}$$

A large jar of coffee has a mass of 280 g. A smaller jar has a mass of 130 g. How much heavier is the larger jar than the smaller jar?   150 g

$$\begin{array}{r} 280 \text{ g} \\ - 130 \text{ g} \\ \hline 150 \text{ g} \end{array}$$

There are 7 shelves of books. 5 shelves are 1.2 m long. 2 shelves are 1.5 m long. What is the total length of the 7 shelves?   9 m

$$\begin{array}{r} 1.2 \\ \times 5 \\ \hline 6.0 \end{array} \qquad \begin{array}{r} 1.5 \\ \times 2 \\ \hline 3.0 \end{array}$$
$$6 + 3 = 9$$

A rock star can sign 36 photographs in a minute. How many can he sign in 30 seconds?   18 photographs

$$\begin{array}{r} 18 \\ 2)\overline{36} \\ 2 \\ \hline 16 \\ 16 \\ \hline 0 \end{array}$$

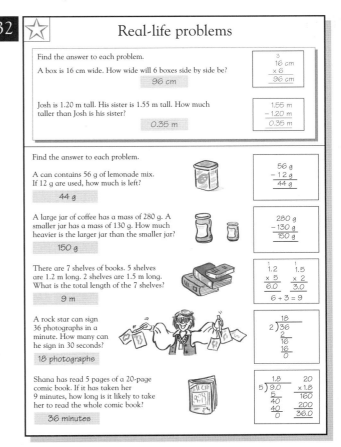

Shana has read 5 pages of a 20-page comic book. If it has taken her 9 minutes, how long is it likely to take her to read the whole comic book?   36 minutes

$$\begin{array}{r} 1.8 \\ 5)\overline{9.0} \\ 5 \\ \hline 40 \\ 40 \\ \hline 0 \end{array} \qquad \begin{array}{r} 20 \\ \times 1.8 \\ \hline 160 \\ 200 \\ \hline 36.0 \end{array}$$

This page continues with real-life problems but with units other than money. Note that children must perform three operations to solve the third problem.

Problems involving time ⭐

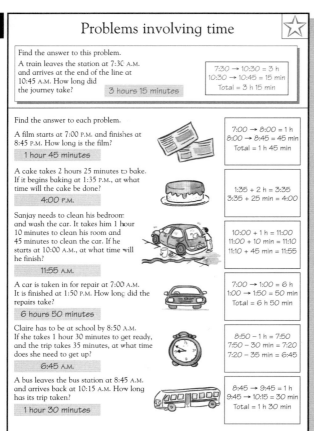

Find the answer to this problem.
A train leaves the station at 7:30 A.M. and arrives at the end of the line at 10:45 A.M. How long did the journey take?

7:30 → 10:30 = 3 h
10:30 → 10:45 = 15 min
Total = 3 h 15 min

3 hours 15 minutes

Find the answer to each problem.

A film starts at 7:00 P.M. and finishes at 8:45 P.M. How long is the film?
1 hour 45 minutes

7:00 → 8:00 = 1 h
8:00 → 8:45 = 45 min
Total = 1 h 45 min

A cake takes 2 hours 25 minutes to bake. If it begins baking at 1:35 P.M., at what time will the cake be done?
4:00 P.M.

1:35 + 2 h = 3:35
3:35 + 25 min = 4:00

Sanjay needs to clean his bedroom and wash the car. It takes him 1 hour 10 minutes to clean his room and 45 minutes to clean the car. If he starts at 10:00 A.M., at what time will he finish?
11:55 A.M.

10:00 + 1 h = 11:00
11:00 + 10 min = 11:10
11:10 + 45 min = 11:55

A car is taken in for repair at 7:00 A.M. It is finished at 1:50 P.M. How long did the repairs take?
6 hours 50 minutes

7:00 → 1:00 = 6 h
1:00 → 1:50 = 50 min
Total = 6 h 50 min

Claire has to be at school by 8:50 A.M. If she takes 1 hour 30 minutes to get ready, and the trip takes 35 minutes, at what time does she need to get up?
6:45 A.M.

8:50 − 1 h = 7:50
7:50 − 30 min = 7:20
7:20 − 35 min = 6:45

A bus leaves the bus station at 8:45 A.M. and arrives back at 10:15 A.M. How long has its trip taken?
1 hour 30 minutes

8:45 → 9:45 = 1 h
9:45 → 10:15 = 30 min
Total = 1 h 30 min

Children must remember that hours are based on units of 60 rather than of 10, so when they regroup, they will add 60 to the minutes instead of the 10 they would add when regrouping numbers.

⭐ Elapsed time

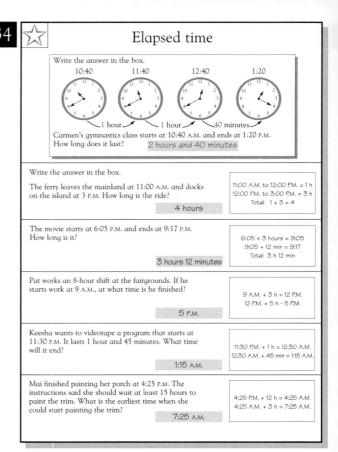

Write the answer in the box.

10:40   11:40   12:40   1:20

← 1 hour → ← 1 hour → ← 40 minutes →

Carmen's gymnastics class starts at 10:40 A.M. and ends at 1:20 P.M. How long does it last?
2 hours and 40 minutes

Write the answer in the box.

The ferry leaves the mainland at 11:00 A.M. and docks on the island at 3 P.M. How long is the ride?
4 hours

11:00 A.M. to 12:00 P.M. = 1 h
12:00 P.M. to 3:00 P.M. = 3 h
Total 1 + 3 = 4

The movie starts at 6:05 P.M. and ends at 9:17 P.M. How long is it?
3 hours 12 minutes

6:05 + 3 hours = 9:05
9:05 + 12 min = 9:17
Total 3 h 12 min

Pat works an 8-hour shift at the fairgrounds. If he starts work at 9 A.M., at what time is he finished?
5 P.M.

9 A.M. + 3 h = 12 P.M.
12 P.M. + 5 h = 5 P.M.

Keesha wants to videotape a program that starts at 11:30 P.M. It lasts 1 hour and 45 minutes. What time will it end?
1:15 A.M.

11:30 P.M. + 1 h = 12:30 A.M.
12:30 A.M. + 45 min = 1:15 A.M.

Mai finished painting her porch at 4:25 P.M. The instructions said she should wait at least 15 hours to paint the trim. What is the earliest time when she could start painting the trim?
7:25 A.M.

4:25 P.M. + 12 h = 4:25 A.M.
4:25 A.M. + 3 h = 7:25 A.M.

If children have trouble keeping track of the changes in hours or minutes, have them write down each step as in the diagram.

Recognizing multiples ⭐

Circle the multiples of 10.
14   (20)   25   (30)   47   (60)

Circle the multiples of 6.
20   (48)   56   (72)   25   35
1   3   (6)   16   26   (36)

Circle the multiples of 7.
(14)   24   (35)   27   47   (49)
(63)   (42)   52   37   64   71

Circle the multiples of 8.
25   31   (48)   84   (32)   (8)
18   54   (64)   35   (72)   28

Circle the multiples of 9.
17   (81)   (27)   35   92   106
(45)   53   (108)   (90)   33   95
64   (9)   28   (18)   (36)   98

Circle the multiples of 10.
15   35   (20)   46   (90)   (100)
44   37   (30)   29   (50)   45

Circle the multiples of 11.
24   (110)   123   54   (66)   90
45   (33)   87   98   (99)   (121)
43   (44)   65   (55)   21   (22)

Circle the multiples of 12.
136   134   (144)   109   (108)   (132)
(24)   34   58   68   (48)   (60)
35   29   (72)   74   (84)   94

Success on this page basically depends on knowledge of multiplication tables. Where children experience difficulties, it may be necessary to reinforce multiplication tables.

⭐ Bar graphs

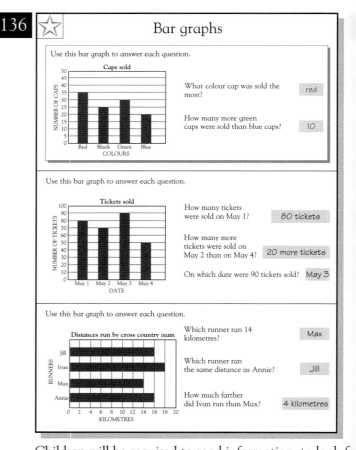

Use this bar graph to answer each question.

Caps sold

What colour cap was sold the most?
red

How many more green caps were sold than blue caps?
10

Use this bar graph to answer each question.

Tickets sold

How many tickets were sold on May 1?
80 tickets

How many more tickets were sold on May 2 than on May 4?
20 more tickets

On which date were 90 tickets sold?
May 3

Use this bar graph to answer each question.

Distances run by cross country team

Which runner ran 14 kilometres?
Max

Which runner ran the same distance as Annie?
Jill

How much farther did Ivan run than Max?
4 kilometres

Children will be required to read information, to look for specific information, and to manipulate the information they read on a bar graph, to answer the questions. They may need to be reassured that a horizontal bar graph can be read in much the same way as a vertical bar graph.

Triangles

Look at these different triangles.

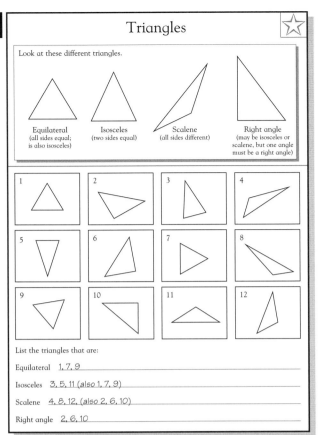

Equilateral
(all sides equal;
is also isosceles)

Isosceles
(two sides equal)

Scalene
(all sides different)

Right angle
(may be isosceles or
scalene, but one angle
must be a right angle)

1	2	3	4
5	6	7	8
9	10	11	12

List the triangles that are:

Equilateral   1, 7, 9

Isosceles   3, 5, 11 (also 1, 7, 9)

Scalene   4, 8, 12, (also 2, 6, 10)

Right angle   2, 6, 10

This page will highlight any gaps in children's ability to recognize and name triangles. Make sure that children can identify the triangles that have been rotated.

Place value to 10 000 000

How many hundreds are there in 7000?   70   hundreds
(70 × 100 = 7000)

What is the value of the 9 in 694?   90   (because the 9 is in the tens column)

Write how many tens there are in:

400	40	tens	600	60	tens	900	90	tens
200	20	tens	1300	130	tens	4700	470	tens
4800	480	tens	1240	124	tens	1320	132	tens
2630	263	tens	5920	592	tens	4350	435	tens

What is the value of the 7 in these numbers?

| 76 | 70 | | 720 | 700 | | 137 | 7 |
| 7122 | 7000 | | 74 301 | 70 000 | | 724 | 700 |

What is the value of the 3 in these numbers?

| 324 126 | 300 000 | | 3 927 141 | 3 000 000 | | 214 623 | 3 |
| 8 254 320 | 300 | | 3 711 999 | 3 000 000 | | 124 372 | 300 |

Write how many hundreds there are in:

6400	64	hundreds	8500	85	hundreds
19 900	199	hundreds	36 200	362	hundreds
524 600	5246	hundreds	712 400	7124	hundreds

What is the value of the 8 in these numbers?

| 8 214 631 | 8 000 000 | | 2 398 147 | 8000 | | 463 846 | 800 |
| 287 034 | 80 000 | | 8 110 927 | 8 000 000 | | 105 428 | 8 |

Explain to children that finding how many tens there are in a number is the same as dividing by 10. In the number 400, for example, there are 40 tens, because 400 divided by 10 is 40.

Multiplying and dividing by 10

Write the answer in the box.

37 × 10 =   370   58 ÷ 10 =   5.8

Write the product in the box.

94 × 10 =	940	13 × 10 =	130	37 × 10 =	370
36 × 10 =	360	47 × 10 =	470	54 × 10 =	540
236 × 10 =	2360	419 × 10 =	4190	262 × 10 =	2620
531 × 10 =	5310	674 × 10 =	6740	801 × 10 =	8010

Write the quotient in the box.

92 ÷ 10 =	9.2	48 ÷ 10 =	4.8	37 ÷ 10 =	3.7
18 ÷ 10 =	1.8	29 ÷ 10 =	2.9	54 ÷ 10 =	5.4
345 ÷ 10 =	34.5	354 ÷ 10 =	35.4	723 ÷ 10 =	72.3
531 ÷ 10 =	53.1	262 ÷ 10 =	26.2	419 ÷ 10 =	41.9

Find the missing factor.

23	× 10 = 230	75	× 10 = 750	99	× 10 = 990
48	× 10 = 480	13	× 10 = 130	25	× 10 = 250
52	× 10 = 520	39	× 10 = 390	27	× 10 = 270
62	× 10 = 620	86	× 10 = 860	17	× 10 = 170

Find the dividend.

47	÷ 10 = 4.7	68	÷ 10 = 6.8	124	÷ 10 = 12.4
257	÷ 10 = 25.7	362	÷ 10 = 36.2	314	÷ 10 = 31.4
408	÷ 10 = 40.8	672	÷ 10 = 67.2	809	÷ 10 = 80.9
924	÷ 10 = 92.4	327	÷ 10 = 32.7	563	÷ 10 = 56.3

Remind children that multiplying by 10 adds a 0 to the original figure. Dividing by 10 moves the decimal one place to the left. Whole numbers can be written with a decimal point (e.g. 16 as 16.0). Inverse operations in the later sections give the number that begins the equation.

Appropriate units of measure

Choose the best units to measure the length of each item.

| millimetres | centimetres | metres |

desk   tooth   swimming pool
centimetres   millimetres   metres

Choose the best units to measure the length of each item.

| centimetres | metres | kilometres |

bed   bicycle   toothbrush   football field
centimetres   centimetres   centimetres   metres

shoe   driveway   sailboat   highway
centimetres   metres   metres   kilometres

The height of a door is about 2   metres   .

The length of a pencil is about 17   centimetres.

The height of a flagpole is about 7   metres   .

Choose the best units to measure the mass of each item.

| grams | kilograms | tonnes |

train   kitten   watermelon   tennis ball
tonnes   grams   kilograms   grams

shoe   bag of potatoes   elephant   washing machine
grams   kilograms   tonnes   kilograms

The mass of a hamburger is about 26   grams   .

The mass of a bag of apples is about 2   kilograms   .

The mass of a truck is about 4   tonnes   .

Children might come up with their own examples of items that measure about 1 centimetre, 1 metre, and 1 kilometre, as well as items that have a mass of about 1 gram, 1 kilogram, and 1 tonne. They can use these as benchmarks to find the appropriate unit.

Identifying patterns ★

Continue each pattern.

| Intervals of 6: | 1 | 7 | 13 | 19 | 25 | 31 | 37 |
| Intervals of 3: | 27 | 24 | 21 | 18 | 15 | 12 | 9 |

Continue each pattern.

0	10	20	30	40	50	60
15	20	25	30	35	40	45
5	7	9	11	13	15	17
2	9	16	23	30	37	44
4	7	10	13	16	19	22
2	10	18	26	34	42	50

Continue each pattern.

44	38	32	26	20	14	8
33	29	25	21	17	13	9
27	23	19	15	11	7	3
56	48	40	32	24	16	8
49	42	35	28	21	14	7
28	25	22	19	16	13	10

Continue each pattern.

36	30	24	18	12	6	0
5	14	23	32	41	50	59
3	8	13	18	23	28	33
47	40	33	26	19	12	5
1	4	7	10	13	16	19

Point out that some of the patterns show an increase and some a decrease. Children should see what operation turns the first number into the second, and that the same operation turns the second number into the third. They can then continue the pattern.

Factors of numbers from 31 to 65

The factors of 40 are 1 2 4 5 8 10 20 40
Circle the factors of 56.
(1) (2) 3 (4) 5 6 (7) (8) (14) (28) 32 (56)

Find all the factors of each number.

The factors of 31 are	1, 31
The factors of 47 are	1, 47
The factors of 60 are	1, 2, 3, 4, 5, 6, 10, 12, 15, 20, 30, 60
The factors of 50 are	1, 2, 5, 10, 25, 50
The factors of 42 are	1, 2, 3, 6, 7, 14, 21, 42
The factors of 32 are	1, 2, 4, 8, 16, 32
The factors of 48 are	1, 2, 3, 4, 6, 8, 12, 16, 24, 48
The factors of 35 are	1, 5, 7, 35
The factors of 52 are	1, 2, 4, 13, 26, 52

Circle all the factors of each number.
Which numbers are factors of 39?
(1) 2 (3) 4 5 8 9 10 (13) 14 15 20 25 (39)
Which numbers are factors of 45?
(1) (3) 4 (5) 8 (9) 12 (15) 16 21 24 36 40 44 (45)
Which numbers are factors of 61?
(1) 3 4 5 6 10 15 16 18 20 26 31 40 (61)
Which numbers are factors of 65?
(1) 2 4 (5) 6 8 9 10 12 (13) 14 15 30 60 (65)

Some numbers have only factors of 1 and themselves. They are called prime numbers.
Write all the prime numbers between 31 and 65 in the box.

31, 37, 41, 43, 47, 53, 59, 61

Children often miss some of the factors of a number, especially when the number is large. Encourage a systematic method of finding factors. Children may forget that 1 and the number itself are factors of the number. If needed, discuss prime numbers with them.

Greatest common factor ★

Circle the common factors.
Write the greatest common factor (GCF).
24: (1) (2) (3) 4 (6) 8 12 24
60: (1) (2) (3) 4 5 (6) 8 10 12 60   The GCF is 6
42: (1) (2) (3) (6) 7 14

Find the factors. Circle the common factors.

45: (1) (3) 5 (9) 15 45
36: (1) 2 (3) 4 6 8 (9) 12 18 36

28: (1) (2) 4 7 14 28
54: (1) (2) 3 6 9 18 54

Find the factors. Write the GCF.

35: (1) (5) 7 35
80: (1) 2 4 (5) 8 10 20 40 80
The GCF is 5

32: (1) (2) (4) (8) (16) (32)
64: (1) (2) (4) (8) (16) (32) 64
The GCF is 32

12: (1) 2 (3) 4 6 12
24: (1) 2 (3) 4 6 8 12, 24
15: (1) (3) 5 15
The GCF is 3

54: (1) (2) (3) (6) (9) (18) 27, 54
72: (1) (2) (3) 4 6 8, (9) 12 (18) 24, 36
18: (1) (2) (3) (6) (9) (18)
The GCF is 18

It is common for children to skip some of the factors of a number. Have them test factors systematically, beginning with 2, and then 3, and so on.

Writing equivalent fractions

Make these fractions equal by writing the missing number.
$$\frac{20}{100} = \frac{2}{10} = \frac{1}{5}$$
$$\frac{5}{15} = \frac{1}{3}$$

Make these fractions equal by writing a number in the box.

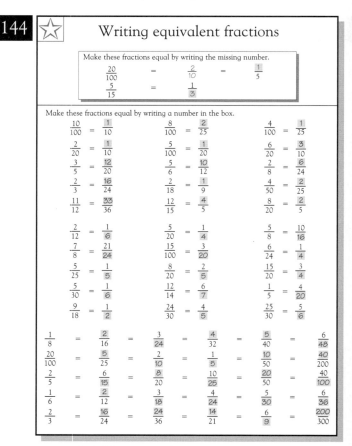

$\frac{10}{100} = \frac{1}{10}$	$\frac{8}{100} = \frac{2}{25}$	$\frac{4}{100} = \frac{1}{25}$
$\frac{2}{20} = \frac{1}{10}$	$\frac{5}{100} = \frac{1}{20}$	$\frac{6}{20} = \frac{3}{10}$
$\frac{3}{5} = \frac{12}{20}$	$\frac{5}{6} = \frac{10}{12}$	$\frac{2}{8} = \frac{6}{24}$
$\frac{2}{3} = \frac{16}{24}$	$\frac{2}{18} = \frac{1}{9}$	$\frac{4}{50} = \frac{2}{25}$
$\frac{11}{12} = \frac{33}{36}$	$\frac{12}{15} = \frac{4}{5}$	$\frac{8}{20} = \frac{2}{5}$

$\frac{2}{12} = \frac{1}{6}$	$\frac{5}{20} = \frac{1}{4}$	$\frac{5}{8} = \frac{10}{16}$
$\frac{7}{8} = \frac{21}{24}$	$\frac{15}{100} = \frac{3}{20}$	$\frac{6}{24} = \frac{1}{4}$
$\frac{5}{25} = \frac{1}{5}$	$\frac{8}{20} = \frac{2}{5}$	$\frac{15}{20} = \frac{3}{4}$
$\frac{5}{30} = \frac{1}{6}$	$\frac{12}{14} = \frac{6}{7}$	$\frac{1}{5} = \frac{4}{20}$
$\frac{9}{18} = \frac{1}{2}$	$\frac{24}{30} = \frac{4}{5}$	$\frac{25}{30} = \frac{5}{6}$

$$\frac{1}{8} = \frac{2}{16} = \frac{3}{24} = \frac{4}{32} = \frac{5}{40} = \frac{6}{48}$$
$$\frac{20}{100} = \frac{5}{25} = \frac{2}{10} = \frac{1}{5} = \frac{10}{50} = \frac{40}{200}$$
$$\frac{2}{5} = \frac{6}{15} = \frac{8}{20} = \frac{10}{25} = \frac{20}{50} = \frac{40}{100}$$
$$\frac{1}{6} = \frac{2}{12} = \frac{3}{18} = \frac{4}{24} = \frac{5}{30} = \frac{6}{36}$$
$$\frac{2}{3} = \frac{16}{24} = \frac{24}{36} = \frac{14}{21} = \frac{6}{9} = \frac{200}{300}$$

Remind children that fractions retain the same value if you multiply both the numerator and denominator by the same number or divide the numerator and denominator by the same number.

Fraction models

Write the missing numbers to show what part is shaded.

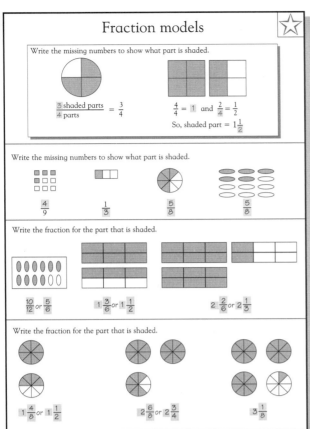

$\dfrac{3 \text{ shaded parts}}{4 \text{ parts}} = \dfrac{3}{4}$

$\dfrac{4}{4} = 1$ and $\dfrac{2}{4} = \dfrac{1}{2}$

So, shaded part $= 1\dfrac{1}{2}$

Write the missing numbers to show what part is shaded.

$\dfrac{4}{9}$ $\dfrac{1}{3}$ $\dfrac{5}{8}$ $\dfrac{5}{8}$

Write the fraction for the part that is shaded.

$\dfrac{10}{12}$ or $\dfrac{5}{6}$ $1\dfrac{3}{6}$ or $1\dfrac{1}{2}$ $2\dfrac{2}{6}$ or $2\dfrac{1}{3}$

Write the fraction for the part that is shaded.

$1\dfrac{4}{8}$ or $1\dfrac{1}{2}$ $2\dfrac{6}{8}$ or $2\dfrac{3}{4}$ $3\dfrac{1}{8}$

Some children may need further explanation of the models of mixed numbers. Point out that when all the parts of a model are shaded, the model shows the number 1.

Multiplying by one-digit numbers

Find each product. Remember to regroup.

1 1	3	3 4
465	391	278
x 3	x 4	x 5
1395	1564	1390

Find each product.

563	910	437	812
x 3	x 2	x 3	x 2
1689	1820	1311	1624

572	831	406	394
x 4	x 3	x 5	x 6
2288	2493	2030	2364

Find each product.

318	223	542	217
x 3	x 4	x 4	x 3
954	892	2168	651

127	275	798	365
x 4	x 5	x 6	x 6
508	1375	4788	2190

100	372	881	953
x 5	x 4	x 4	x 3
500	1488	3524	2859

Solve each problem.

A middle school has 255 students. A high school has 6 times as many students. How many children are there at the high school?

1530 students

| 3 3 |
| 255 |
| x 6 |
| 1530 |

A train can carry 365 passengers. How many could it carry on

four trips? 1460 passengers

six trips? 2190 passengers

2 2	3 3
365	365
x 4	x 6
1460	2190

Make sure children understand the convention of multiplication, i.e. multiply the ones first and work left. Problems on this page may result from gaps in knowledge of the 2, 3, 4, 5, and 6 times tables. Errors will also occur if children neglect to regroup.

Multiplying by one-digit numbers

Find each product. Remember to regroup.

3 3	1 2	4 4
456	823	755
x 6	x 8	x 9
2736	6584	6795

Find each product.

394	736	827	943
x 7	x 7	x 8	x 9
2758	5152	6616	8487

643	199	821	547
x 6	x 6	x 7	x 8
3858	1194	5747	4376

501	377	843	222
x 7	x 8	x 8	x 9
3507	3016	6744	1998

471	223	606	513
x 9	x 8	x 6	x 7
4239	1784	3636	3591

500	800	900	200
x 9	x 9	x 8	x 9
4500	7200	7200	1800

Solve each problem.

A crate holds 550 apples. How many apples are there in 8 crates?

4400 apples

| 4 |
| 550 |
| x 8 |
| 4400 |

Keyshawn swims 760 laps each week. How many laps does he swim in 5 weeks?

3800 people

| 3 |
| 760 |
| x 5 |
| 3800 |

Problems encountered will be similar to the previous page. Gaps in knowledge of the 6, 7, 8, and 9 times table will result in children's errors.

Real-life problems

Find the answer to each problem.

Jacob spent $4.68 at the store and had $4.77 left. How much did he have to start with?

$9.45

| 1 1 |
| 4.77 |
| + 4.68 |
| 9.45 |

Tracy receives a weekly allowance of $3.00 a week. How much will she have if she saves all of it for 8 weeks?

$24.00

| 3.00 |
| x 8 |
| 24.00 |

Find the answer to each problem.

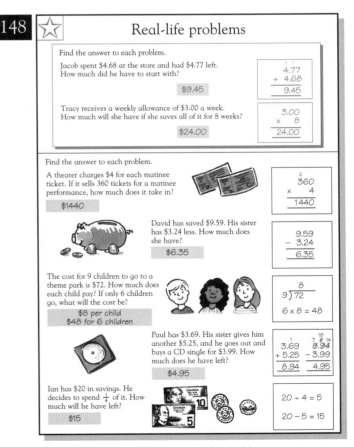

A theater charges $4 for each matinee ticket. If it sells 360 tickets for a matinee performance, how much does it take in?

$1440

| 2 |
| 360 |
| x 4 |
| 1440 |

David has saved $9.59. His sister has $3.24 less. How much does she have?

$6.35

| 9.59 |
| − 3.24 |
| 6.35 |

The cost for 9 children to go to a theme park is $72. How much does each child pay? If only 6 children go, what will the cost be?

$8 per child
$48 for 6 children

| 8 |
| 9)72 |
| 6 x 8 = 48 |

Paul has $3.69. His sister gives him another $5.25, and he goes out and buys a CD single for $3.99. How much does he have left?

$4.95

1	7 18
3.69	8.94
+ 5.25	− 3.99
8.94	4.95

Ian has $20 in savings. He decides to spend $\frac{1}{4}$ of it. How much will he have left?

$15

| 20 ÷ 4 = 5 |
| 20 − 5 = 15 |

This page and the next provide children an opportunity to apply the skills they have practiced. They will need to select the appropriate operation. If they are unsure, discuss whether the answer should be larger or smaller. This can help them decide on the operation.

Real-life problems

Find the answer to each problem.

Nina has an hour to do her homework. She plans to spend $\frac{1}{3}$ of her time on math. How many minutes will she spend doing math?

20 minutes

1 hour is 60 minutes

$$3\overline{)60}^{20}$$

In gym class, David makes 2 long jumps of 1.78 m and 2.19 m. How far does he jump altogether?

3.97 m

$$\begin{array}{r} 1 \\ 1.78 \text{ m} \\ + 2.19 \text{ m} \\ \hline 3.97 \text{ m} \end{array}$$

Find the answer to each problem.

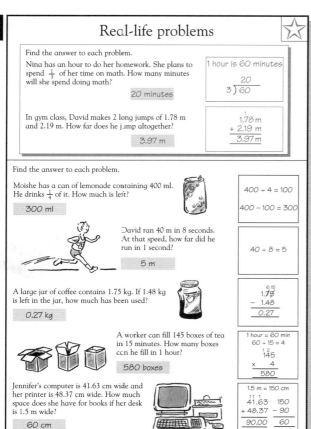

Moishe has a can of lemonade containing 400 ml. He drinks $\frac{1}{4}$ of it. How much is left?

300 ml

$400 \div 4 = 100$

$400 - 100 = 300$

David ran 40 m in 8 seconds. At that speed, how far did he run in 1 second?

5 m

$40 \div 8 = 5$

A large jar of coffee contains 1.75 kg. If 1.48 kg is left in the jar, how much has been used?

0.27 kg

$$\begin{array}{r} 6\;15 \\ 1.7\cancel{5} \\ - 1.48 \\ \hline 0.27 \end{array}$$

A worker can fill 145 boxes of tea in 15 minutes. How many boxes can he fill in 1 hour?

580 boxes

1 hour = 60 min
60 ÷ 15 = 4

$$\begin{array}{r} 1\,2 \\ 145 \\ \times \quad 4 \\ \hline 580 \end{array}$$

Jennifer's computer is 41.63 cm wide and her printer is 48.37 cm wide. How much space does she have for books if her desk is 1.5 m wide?

60 cm

1.5 m = 150 cm

$$\begin{array}{rr} 1\,1 \\ 41.63 & 150 \\ + 48.37 & - 90 \\ \hline 90.00 & 60 \end{array}$$

This page deals with units other than money. Note that solving the final problem requires two operations.

Problems involving time

Find the answer to each problem.

Caitlin spends 35 minutes on her homework each day. How many minutes does she spend on her homework in one week from Monday through Friday?

175 minutes

$$\begin{array}{r} 2 \\ 35 \\ \times \;\; 5 \\ \hline 175 \end{array}$$

Jenny spends 175 minutes on her homework from Monday through Friday. How much time does she spend on homework each day?

35 minutes

$$5\overline{)175}^{35}$$

Find the answer to each problem.

Amy works from 9 A.M. until 5 P.M. She has a lunch break from noon until 1 P.M. How many hours does she work in a 5-day week?

35 hours

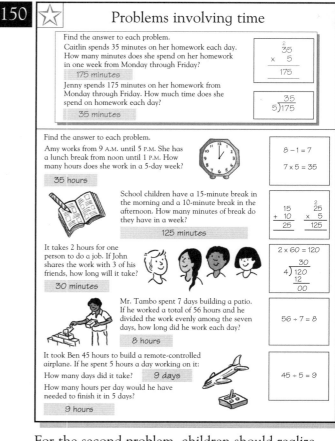

$8 - 1 = 7$

$7 \times 5 = 35$

School children have a 15-minute break in the morning and a 10-minute break in the afternoon. How many minutes of break do they have in a week?

125 minutes

$$\begin{array}{r} 15 \\ + 10 \\ \hline 25 \end{array} \qquad \begin{array}{r} 2 \\ 25 \\ \times \;\; 5 \\ \hline 125 \end{array}$$

It takes 2 hours for one person to do a job. If John shares the work with 3 of his friends, how long will it take?

30 minutes

$2 \times 60 = 120$

$$4\overline{)120}^{30}$$
$$\begin{array}{r} 12 \\ \hline 00 \end{array}$$

Mr. Tambo spent 7 days building a patio. If he worked a total of 56 hours and he divided the work evenly among the seven days, how long did he work each day?

8 hours

$56 \div 7 = 8$

It took Ben 45 hours to build a remote-controlled airplane. If he spent 5 hours a day working on it:

How many days did it take? **9 days**

How many hours per day would he have needed to finish it in 5 days?

9 hours

$45 \div 5 = 9$

For the second problem, children should realize that a school week is 5 days. For the third problem, check that children divide by 4 rather than 3.

Multiplying and dividing

Write the answer in the box.

26 × 10 = **260**	26 × 100 = **2600**	
400 ÷ 10 = **40**	400 ÷ 100 = **4**	

Write the product in the box.

33 × 10 = **330**	21 × 10 = **210**	42 × 10 = **420**
94 × 100 = **9400**	36 × 100 = **3600**	81 × 100 = **8100**
416 × 10 = **4160**	204 × 10 = **2040**	513 × 10 = **5130**
767 × 100 = **76 700**	821 × 100 = **82 100**	245 × 100 = **24 500**

Write the quotient in the box.

120 ÷ 10 = **12**	260 ÷ 10 = **26**	470 ÷ 10 = **47**
300 ÷ 100 = **3**	800 ÷ 100 = **8**	400 ÷ 100 = **4**
20 ÷ 10 = **2**	30 ÷ 10 = **3**	70 ÷ 10 = **7**
500 ÷ 100 = **5**	100 ÷ 100 = **1**	900 ÷ 100 = **9**

Write the number that has been multiplied by 100.

59 × 100 = 5900	**714** × 100 = 71 400
721 × 100 = 72 100	**234** × 100 = 23 400
11 × 100 = 1100	**470** × 100 = 47 000
84 × 100 = 8400	**441** × 100 = 44 100

Write the number that has been divided by 100.

200 ÷ 100 = 2	**800** ÷ 100 = 8
2100 ÷ 100 = 21	**1800** ÷ 100 = 18
8600 ÷ 100 = 86	**2100** ÷ 100 = 21
1000 ÷ 100 = 10	**5900** ÷ 100 = 59

Children should realize that multiplying a whole number by 10 or 100 means writing one or two zeros at the end of the number. To divide a multiple of ten by 10, simply take the final zero off. In the two final sections, solve by using the inverse operation.

Identifying patterns

Continue each pattern.

Steps of 2:	$\frac{1}{2}$	$2\frac{1}{2}$	$4\frac{1}{2}$	$6\frac{1}{2}$	$8\frac{1}{2}$	$10\frac{1}{2}$
Steps of 5:	3.5	8.5	13.5	18.5	23.5	28.5

Continue each pattern.

$5\frac{1}{2}$	$10\frac{1}{2}$	$15\frac{1}{2}$	$20\frac{1}{2}$	$25\frac{1}{2}$	$30\frac{1}{2}$
$1\frac{1}{4}$	$3\frac{1}{4}$	$5\frac{1}{4}$	$7\frac{1}{4}$	$9\frac{1}{4}$	$11\frac{1}{4}$
$8\frac{1}{3}$	$9\frac{1}{3}$	$10\frac{1}{3}$	$11\frac{1}{3}$	$12\frac{1}{3}$	$13\frac{1}{3}$
$55\frac{3}{4}$	$45\frac{3}{4}$	$35\frac{3}{4}$	$25\frac{3}{4}$	$15\frac{3}{4}$	$5\frac{3}{4}$
$42\frac{1}{2}$	$38\frac{1}{2}$	$34\frac{1}{2}$	$30\frac{1}{2}$	$26\frac{1}{2}$	$22\frac{1}{2}$
7.5	6.5	5.5	4.5	3.5	2.5
28.4	25.4	22.4	19.4	16.4	13.4
81.6	73.6	65.6	57.6	49.6	41.6
6.3	10.3	14.3	18.3	22.3	26.3
12.1	13.1	14.1	15.1	16.1	17.1
14.6	21.6	28.6	35.6	42.6	49.6
$11\frac{1}{2}$	$10\frac{1}{2}$	$9\frac{1}{2}$	$8\frac{1}{2}$	$7\frac{1}{2}$	$6\frac{1}{2}$
8.4	11.4	14.4	17.4	20.4	23.4
$7\frac{3}{4}$	$13\frac{3}{4}$	$19\frac{3}{4}$	$25\frac{3}{4}$	$31\frac{3}{4}$	$37\frac{3}{4}$
57.5	48.5	39.5	30.5	21.5	12.5

The patterns on this page are formed by adding or subtracting whole numbers but the items in each row are mixed numbers or decimals. Children should see what operation turns the first number into the second, and the second into the third, and then continue the pattern.

Products with odd and even numbers ☆

Find the products of these numbers.

3 and 4 The product of 3 and 4 is 12.   6 and 8 The product of 6 and 8 is 48.

Find the products of these odd and even numbers.

5 and 6	The product of 5 and 6 is 30.	3 and 2	The product of 3 and 2 is 6.
7 and 4	The product of 7 and 4 is 28.	8 and 3	The product of 8 and 3 is 24.
6 and 3	The product of 6 and 3 is 18.	2 and 9	The product of 2 and 9 is 18.
10 and 3	The product of 10 and 3 is 30.	12 and 5	The product of 12 and 5 is 60.

What do you notice about your answers? The product of odd and even numbers is always an even number.

Find the products of these odd numbers.

5 and 7	The product of 5 and 7 is 35.	3 and 9	The product of 3 and 9 is 27.
5 and 11	The product of 5 and 11 is 55.	7 and 3	The product of 7 and 3 is 21.
9 and 5	The product of 9 and 5 is 45.	11 and 7	The product of 11 and 7 is 77.
13 and 3	The product of 13 and 3 is 39.	1 and 5	The product of 1 and 5 is 5.

What do you notice about your answers? The product of two odd numbers is always an odd number.

Find the products of these even numbers.

2 and 4	The product of 2 and 4 is 8.	4 and 6	The product of 4 and 6 is 24.
6 and 2	The product of 6 and 2 is 12.	4 and 8	The product of 4 and 8 is 32.
10 and 2	The product of 10 and 2 is 20.	4 and 10	The product of 4 and 10 is 40.
6 and 10	The product of 6 and 10 is 60.	6 and 8	The product of 6 and 8 is 48.

What do you notice about your answers? The product of two even numbers is always an even number.

Can you write a rule for the products with odd and even numbers?
The product of two numbers will always be even unless both numbers are odd.

Children may need help answering the questions on what they notice about the products. Accept any rule about products that children write, as long as it indicates that they have grasped the concept.

☆ Factors of numbers from 66 to 100

The factors of 66 are   1   2   3   6   11   22   33   66
Circle the factors of 94. ① ② 28 32 43 ㊼ 71 86 ㉙₄

Write the factors of each number in the box.

The factors of 70 are 1, 2, 5, 7, 10, 14, 35, 70
The factors of 85 are 1, 5, 17, 85
The factors of 69 are 1, 3, 23, 69
The factors of 83 are 1, 83
The factors of 75 are 1, 3, 5, 15, 25, 75
The factors of 96 are 1, 2, 3, 4, 6, 8, 12, 16, 24, 32, 48, 96
The factors of 63 are 1, 3, 7, 9, 21, 63
The factors of 99 are 1, 3, 9, 11, 33, 99
The factors of 72 are 1, 2, 3, 4, 6, 8, 9, 12, 18, 24, 36, 72

Circle the factors of 68.
① ② 3 ④ 5 6 7 8 9 11 12 ⑰ ㉞ 35 62 ㊽

Circle the factors of 95.
① 2 3 4 ⑤ 15 16 17 ⑲ 24 37 85 90 ㊾ 96

Circle the factors of 88.
① ② 3 ④ 5 6 ⑧ 10 ⑪ 15 ㉒ 25 27 ㊹ 87 ㊰

Circle the factors of 73.
① 2 4 5 6 8 9 10 12 13 14 15 30 60 ㉒

A prime number only has two factors, 1 and itself.
Write all the prime numbers between 66 and 100 in the box.

67, 71, 73, 79, 83, 89, 97

Children often miss some of the factors of a number, especially for large numbers . Encourage a systematic method of finding factors. Children may forget that 1 and the number itself are factors of a number. If necessary, discuss prime numbers with children.

Multiplying by two-digit numbers ☆

Write the product for each problem.

56	45
x 32	x 43
112	135
1680	1800
1792	1935

Write the product for each problem.

56	23	47	84
x 23	x 24	x 25	x 22
168	92	235	168
1120	460	940	1680
1288	552	1175	1848

73	52	64	51
x 34	x 35	x 33	x 32
292	260	192	102
2190	1560	1920	1530
2482	1820	2112	1632

Write the product for each problem.

41	65	72	84
x 62	x 54	x 68	x 71
82	260	576	84
2460	3250	4320	5880
2542	3510	4896	5964

92	57	38	26
x 63	x 82	x 94	x 75
276	114	152	130
5520	4560	3420	1820
5796	4674	3572	1950

Children should understand that multiplying a number by 32 is the same as multiplying the number by 2 and then by 30, and adding the two products.

☆ Multiplying by two-digit numbers

Write the product for each problem.

39	68
x 87	x 98
273	544
3120	6120
3393	6664

Write the product for each problem.

87	76	99	85
x 98	x 78	x 69	x 98
696	608	891	680
7830	5320	5940	7650
8526	5928	6831	8330

88	67	94	89
x 95	x 76	x 69	x 47
440	402	846	623
7920	4690	5640	3560
8360	5092	6486	4183

Write the product for each problem.

87	46	58	73
x 79	x 67	x 59	x 98
783	322	522	584
6090	2760	2900	6570
6873	3082	3422	7154

95	58	78	96
x 67	x 88	x 97	x 79
665	464	546	864
5700	4640	7020	6720
6365	5104	7566	7584

This page gives further practice of multiplication as on the previous page. Make sure that children do not neglect to regroup when necessary.

EDITOR, CANADA   Julia Roles

PRODUCTION   Erica Rosen

EDITOR, INDIA   Aekta Jerath

DTP, INDIA   Balwant Singh

MANAGER, INDIA   Aparna Sharma

First Canadian Edition, 2005

Library and Archives Canada Cataloguing in Publication

Math made easy grade 5 : math workbook / Marilyn Wilson,
Canadian editor. -- Canadian ed.

"Ages 10-11".
ISBN 978-1-55363-053-1

1. Mathematics--Problems, exercises, etc.--Juvenile literature.
I. Wilson, Marilyn

QA107.2.M3886 2005   510'.76   C2004-906903-9

Colour reproduction by Colourscan
Printed and bound in China by L.Rex
11 12 13 10 9 8 7 6 5 4
004-MD276-Oct/04

The publisher would like to thank
Chris Houston for his illustrations of Canadian money.

Discover more at
www.dk.com